THE VOICE OF JAMES M. CAIN

FICTION BY DAVID MADDEN
The Beautiful Greed
Cassandra Singing
The Shadow Knows (stories)
Brothers in Confidence
Bijou
The Suicide's Wife
The New Orleans of Possibilities (stories)
Pleasure-Dome
On the Big Wind
Sharpshooter
Abducted by Circumstance
London Bridge in Plague and Fire
The Last Bizarre Tale (stories)
Marble Goddesses and Mortal Flesh (4 novellas)

SELECTED WORKS OF NONFICTION
Wright Morris
Proletarian Writers of the Thirties
Tough Guy Writers of the Thirties
James M. Cain
Cain's Craft
Rediscoveries I
Rediscoveries II
The Poetic Image in Six Genres
Harlequin's Stick, Charlie's Cane
American Dreams, American Nightmares
Remembering James Agee
The Legacy of Robert Penn Warren
Nathanael West: The Cheaters and the Cheated
Touching the Web of Southern Novelists
Thomas Wolfe's Civil War
The Tangled Web of the Civil War and Reconstruction

THE VOICE OF JAMES M. CAIN

A Biography

DAVID MADDEN

Guilford, Connecticut

To Robbie, six decades an activist for the ERA and other causes.

An imprint of The Rowman & Littlefield Publishing Group, Inc.
4501 Forbes Blvd., Ste. 200
Lanham, MD 20706
www.rowman.com

Distributed by NATIONAL BOOK NETWORK

British Library Cataloguing in Publication Information available

Library of Congress Cataloging-in-Publication Data available

ISBN 978-1-4930-4812-0 (hardcover)
ISBN 978-1-4930-4813-7 (e-book)

Contents

Acknowledgments

I have great gratitude to the estate of James M. Cain via Folio Management to quote from Cain's works and letters.

NOTE

Unlike *Cain*, the journalist Roy Hoopes's 1982 excellent, massive, thoroughly researched and documented biography, *The Voice of James M. Cain* is the work of a novelist. It is innovative in style and technique. It does not include footnotes, bibliography, or an index. It is a story.

For over seventeen years, through visits, frequent phone calls, and a great many letters, James M. Cain cooperated with me intimately, somewhat collaboratively, each step of the way as I wrote a literary study of his works nearly fifty years ago, published in 1970.

During that time our relationship was one of two writers of fiction, interacting, sharing with each other. That relationship, intricate, complex, sometimes a little contentious, is a relevant part of the story, with the result that this book, especially in the last third, is simultaneously a biography of an old master in decline and a memoir of a young novelist on the rise.

Cain provided me with an unsolicited 125-page autobiographical narrative of his life, telling me on the phone and in writing that he had written it for me so that I could use it in any way I saw fit. Then he read and approved the innovative use to which I put his words in that first book and I use them again now in this book.

Because I want Cain's own distinctively tough, frank, slangy voice to convey a sense of his life as a storyteller, I have employed three very unorthodox methods.

First, I have restructured, pruned, and sometimes rephrased the pages he sent me and blended his words with my own phrases to give an impression of his voice throughout the book. To avoid a tedious and unsightly briar-patch effect of quotations, paraphrases, and endless footnotes, I have not enclosed his wording in quotation marks.

Drawing upon my long-time intimate knowledge of his personality and of his writings, I have created, as a second major feature of this biography, an imaginative impression of his creative process as a writer in the very act of writing, both fiction and nonfiction.

A third major feature is my use of the technique that I have often used in my own fiction, whereby the point of view is confined strictly to what Cain remembers and perceives at any given moment in the strict chronology of his life, never alluding to anything in his future.

The result is an innovative biography, an unusual, complex and, I hope, an effective and interesting collaboration that gives the reader a unique sense of a writer's life as a storyteller that could not otherwise be conveyed.

1

Young Man on a Park Bench

"CAIN, YOU'RE TWENTY-TWO YEARS OLD, YOU'VE JUST QUIT YOUR FIFTH job, your wish to become a great opera singer will never come true. So how do you intend to spend the rest of your life?" he said to himself, sitting on a Lafayette Park bench in the fall of 1914, the White House at his back.

"You're going to be a writer," said a voice out of the blue.

Was he about to take another preposterous plunge, as he had when he set out to become an opera singer? Or were there discernible forces that brought him to this seemingly gratuitous decision? Taking stock was a habit. Though he looked Jewish, only Irish blood ran in his veins, so he might assume a likely propensity for talking well and telling stories effectively. But only his reports for the Maryland Road Commission suggested he could write effectively.

As president of Washington College, his father had proven how charmingly he could talk. His mother, trained to sing opera, had inspired his own ambition. She had also taught him how to speak and write with clarity, correct grammar, and brevity. Of his three sisters, only Virginia showed any literary talent. His brother Edward was the family's bright star, athletic, handsome, and charming, like his father, good at everything his father understood and admired, and a proficient musician, like his mother.

Neither his father nor his mother seemed to think Jamie would amount to much.

But from early years to this moment of decision, he had developed a prospective writer's background in reading. Literature was his favorite

James M. Cain and Gilbert Malcolm in uniform. PHOTOGRAPHER UNKNOWN

subject. His favorite work of fiction was *Alice in Wonderland*. Other favorite books were *The Adventures of Sherlock Holmes, The Last of the Mohicans, The Virginian, Vanity Fair, Treasure Island, The Three Musketeers* (he'd taught himself French so he could read Dumas' *The Black Tulip* in the original)—and *Who's Who in America*.

During the uneventful first twelve years of his life in Annapolis and the next six across Chesapeake Bay in Chestertown, he had produced no dramatic evidence of an inclination toward writing. Rebellion, especially against religion, might be considered a telling factor in the background of a writer. At thirteen, when he realized he was faking it, he had broken with the Catholic Church, which was a "hick operation" in Chestertown. Writers usually had memories of interesting characters and buddies from their childhoods. He had Ike Newton, town storyteller, and boyhood friend Bushrod Howard, rebel against authority. As superintendent of Annapolis schools, his father had unwisely honored his request that he skip from third to fifth grade, making him ever-after a midget among giants in school.

As a precocious fifteen-year-old student at Washington College, he had taken no part in athletic or other extracurricular activities, belonged to no organizations, held no jobs, and declined to edit the campus magazine. His father had looked with wholehearted disapproval upon his complete indifference to campus affairs. When he graduated in 1910 at eighteen without distinction, he knew he had already failed to live up to his father's expectations.

After graduation, the realization hit him that, contrary to the atmosphere of the grand style in which he had been raised, life was hard, that work was every man's daily lot. Growing up, he'd had no idea at all that a man was supposed to "do something" with his life. Having assessed the visible choices, he didn't want to do anything, though he had a vague intention of becoming "somebody" and showing up in *Who's Who*.

His high-toned college girlfriend, Mary Clough, who was teaching school, treated him now with a lofty disdain.

It pained him now to look back over four years on a series of jobs whose only object was to make a living. The mumps had released him from a six-month stretch with Consolidated Gas and Light of Baltimore, secured through his father's connections, performing hateful routine tasks with ledgers. Inspecting roads and writing reports for the Maryland Road Commission had been enjoyable, but getting laid off was humiliating. As principal of the high school in the little village of Vienna, Maryland, on the Eastern Shore, he'd learned a few things about teaching.

When he suddenly decided to quit to take singing lessons, his mother was shocked. "You have no voice, no looks, no stage personality. You have some musical sense, but it's not enough." What he did have was the first big decision he'd made on his own, and he'd gone ahead with it. To make a living while taking lessons from a teacher who seemed to share his mother's assessment, he tried to sell insurance. He failed. Facing the fact that his singing talent was minimal, that his enthusiasm for practicing was faint, he "quituated."

Kann's department store hired him to sell Victor records and Victrolas. Meeting some of the fine singers who came to Washington was exciting, but he had to have a raise. Kann's disagreed.

He had discovered that he had a certain incompetence in several fields of work. The only one who lacked the Cain-Mallahan good looks, physically weak and uncoordinated, he was unsuccessful in love and lust. But the lunge at music had been at least an action in the right direction, for his mind was mainly aesthetic. And singing, which his gifted mother had given up for marriage, had been a rebellion against his father, who saw a law career for him. He had failed to win his father's approval and so to remove the barrier between them. He had even failed to impress his mother, to whom he had always felt very close. Sitting on the bench, he had the feeling he'd just awarded himself a consolation prize for his failure to become an opera singer. But the years of indecisiveness, of searching, were past, now that God had made up his mind for him.

Some things were over now. He had, in a way, come through.

Expecting to astonish his parents with his firm resolve, they astonished him by seeing it as the wish most likely to come true for James Mallahan Cain, their firstborn.

He went down to Richmond to seek the advice of his favorite living writer, Henry Sydnor Harrison, author of the bestseller *Queed*, but he was not at home.

Living with his parents in Chestertown, he secretly wrote short stories, mainly out of a desire to project local color and background. Passages memorized from Harrison's highly successful novels provided stylistic models: "his tongue un-locked and he began to speak his heart. It was not speech as he had always known speech. In all his wonderful array of terminology there were no words fitted to this undreamed need. He had to discover the words somehow, by main strength make them up for himself. They came out stammering, hard-wrung, bearing new upon their rough faces the mint-mark of his own heart. Perhaps she did not prize them any the less on that account." As his stories came back from the magazines, he suspected that they lacked narrative thrust. At least, he was learning to type, practicing on the machine in his father's office at the college. The look of x-outs made him feel uneasy, so the method he developed was to type neat copies of all drafts after the first. But even as he set about working out his self-assigned destiny, his father drew him into another in that series of interim jobs.

When his father asked him to fill in for a teacher who was ill, he accepted the offer. The classes were in English and mathematics in the preparatory school across the road from the college. Although he had taught a year in high school, he now became even more convinced that teaching was mainly a matter of preparation, of knowing what you intend to try to teach today. The only way he could face those boys was to become an expert on grammar, syntax, rhetoric, and especially punctuation. He performed so well that when the instructor took a job elsewhere, his father asked him to manage the entire preparatory department. That meant that he had to live in the dormitory and discipline the boys.

Knowing that for many years the boys had kept the dormitory looking like a pig sty with their pranks, overworking the black cleanup men, he called them together on his first night. "I intend to live in a place that my mother, my sisters, or any woman can drop in on any time, and find fit for them to visit. I assume you do too, that that's the kind of place you would maintain if it weren't for a few clowns trying to be funny. Well, that's the kind of place we're going to have. I'm telling you, not asking you. This isn't an invitation for you to vote on *whether*. We're going to *have* that kind of place, and the only question is, *how*. If you want to cooperate, I'm

willing, even glad, to let you, and we can adjust the rules to that cooperation, so you have certain liberties you don't now enjoy. If you don't want
to cooperate, we're going to have that kind of place anyhow, but you'll
find the screws tightened in a way you may not enjoy. So I'm leaving the
room now for a few minutes, and you can talk it over, and then we'll all
talk together."

They talked, and by unanimous vote, except for one mischievous but
bright boy who finally came around, agreed to cooperate. As the look
of the dormitory continued to reflect that agreement, he observed with
some astonishment that teenagers apparently liked the "iron mike." Being
told what they ought to do let them know where they stood, and they got
the point without resentment. They learned that cooperation meant being
allowed to participate and that pride was a good substitute for pranks.

As he began to realize that students seek not knowledge but grades,
he set up the rule in his math classes that he would give only two marks:
perfect or zero. "There's no such thing in math as being pretty nearly
right. It's all right or it's all wrong." His students seemed to accept his
dictum. Every day he posted their marks on his door, so that at the end
of the month, each student could figure the same grade the school would
send his parents.

Examining the marks sent in, his father complained sharply, "One
hundred is an awfully high mark for a boy to be getting in solid geometry."

"He earned one hundred. Two or three boys made zero for the month,
which to my mind is a bit cruel, and I'd like to fudge it a little, so they
had something to show for their time. But zero is what they earned, and
zero is what they'll get." Then, looking his father in the eye, he said, "It's
not me, but you, who're too lenient with the marks. You grade your students up, and all your students know it, for the simple reason you fake
your marks. You tote up your books every week or so by approximation,
guesswork, and kindness, and that's why they cheat on you, every exam
you give, and don't feel they owe you honor. It's why cheating on exams is
an academic disease in American colleges. The students know the professor cheats first—he pretends to a fairness in grades that he doesn't actually have. And they don't see any reason why they owe a higher degree of
honor than the degree of honor they get."

His father, somewhat annoyed, refused to get the point, but he kept his own Spartan system of teaching and grading in force. The skills and attitudes he was transmitting to his boys, he was simultaneously instilling in himself. Fine writing could not be taught; the mechanics could. If his short stories were getting slightly sidetracked, he was thoroughly learning and teaching sound principles of English composition and punctuation no less than the general principles of rhetoric. "When you learn how to punctuate, you'll be free to be yourselves. Instead of being in a straitjacket of what can be put between commas with a period at the end, you can write as freely as you talk, and know that you can set it up so it reads."

He put together a little book on punctuation, with illustrations from the world's literature. Drilling the boys, he assured them, "Writing is like football: It's all fundamentals, there are no higher branches." And to put a little reality and excitement into their exercises, he directed them to get jobs as correspondents for their hometown papers, covering college athletic events, featuring the fears of the hometown boys involved.

After three years at this job, he looked back with some satisfaction on competence demonstrated and confidence gained. Charles Louis Townsend, professor of French at the college, encouraged his writing aspirations. On one of their long walks across the bridge over the Chester River, Townsend responded with enthusiasm to his tale of a famous singer who commits a murder, escapes, but can no longer sing for fear of giving himself away. Townsend's fascination with the idea had lingered with him.

Townsend insisted that he get his master's while at Washington College. Reluctantly, he did the work, some of it under Townsend, majoring in history and minoring in drama. Teaching and working on a master's degree distracted him from his intention to become a writer. Also, he worried about the troubles his father was having with the faculty and the board of governors, problems aggravated by his drinking and the burning in January 1916 of the most historic building on this eleventh oldest campus in the United States, for which President Washington had been a trustee.

And he was dangerously in love with a fourteen-year-old girl while also seeing Mary Clough again. Mary, an intellectual whose mother was related to Stephen Crane, was impressed that his goal was to become a writer, displeased, on the other hand, with his arguments that *The Red Badge of Courage* was one of the most dreadful novels ever overpraised by the literati.

An offer from a high school in Easton, Pennsylvania, to teach math was a way of striking out on his own finally, at the age of twenty-five, but the draft seemed to offer a more interesting way, although he was not enthusiastically behind the nation's reasons for war.

Meanwhile, he received his master's degree with a sense of having wasted energy better spent on short stories. Each rejection was an assault on his self-respect, so he decided to give up writing.

On impulse, he set out to get a summer job in one of the war factories. But when he saw the long lines, he stayed on the streetcar. Back in his boarding house, he took stock, and imposed on himself the kind of discipline he had refined in talking with his students: "The first possible place that might have a job, you're going in there and get it." That place was Swift and Company. He pleased the management and himself with his work as weigh master in the cold storage room, but he could take only a week of clocking in at 3:00 a.m.

While looking for another job, he noticed Baltimore *American* printed across a building. Ignorant of the qualifications, he audaciously offered himself to the city editor, who put him on one of the police beats. Having just read Cain's first article, an account of a drowning, the night city editor declared, "You're in the right business, Cain. You'll go far." He didn't ask why. He took it on faith.

In the fall, he was also teaching math at Easton where a twelve-year-old girl aroused two emotions in him, the second of which was a sense of the proximity of the Pennsylvania State Penitentiary. He fled Easton, and the *American* took him back as financial reporter, covering war bond drives, large financial "combos," and war conferences. But early in 1918, the *Sun*, Baltimore's best paper, offered him a higher salary, and he went back on the police beat. He also managed to interview several opera singers.

Mary Clough now paid him more attention.

Even though the draft had turned him down, he began to doubt the motives behind his anti-war, somewhat anti-Allies sentiments. From childhood, his physical appearance had been deceptive. Large for his age, he looked strong, but his soft muscle lacked tone and potential. He was kinetically a weakling. He tried to enlist, but was rejected. Finally, he persuaded a doctor to qualify him for the draft, despite the possible gestation of incipient TB. Just as he was settling into a profession that enabled him to write, he had to take another interim job—service in the Army.

Before reporting to the draft board, he visited his parents. The discovery that his father, whose talent for politicking had made a success of sleepy, pastoral Washington College, had been fired from the presidency under rather mysterious circumstances at the age of fifty-eight, distressed Cain more than the prospect of war's hazards.

At Camp Meade, Maryland, he heard of an outfit going overseas that needed men. He rode another wave of audacity to the desk of Captain Edward O. Madeira and misrepresented himself as being able to do all sorts of things he could do a little, but not well—speak French, ride a horse. Transferred to First Headquarters Infantry Troop, Seventy-Ninth Division, a private in the rear rank, he met another man who had misrepresented his qualifications—Gilbert Malcolm, a tall, rawboned, red-haired graduate of Dickinson Law School, who had some newspaper experience. If, despite their misgivings about its justifications, they were to go to the war, they didn't want to watch the show, but to play a role in it.

He boarded the USS *Leviathan* with a sense of commitment to marry Mary Clough after the war, and with a sense of relief that his father had gotten a high-level job in an insurance company in Baltimore.

The several weeks Cain served in an observation tower on the front in France gave him confidence when Captain Madeira ordered him to deliver a message. But he got lost among the trenches in the most humiliating nightmare of his life.

Two months after the Armistice, he woke up to a dream job that saved him from boredom and KP: He was assigned to special duty as editor of the *Lorraine Cross*, the division's limping, two-column, four-page newspaper. His buddy Malcolm was made sports editor. Their orders were to put some life into the paper. Cain cast Malcolm in the role of big brother, whose judgment he respected and whose approval he craved.

By the second week, Cain, Malcolm, and an aggressive circulation manager were putting out a six-page, five-column "sock-dollinger," made up in big-city style, with attention-getting headlines and much division news.

Cain and his younger brother Edward exchanged letters that were deliberate imitations of Jack Keefe's army letters to his "old pal" in Ring Lardner's popular *You Know Me Al* and *Treat 'Em Rough*.

In February 1919, Cain received from home the shocking news that Edward had been taking a farewell spin just before a luncheon in honor of his discharge from the Marine Air Corps in Miami when his plane crashed. His brother's death was a dreadful blow to the family, and Cain needed Malcolm's "big-brother" compassion and the distraction of work on the paper.

Cain's sometimes larcenous and highly ingenious maneuvers to get paper, stamps, and other necessities made the *Cross* one of the most successful weeklies of the American Expeditionary Force, prompting Sergeant Alexander Woollcott, who wrote for the *Stars and Stripes*, to refer to it as "a snappy young journal." Except for the identifiable contributions of occasional outsiders, Cain wrote the whole paper. Writing for the paper had enabled him to put into practice the rules of rhetoric he had taught himself at Washington College. As an Army newspaperman, Cain had enjoyed the pure act of recording the facts, especially when they obviously contributed to history. He had earned Malcolm's respect.

With the division preparing in May 1919 to return to the States, he and Malcolm were again placed on the KP roster, but they avoided it by again making themselves indispensable, as press agents for the returning division. Together they wrote a history of the division, and it was published that year, with part of it appearing in the *New York Times* on June 8 with no byline. He took pride in it.

He moved in with his parents in a suburb of Baltimore and returned to the *Sun*, at $30 a week, $20 more than when he started newspaper work in 1917. As a junior copy editor among eight others, he handled state copy, a dull job that he transformed into a circulation asset, winning the praise of the management. But only his sense of learning more about language kept him from being depressed over the fact that his aspiration to become a novelist or a playwright was going nowhere.

In January 1920, with reluctance but the best of intentions, he honored his pledge to marry Miss Clough. That her beauty lacked sexual voltage became immediately apparent, and there was an incompatibility between her schoolmarmish highbrow tastes, evolving out of her Eastern Shore squirearchy background, and his attitudes toward life, letters, love, and alcohol.

A visit late in 1920 from Gilbert Malcolm, who had become a very successful broker in Harrisburg, Pennsylvania, made Cain restless. An investment banker friend assured him that doom was the reverse side of Malcolm's brokerage boom. Cain got an offer from the president of the Baltimore Steamship Company who wanted him to go to Puerto Rico and concoct exposé articles on the governor. Realizing that he wouldn't be free to write as he felt, he declined, and stayed with the *Sun*, where he was assigned to cover developments in the volatile labor movement. Fascination with political and industrial strife qualified him to read about it, but not to write about it, so he took courses in labor problems at Johns Hopkins University.

He was required to read *Das Kapital*, but a writer who hit him much harder than Marx was Mencken, the Sage of Baltimore. One day he started to read a column called "The Clowns March In" with a sense of contempt for H. L. Mencken's pro-German position that had cast a shadow over his reputation during the war. He had long known that Mencken was a columnist on the *Sun*, celebrated beyond the Baltimore city limits, but still a sort of local wunderkind. Cain was so electrified by the style with which Mencken demolished the candidates for the presidential nomination that he went out and bought a copy of *The Smart Set*, edited by Mencken and George Jean Nathan, and began to read Mencken's books. He understood why the man was referred to variously as the American Shaw, Voltaire, or Rabelais.

In Mencken's *A Book of Prefaces*, the phrase "the virulence of the national appetite for bogus revelation" contained a familiar idea, but the style had a witty muscularity he had encountered nowhere else. "To the man with an ear for verbal delicacies—the man who searches painfully for the perfect word, and puts the way of saying a thing above the thing said—there is in writing the constant joy of sudden discovery, of happy accident." Aspiring writer, he grasped that passage fully. "The public . . . demands certainties. It must be told definitely and a bit raucously that this is true and that is false. But there are no certainties."

In *Prejudices, First Series*, 1919, the practicing journalist heard a powerful voice directly. With a few acrid phrases, Mencken liberated Cain the novelist from the inverted prose of Henry Sydnor Harrison's "100,000 word Christmas cards . . . simply sentimental bosh," and enthralled Cain the social commentator in the metallic prose of the enemy of the "booboisie." Mencken's prose complemented the colloquial fictional style of the only other writer Cain had consciously imitated: Ring Lardner. "She maybe ain't as pretty as Violet and Hazel but as they say beauty isn't only so deep."

For a Christmas present, Cain's mother had framed the copies of the *Lorraine Cross* that she had found in his rucksack. He hung them up with pride, but not until after he had felt the first impact of Mencken's style was he arrested one day by the syntax of one of his own framed pieces. It closely resembled the mannerisms of the man he vastly admired and now suspected himself of aping. But back in 1919, he had not yet read the Baltimore iconoclast. He decided that he and Mencken had been reading and assimilating the same books on theoretical rhetoric, Cain to prepare himself to teach, Mencken to ridicule professional rhetoricians in *The American Language*, which in turn was now a ready reference tool for Cain.

The articles and ideas he submitted to *The Smart Set* were rejected, but their correspondence made him feel Mencken was keeping him.

Typhoid fever serious enough nearly to paralyze him put Cain in a Baltimore hospital. Discharged from the hospital, still afflicted with debilitating side effects, he was attracted to what struck him as one of the most significant issues since the war: the question of treason as posed in the trial of twenty-three United Mine Workers in, ironically enough, the town where John Brown was tried, Charles Town, West Virginia. He questioned whether a riot provoked by mine owners qualifies as an act of treason against the state. He persuaded his editors to let him cover the trial. His series of reports and signed articles for the *Sun*'s editorial page made him a well-known figure in West Virginia and Maryland during the six months of the trial. The mine owners tried to get him fired for biased reporting, but an editor for the *Sun* verified, on the scene, Cain's facts. Despite threats from the state police, he stayed on the job, gathering facts that proved collusion between the state and the mine owners in their war with the union.

Encouraged by the reputation he had made for the quality of his writing for the paper on a major issue, he felt ready to get up from that iron park bench at the age of thirty and become a writer at last. Back in Baltimore, in June 1922, he queried the major magazines, but got the go-ahead only from Ellery Sedgwick at the *Atlantic Monthly*, who looked upon the *Sun*'s treatment, especially in Cain's pieces, of West Virginia's "difficult and dangerous" mining situation "as a public service of a high order."

Sitting well forward on the edge of the bench, about to plunge into an article for the nation's oldest and most prestigious publication, he felt this was his main chance to prove himself to his parents, to himself. The resources on which he drew were the styles and techniques of Doyle, Lardner, and Mencken. He had a confident grasp of the facts as they related to two very different men, William Blizzard, the local union official whose trial was the test case for all the other men indicted, and Colonel William Wiley, an enlightened mine owner who understood both sides and wanted an evenhanded justice. And Cain put into play his own convictions on the issues of unionism and treason.

As he wrote, Cain told himself how to talk to his readers, employing the rules of rhetoric, divested of the toga, sporting modern dress. "Listen, I went up there, I saw, I heard, I talked with people, walked around, gathered facts, I was a witness. I got the inside dope. I researched the historical background. Here it all is. I may look more like John L. Lewis than Walter Lippmann, but you can trust me. I may talk tough, out of the side of my mouth, and use slang, but I also can talk and write quite elegantly. This is about war, shootings, about virile union men and mine guards and state troopers," he told himself.

Even for the *Atlantic Monthly* crowd, the style and tone must be true to those tough elements. The title "The Battle Ground of Coal" promised

an account of the conflict of tremendous forces. Place the readers immediately and directly on the scene: "As you leave the Ohio River. . . ." Make
them feel the drama is on a grand scale: "there is being fought the bitterest and most unrelenting war in modern industrial history." Make them
see the setting and hear the voices on both sides speak: "If you get off
the train at Williamson, county seat of Mingo, you will be at the fighting front. People there will tell you that this struggle has been going on
for three years. They will tell you of the bloody day at Matewan, May 19,
1920, when ten men, including the mayor of the town, fell in a pistol
battle that lasted less than a minute. They will tell you of guerilla warfare
that went on for months. How Federal troops had to be called in twice
. . . The operators will tell you of attacks from ambush . . . how witnesses
for trials were mysteriously killed before they could testify." Show them
you can write a sentence: "This peculiarity of the coal market was the
reason for the basic wage-scale arrangement which gave all districts as
nearly equal chances as possible, and precluded the possibility that a mis-
calculated rate might put whole mining fields out of business altogether."
After that feint, let them have it with a city room punch: "The Union
feeds them, clothes them, and buries their dead." Remind the reader that
you are talking directly to him: "Recall that these people . . . had become
. . . picturesque characters in popular fiction." They require statistics: deal
them out. Let facts speak for themselves. Facts are concrete, but create for
them a context not only of relevance but of immediacy, a human urgency.
He wrote almost as if he were on a hot seat, in a witness box: be clear, be
accurate, be brief, be convincing. "This is not theorizing. This is precisely
what happens." Reason well, argue fairly, though the goal is to convince
readers of the necessity for ending industrial feudalism with total union-
ization of mines.

He sent it off, and hoped that the next time he saw it, thousands of
readers would, too.

Cain felt he had not exhausted the subject and that there was a different readership he could inform and persuade. The tone of quiet rea-
sonableness, spiked with occasional rhetorical flourishes to give the piece
dramatic immediacy, appropriate for the *Atlantic Monthly* audience, could
be dropped for the readers of the radical *Nation*. As if raising his voice to

address those in the rear of the courtroom, "Treason-to Coal Operators" laid Cain's position on the line.

He had gone up to Charles Town for the treason trial of Walter Allen. Readers usually begin with only a mild interest, even a certain reluctance. Galvanize them. "By a jury of his peers, packed against him and bearing instructions virtually proclaiming his guilt. On the flimsiest sort of evidence and with not the ghost of a chance at a fair trial from start to finish, Walter Allen, union miner, has been solemnly adjudged to be a traitor to that section of coal operator's real estate known as the sovereign State of West Virginia. . . . The selection of a jury was a farce." *Nation* readers would like the sound of this ending: "the prediction is hereby made that the conviction of Walter Allen will become one of the greatest issues, political, moral, and industrial, that the State of West Virginia has ever known."

When the October *Atlantic* came in, he felt the unique excitement every writer feels seeing his first important work in print. Writing the two articles on West Virginia mine wars had frustrated him, for fiction was what he urgently wanted to write. But they helped him learn to conceptualize, to reach for vivid detail, to remember, and they gave him opportunities to describe landscapes and people.

Now that he had the attention of some influential people, Cain felt the time was right to go to work on a novel. Firsthand observation of life in the minefields during a crisis convinced him that a conflict there might focus certain aspects of American life out of which he might fashion that great American novel people were talking about. And he liked the mountain people.

But Colonel Wiley had told him that a few weeks working in the mines would show him what a fool he had made of himself in his articles. So he felt he had to have been a miner to write about them. He decided to take a leave from the paper and go down there.

But first he sought the advice of his hero, Mencken. They had corresponded but had never met. Mencken came down to the city desk to talk with Cain. Since he had not written a novel himself, he didn't seem to have much to say. Cain felt Mencken had given him his "No. 5 act for young writers."

By November 1922, Cain was digging coal in Ward, West Virginia, proudly packing a United Mine Workers card. A miner saved him from an accident, but Cain's in with the management finally made him an outcast.

He left the minefields with an inside knowledge of both points of view, but an even stronger commitment to the miner's cause.

Back in Baltimore, he wrote three drafts of a novel that dealt not only with controversial political but sexual issues, such as incest. As a sort of literary model, he had Dos Passos's *Three Soldiers* in mind. The hero was a radical union organizer who was active in the march on Mingo in 1921. But he realized that the seasoned journalist's concern for authenticity, background, and inside dope had overwhelmed the novelist's desire to create and tell a story. He imagined that the grotesque speech of his homespun characters would wear out the patience of his readers, who would not share the intellectual's interest in labor themes anyway. "I simply cannot write a novel," he decided, and slunk back to the city desk, hoping nobody would bring up the subject of the great American novel.

But he was not certain that newspaper work was to be his fate at all. His attitude that facts in themselves lacked a certain dramatic emphasis made him a second-rate newspaperman. And he was going nowhere on the *Sun*, whose management treated him badly, though he felt he was making friends he would want to keep for life.

While he was looking around for new fields to conquer or to fail in, he launched upon another essay for the *Nation*. His changing attitudes about the minefields, his failure as a novelist, his disaffection as a straight newspaperman led him to take a sardonic approach. He set up his rhetorical strategy in the title, "West Virginia: A Mine-field Melodrama." Now he would develop his interest in the pure drama of events. His frustrated interest in opera predisposed him to see opera motifs. "A setting for a Nibelungen epic, revealing instead a sordid melodrama." His own appetite for and personal shrinking from drama led him to examine that element in the common man. He took a position aligned with the readership of neither the *Atlantic Monthly* nor the *Nation*. The technique objectified his material and theme, and the effect was that both labor and management looked ludicrous. "Mine guards ... were dubbed thugs, and took their places as permanent members of the cast, upstage, right, striding scowlishly about slapping their holsters while the trembling miner signed the open shop agreement. . . . Mr. Chafin's deputies did their work thoroughly, and soon a wail drifted down the stage. . . . 'They're a-murderin' the women an' children!' This is a very important line in the West Virginia libretto. It is always the cue for the big scene. . . . So far as I know the deputies have never murdered any women or children, but art is art, and it is a good line. Why sacrifice it?" Vary the pace. When it lags, up the voltage. "You arise in your seat. Stay. There is another act, the great courtroom scene." Climax: Give West Virginia "a century or so. Then possibly it will shoot the pianist and call for a new score."

The essay was accepted, and published June 1923, thirty-second in the *Nation's* "These United States" series.

2

Occupation: Newspaperman

As he felt his own career as a fiction writer go slack, Cain watched his aging father's second career, insurance, soar. As a member of the Board of Governors of St. John's College, Cain's father brought him together with Major Enoch Barton Garey, who was taking over as president and who offered Cain a job teaching two courses in journalism, one in English, at double his *Sun* salary. Cain suspected that what Garey really wanted was a press agent. Garey said, No, he wanted strictly a teacher, and Cain accepted.

Cain and Mary moved to Annapolis and lived on the campus in a faculty apartment, near the house where he was born and had lived until he was eleven, but the change of scene had no effect on the factors that made them an incompatible couple. Cain felt that she had come to see him as decidedly boorish with his city room bark and indiscreet flirtations with women, and to him she was a sexually cold snob. Nobody he knew could understand what they had seen in each other.

Just before he started teaching, Cain met Mencken for lunch in Baltimore, where they discussed a magazine called the *American Mercury* that Mencken, George Jean Nathan, and Alfred A. Knopf planned to start. Mencken wanted something from Cain for the premier issue. What Cain promised him was another piece out of his mine war experience. It was to be the first in a series called "American Portraits." Cain chose the labor leader, and wrote it while enjoying teaching journalism at St. John's.

Cain's attitude had developed from a wary admiration of the union leader in his first essay to the satirical tone in the third, to an almost farcical and decidedly cynical attitude as he set out in this one to describe the changes in clothes, house, popular culture tastes, and jargon of the laborer who slugs his way into the presidency of the union. He would lay out in comic strip panels a picture of the upper-lower-class workingman and his environment.

The device he had used intermittently in the first three essays, he would sustain throughout this one: He would render his criticisms through a mocking paraphrase of the coarse argot of his subject, giving it a ring of authenticity and authority, with the effect that the reader could hear Cain the expert on the subject and the subject himself speak in a single voice, while making distinctions between the two. "Most of the candidates will go around saying that this here committee is an important thing, now, and they had better git some fellers that know what they are doing and not none of this no-account element that is trying all the time to run things to suit theirself and don't know what they want nohow. . . ." By use of the old parallel structure and repetition of phrase device, he set up a tempo and pace that felt good as he typed. "They are of the sort that mop up the plate with bread" enabled him to get into and out of five sentence fragments very quickly by repeating the "that" syntax. "Whose women folk . . ." set up more "whose" phrases. "It is part of their nature" and "so this is he who" set up two more rhetorical beats that ended the riff. Anticipating the incredulous reader's objections, Cain spoke directly: "You may think I exaggerate," and gave testimony from personal experience. He had written a tour de force, still in the Lardner mode, with the Mencken bite.

The typesetter refused to set the essay. The cynical note on which Cain ended the piece—"Well, hell," the labor leader says, "I can always sell out to the operators"—might have been one stab too many. Seeing the first issue of a magazine that he knew would make literary history without his portrait of a labor leader was a sickening disappointment. What he found in the January 1924 *American Mercury* was "The Lincoln Legend" by Isaac H. Pennypacker, the lead essay, a poem by Theodore Dreiser, an essay by Carl Van Doren, a story by Ruth Suckow, an essay by James Gibbons Huneker, the famous music critic, a dialog on George Moore, a department called "Americana," and an essay that expressed some of his own disdain, "Aesthete: Model 1924" by Ernest Boyd. The editorial set forth the aim of the magazine: to present the truth in new ways, "to keep common sense as fast as they can, to belabor sham as agreeably as possible, to give a civilized entertainment."

When Cain's essay appeared in the second issue in February, he found himself in good company: a long play, *All God's Chillun Got Wings*, by Eugene O'Neill and a story by Sherwood Anderson, "Caught." The contributor's note on him misplaced him at the University of Maryland and called him a newspaperman specializing in labor news. Mencken told him that Sinclair Lewis had written from London: "Christ, that was a lovely article by Mr. James Cain."

Cain was satisfied with the quality of his teaching, but he was having trouble both in the halls of academe and in the bowers of domesticity. President Garey caused a student strike when he expelled four boys without a hearing of the evidence. Cain insisted that an injustice had been done, and that faculty should have by right participated. "I'm a member of the faculty, and the charter of the college says he runs it with the faculty's assistance. I don't stand for it." Although he rallied the faculty to do their duty under the charter to oppose such high-handed tactics, he tried in other ways to restore calm. He resigned, but agreed to serve out the year. Something about the way he had conducted himself made him have serious misgivings about himself. He wondered whether his convictions and the storm of controversy they aroused balanced out. Otherwise, it had been a good year.

Cain's attraction to women had produced no ongoing love affairs. His marital status had scared off several women. But he met one in New York that he wanted to continue seeing: Elina Tyzsecka, a Finnish woman who spoke no English.

On February 18, 1924, he told Mary he was leaving her. Cain's father came down to reason with him, but his mission failed.

Facing the end of his interim job at St. John's, Cain turned to his typewriter and sketched another portrait in acid. What happens when a reporter metamorphoses into an editorial writer? How does the editorial writer's idealism evolve out of the reporter's cynicism? Cast the reader right off in the role of a reporter and speak directly to the reader through him. "You are, I shall suppose, a cub reporter on a newspaper."

Work it from that angle, as an editor would say. Give impressions of the reporter's routine life on a paper. You wonder who that man wearing the green eyeshade is. You start to ask. "Well, Well, save your breath. Pull up your chair and I shall tell you who he is. The man is a Priest. He is Keeper of the Soul of the American People. He sits alone in his office, high above the madding crowd, and as he sits, soft voices rise from below. When he hears them, he passes into a long, long dream, and as he dreams, his hand (which holds a pencil) begins to write and write and write. . . ." He is the man who writes the editorials. "Like yourself, he started as a cub." He slowly developed a veneer of wisdom, a posture of cynicism, a hard-boiled manner. Now take them through the development of this cub reporter stage by stage into an editorial writer, using cliché expressions of the newspaper world as the milieu, until "he finds it pays better to be Constructive than Cynical, or even Hard-boiled. . . . So he begins to orient things with a view to the Public Interest involved . . . By now he is a real expert on all public matters." Now posit a typical news story and contrast the way the cub reporter would have written it up as a cynic, his honest reactions, with the way he must write it up as in an editorial. This way readers will follow the mental process and the strategy that produce an editorial. Now drop the role-playing, and wind up by talking directly, as Cain, as a reporter who has remained a hard-boiled cynic, to the reader. "If you find a single editorial that rises above this general level cut it out and paste it in your hat. You won't find it again." "Composing in his own right, his tempo may be sizzling fast, but his editorials will move at a decorous *andantino*." The subject was language and writing. On the assumption that one's writing style should never depart very far from one's talking style, Cain pointed out that "certainly he never talks any such ponderous blather." The distance is greatest in editorials. Cain was aware of his own inclination to lecture in the editorial mode, and that his hard-boiled manner helped him keep his balance.

Even as the first two portraits were appearing in the *Mercury*, Cain was writing another, aware of his contribution to a new voice shaping American opinion and attitudes. He had found the mere facts of reporting wanting. He had found editorial commentary on the facts wanting.

He had found the scholastic appraisal of life wanting. Self-doubt, self-appraisal were the impetus to doubt everything around him, to analyze, size up, and judge. The interrogative rhetorical device was appropriate.

Reading *Who's Who* as a child had made him always keenly aware of the look, speech, and behavior of professional types. Why had he expected so much of each subject, and why had they delivered so little? Did each appeal to him because each was a facet of his own personality? He knew each subject so well, he could get the subject's stream of consciousness going and ride with it, while maintaining his own distance, so that when he spoke in his own "I," he jolted the reader to attention and socked home his own attitude and point.

Having looked back at labor leaders and editorial writers, he looked right under his nose at the pedagogue, using "a perfect type" at St. John's. Go easy at first. Many *Mercury* readers will be *Atlantic* readers taking a peek at the brash new kid on the block. Open with a gently satirical physical description of the subject, of his routine ways. Let me introduce you to him. "When you meet him" this is what you experience. Show how he can numb the mind with charming equivocation on any subject. Spin off as much of his language as will give a sense of his mind, his sensibility, for the subject's own language is the raw material of these portraits, the delineation comes out of the subject's own mouth. If the reader first hears him clearly, he will see him clearly, know him deeply. When you leave him, "You inhale deeply, blow a cobwebby sensation from your nose and cheeks, and pray that you may meet some ribald lout who will hie with you to the bootlegger's and tell you in plain language, without syllogisms, that you are full of fleas."

"Why is he such a disappointment? Why does he blight every subject with his moldy, cobwebby logic? Why so much dialectic and so little sense?" Let that sink in. Open Section III with: "Possibly I presume in diagnosing his trouble, but I think it is his incurable hankering for the posture of wisdom." Mimicking a typical faculty meeting, Cain conveyed his criticism through the catalog of academic clichés. Was this an attack on his father, masked as an attack on the type who had expelled his father, on the types from which Cain himself was fleeing? Cain imagined "Pedagogue: Old Style" appearing in the *Mercury*.

The trace of tuberculosis detected before he went into the Army had continued to be a problem, exacerbated by alcohol. A bad mustard-gas attack had aggravated his incipient TB, and in the summer of 1924, he had to go into a sanatorium at Sabillasville. But the St. John's controversy, the breakup of his marriage, and the aggravation of his lung problem left him feeling he was on the end of the plank. He came out of another major seminar of stocktaking with the feeling that he was at a turning point in his life. Until then, he had a driving compulsion to avoid being a failure, to amount to something, to be a credit to his father, to win admiration from his mother. But learning he had TB had relieved him of that. Who can hold a lunger to high ambition? Thinking he had so little time to live, no longer envisioning some high-pressure career, he began doing what he wanted to do. What he wanted to do was write. While Mencken was still accepting and publishing his portraits, he would continue with those for a while. He wrote two in the sanatorium with little diminution of energy.

In "Politician Female," speaking as himself directly to the reader, Cain used no overall strategy as he had in the first three essays. He stated a thesis that applied to all his subjects so far in various ways. "Though I can't comprehend what good a woman politician accomplishes, I am thoroughly sensitive to how she looks while she goes about her business. If I am blind to her as a public force, I nevertheless vibrate to her every glance and posture as a mime in the great American drama. It is this glancing and posturing that I wish to discuss—not the inner phenomena, but the outer." Her mind is on her "trappings and outer show, as every other sane person's mind is." Cain did not exclude himself. "Well, this outer show is precisely what I want to inquire into."

This was another target of his fascination with the explicit, not the implicit in all things, with his compulsion to examine exteriors, surfaces. The best model for the outer show is opera. Here was a chance to express some of his attitudes about women. "Her appeal to the imagination . . . must carry something of the sinister in it." "We women! What a hideous phrase . . . Females in wholesale lots!" "Woman . . . shines best as a solo instrument." To prove his point, he described an exception to his charges against female politicians, a lady on the Washington political stage, "a twenty minute egg, "who is completely effective dramatically," because "she plays a solo game," as Cain's mother always had, as Mary never had.

And while he was at it, he had might as well demolish politicians altogether. He opened "High Dignitaries of State" with the declaration: "It is clear that politics under democracy, on its visible levels, is an impossible trade for heroes. The man who seeks romance there is doomed to disappointment." Let others appraise their substance, Cain would deal with the "way they look and sound, their effectiveness as dramatic figures." How do they look center stage in the spotlight? Do their acts play?

Lacking a well-defined type to bring more and more sharply in focus as the piece developed, Cain put in his own opinions, couched in such key terms as "glamour," "dramatic appeal," "romance," and in vivid phrases and generalizations, enhanced by startling images and metaphors. At center stage, the solo performance was now his. He set two concepts in contrast: power and service. The power of Napoleon, as opposed to the service of the typical American politician. The one was appealingly dramatic, the other totally lacking in drama. Cain admired men who "shoot the bones for the whole pile." Though they had something of the sinister about them, "they were in unusually close touch with brute reality . . . magnificent cynics . . . on a heroic and shocking scale . . . what aglitter, what a hypnotic lure!" The average man would rather be Napoleon with his power than Lincoln with his service. Ironically, the politician in modern democracy is neither. He plays the role of the common man, and the aspiration to serve him raises him only a step above the herd he serves. "I have been after it for sometime now, and I am not sure that I have got it, but I shall try and get down what I think it is."

"The source of all dramatic appeal in public men, I think, is power." "There can be no real magnificence without a foot on somebody's neck." "Service, as an ingredient of drama, is very defective." It "won't develop. It won't orchestrate." One of his central convictions was that "Service can be effective dramatically only when it costs something to perform." The common soldier for instance goes "where the shells were whickering." Only the political boss has "glamor, a pure incandescent glow," that derives from power. "It is the irony of drama that such men, who think nothing of Humanity and only of themselves, should have such incomparable appeal." Leave readers pondering the fact that "Harding has a memorial!"

Though he was consciously a debunker in the Mencken manner, Cain felt a compulsion to demonstrate a fair-mindedness toward his target, a willingness, even an eagerness, to acknowledge the earned possibilities of the most negative situation.

During the summer "seminar" of "taking the cure" at the sanatorium, Cain was compelled once more to think over his life and to look realistically at his future.

Wasn't he still sitting on that park bench telling himself he would be a writer? But despite the domestic, professional, and physical deterioration that had marked the past few years, a great creative outpouring had produced five major essays, published in a major new magazine, an opinion molder, whose spirit he had caught so well that his essays were a force working in that spirit, among other writers with major reputations at a time when maximum attention was on the magazine. His coalfield essays for the *Atlantic* and the *Nation* were not forgotten. But none of these, he felt, made him the writer the Voice Out of the Blue had in mind. He had proven that he could teach, that he could cover major events as a reporter, and he had learned that neither a teacher nor a reporter was what he was. He had been a good soldier. Had failed as a husband. Had been only now and then a fairly creditable son. What did he want? Money and fame. A write up in *Who's Who*. "If you want to make money," a banker friend had told him, "go where the money is." There was money in New York City. Also in New York was Elina. And maybe fame in the future, perhaps in the theater. If his father could start over at fifty-eight, couldn't Cain at thirty-two?

Released from the sanatorium and free of commitments for the first time in years, he set out to Manhattan.

Instructed by his doctor to seek a sitting-down job, Cain, armed with a letter from Mencken, called on Arthur Krock, assistant to publisher Ralph Pulitzer, at the *World* building, Manhattan's tallest, on Park Row. Cain had evaluated the editorial section, not with the intention of applying for a job writing editorials, but for a job as editor of the page opposite, which he felt was ailing, and he was ready to say why. What it needed was an article-chaser to bring in outside points of view. He wanted to make a distinct contribution to a paper that deserved its reputation as intelligent, witty, and reliable. Herbert Bayard Swope had an impressive reputation. The new man in charge of editorials, Walter Lippmann, was highly respected, and his writers, Maxwell Anderson, Charles Merz, Allan Nevins, John Heaton, and W. O. Scroggs seldom fit Cain's *Mercury* descriptions. The regular columns on the page opposite by Franklin P. Adams, Heywood Broun, and Laurence Stallings were usually excellent.

As Krock took him up to the office of Walter Lippmann under the golden dome, Cain suspected he was getting a genteel brush off. The tall, stocky, handsome, completely self-possessed man, two years younger than Cain, somewhat curtly interviewed him. Feeling a little truculent at being cast in a possible role he had satirized in the *Mercury*, Cain analyzed the editorial section's weaknesses and offered to "orchestrate" the themes of the editorials. Lippmann's request to see some specimen Cain pieces surprised him. But he asked his mother to send up from Baltimore copies of his *Atlantic*, *Nation*, and *Mercury* articles.

He shared an apartment with Malcolm Ross, editorial writer on the *World*, in Greenwich Village. A few days later, he was summoned to Lippmann's office. He told Cain it was as much his ability to talk grammatically and fluently in complete sentences as it was his articles that convinced him Cain could write the kind of editorials he wanted, if Cain was willing to start on a trial basis. He was. Lippman instructed him to write several editorials.

He perused the day's newspapers for a subject, passing up the think pieces on the Teapot Dome Scandals, the tariff, Calvin Coolidge, the coming elections, the crisis in the Ruhr, none of which sparked any ideas. He remembered Lippmann's *Public Opinion* of two years earlier as an attempt to intellectualize a subject not really intellectual, with prose the polar opposite of Lardner's or Mencken's: "I attempt, therefore, to argue that the serious acceptance of the principle that personal representation must be supplemented by representation of the unseen fact would alone permit a satisfactory decentralization, and allow us to escape from the

The *New York World* editorial staff. Seated: Charles Merz, Walter Lippman, John L. Heaton. Standing: William O. Scroggs, Cain, Allan Nevins, Rollin Kirby, L.R.E Paulin. YALE UNIVERSITY

intolerable and unworkable fiction that each of us must acquire a competent opinion about all public affairs."

Like all the working stiffs in the news department of the *Sun*, he had always thought of editorial writers as elderly trained seals who wrote think pieces. "You must be in favor of motherhood," Cain kept telling himself, "and against the man-eating shark." With an imp of the perverse squatting on his shoulder, he got off a bit of gallows humor passionately proclaiming that the man-eating shark *is* motherhood. "She brings her young forth alive, provides their food, minds her own business, keeps quiet, and molests not unless molested." He cut two more editorials from the same cloth, sneaked down the stairs, tossed them into Lippmann's basket, slunk out into the street, and started thinking about other job possibilities. He later told Malcolm Ross he had blown it. But Ross showed him the evening paper, and there was the shark, and Ross was laughing.

Cain reported for work the next day. Unable to imagine anything appropriate, he turned in more "japes," and saw them emerge from the presses. They began to excite those trivial controversies that continue for weeks in letter columns. But Lippmann not only printed them, he told Cain they were exactly what he wanted, now that Maxwell Anderson had quit writing the human interest editorials to write plays full-time. Anderson's and Stallings's play *What Price Glory?* was a smash hit. Cain, the expert on what was wrong with editorials, who also had playwriting aspirations, became an editorialist at $20 a day, taking up these subjects, among others: baseball, a woman matador, truth serum, American opera, the disappearance of two men in the arctic, lighthearted "japes" all aimed at the average man and woman.

But he was still uneasy. He was a fake. Those pieces were only impudent admissions of failure. "If you think you're flopping," said Krock, "you're wrong. You're doing fine, and Lippmann is very pleased." When he got serious, with pieces on politics and international affairs, Cain noticed a slight chill in Lippmann's attitude. Krock set him straight: "Pleasant, light pieces, with enough intellect in them to spike up the letter column and be worth publishing, are tough to get. That's what Lippmann wants from you."

"You mean this nonsense I write is worth something?" Cain asked. "They pay for stuff like that? They actually pay you." They paid Cain $125 a week, giving him a three-year contract on the basis of work well done. Cain, who did not want to write editorials, called "idiotorials" at the *Sun*, told his mother, "You've been proclaiming for years that I don't have a good sense, and events have proved you're right—but in New York they pay you for it."

But he had a job and he had a girl, Elina, who still couldn't speak English but who made Cain very happy. He had been taken by pretty faces before, but he had never encountered the strange quality of Finnish gravity that Elina had. Cain made Elina part of his work-life when he wrote a piece that appeared New Year's Day, 1925 on the op-ed page called "How the Finns Keep Fit" and put her name on it.

Seeing her frequently made the first year in New York all the more exciting. Like Cain, she was not yet divorced. She worked as a governess and kept a home for nurses. Except for a little German, their relationship was uniquely physical, but not just in the sexual sense. Kisses and pats and looks expressed everything. Love with a touch of lunacy. Feeling the need for more privacy, Cain left Malcolm Ross's apartment and moved into three rooms at 11 Van Nest Place in the Village off Seventh Avenue. He liked knowing that his friends saw him living in sin.

To focus more dramatically on American types, Cain decided to use a popular form, the satirical dialogue sketch made popular by such writers as Charles Erskine Scott Wood in the old *Masses* and by Ring Lardner in *What of It?* He had already focused on speech as it revealed character traits and on the function of self-dramatization in American behavior. It seemed more appropriate and effective to give it an objective dramatic setting, with greater attention on the printed page to conversation than to action, which is the major demand of stage plays. It was more like radio than theater. He would continue to put self-incriminating words into the mouths of his characters, otherwise the devices of the dialogue were in total contrast to the techniques of his essays. Cain would have to shut up and listen to his characters talk, give readers a taste of the old Ike Newton colloquialisms that excited him when he was twelve and ever since. The dramatic immediacy of voices inadvertently making points for Cain's criticism appealed to him.

County government was a good target, specifically its commissioners, "Servants of the People." The chairman, the superintendent of the county almshouse, his janitor, and an inmate gather in an office in the courthouse to get to the bottom of these newspaper stories about the burning of dead paupers without proper Christian service, a situation that produced some grim humor. The inmate saw the superintendent and the janitor burn the corpses in the furnace. "I hope Christ may kill me if I didn't find a jawbone down here. I got that jawbone, right here in my coat pocket." It is far less expensive to burn than to bury. "Hope Christ may kill me, I never knew they was news man," says the inmate. The repetition of that phrase as one revelation after another is made would intimate to the reader that the superintendent and the janitor will dispose of the informer himself.

Mencken wanted more "American Portraits" from Cain, although after publishing seven—on two Washington job holders, the medical doctors, a Babbitt emeritus, the advertising agent, one county banker, by Harvey Fergusson and others—the *Mercury* dropped the series title.

Well, the American pastor was ridiculous and contemptible, wasn't he? And wasn't his role dramatically impossible? In his conception of religion and of places of worship, he lacked a sense of poetry, beauty, and imagination. Cain's wit and vicious attitude needed more space for this one. Set them up with a flowing description of the popular attitude. "Of all the roles in which man may be cast, the one least likely to be ridiculous is that of divine service ... the role itself is dramatically solemn and moving." Now, hit them with the contrast. "Wherefore, it is all the more surprising that the typical American man of God in these our days is so loathsome, such a low, greasy buffo, so utterly beneath ridicule, so fit only for contempt. I refer, of course, to the evangelical brother. He is the only authentic American product.... and his role is therefore dramatically impossible." "He did away with beautiful music, and began yowling mean hymns. In short, he did a wholesale trading of beauty for ugliness." The "lyric spirit ... froze up in him." He preached "religion you could wolf down like meat and gravy, religion you didn't have to fast all night to understand." He became "the American hawker and salesman, the man of trade ... he learned the jargon of the advertising man, the go-getter. He learned to laugh the har-har-har of the town boaster, to clap his lay brother on the back.... He stuck electric lights in the steeple cross." "I know where of I speak." "It is simply none of his damn business what happens to my soul." "As to whether there is a God or not, I have no means of knowing and cannot say. But this much I know. If we are to believe in God, the only concept of Him acceptable to imaginative man is a God ... of thunder and ocean, of the hushed forest."

Now make the main point. "Of late years I have come to the conclusion ... either through my own feeling or through watching others that there is almost an identical quality of exaltation in romantic love, in religious experience, and in aesthetic experience." "The pastor bellows about hell, and the same half-frightened half-participatory shiver run all through me as come up stepping into a brothel." As young Cain had. "Excitement fills the air. A trance descends from above—a trance, it is true slightly tinged with the bestial, but still a trance, and everybody is entitled to a trance," including his own readers, one of whom was E. W. Howe, author of the famous novel *Story of a Country Town*, who wondered at Cain's boldness and admired his style, "not excelled by the best magazines at home or abroad."

When his colleagues, including Lippmann, attacked immorality in Eugene O'Neill's *Desire Under the Elms* and other plays, Cain had to get permission, to be noted in the heading of his piece, to vent his outrage elsewhere—in the liberal *Nation*. He enjoyed working both sides of the street, editorializing on editorials. "One of the greatest blows ever struck at the American theater came when the *New York World* turned its guns on current Broadway plays.... Coming from the greatest libertarian newspaper in the country, it has played havoc." The *World* had enunciated two fallacious and intolerable principles: 1. That "the line must be drawn somewhere. 2. That artistic excellence or intent is to be the measure of how much obscenity is permissible in a given instance." Cain's simple aesthetic rule was that "one man's art is another man's poison." His colleagues called him "an immoral reprobate whom nothing can shock," so he used that phrase about himself throughout. He turned the *World*'s own logic against its comic strip, "Mutt and Jeff," which he found offensive. "If a reprobate like me finds it low, then it must be low indeed." But "it is published because it sells papers.... the motive is commercial, pure and simple. Papers have to be sold to make possible the lofty idealism that uniformly marks the editorial pages. So, then, we have a most uncomfortably close analogy between the theatrical business and the newspaper business." "Do we need to be protected by the *World* against our free, white, sovereign, independent, 100 per cent American selves?" The *World* eventually dropped its crusade, its support of a "citizen's jury." He anticipated a reaction from Lippmann. He never got one.

In spite of his aversion to it, Cain realized that he functioned amazingly well in a role apparently inimical to his nature, personality, and interests. The controversies many of his editorials generated, filling the letters columns with reactions pro and con, struck him as foolish. "This Evil Must Cease" was a diatribe against the "Pie Trust," for spiking its products with cornstarch, "so they will stack," instead of putting in honest filling, with free-running juice and fine flavor. Reactions to his items on food indicated a subject of major interest to the popular mind. Cain's simple inquiry as to how hogs are called caused a national furor, chronicled at length in *Literary Digest* and noted on NBC radio. Cain saw the beginning of hog calling as a national institution. "A propos nothing whatever, what does one do on meeting the man-eating tiger?" Many readers offered expert, sometimes contradictory, advice. The delivery from Virginia of a box of six enormous frogs climaxed a prolonged frog-leg debate. "How can a sailor be washed off his ship by a wave, then, by that selfsame wave be washed back aboard?" So many answers came in that Lippmann finally bellowed: "I'm sick of that damned wave! Cut it off!" These inflated, prolonged, ridiculous controversies taught Cain a great deal about ways to stir the popular imagination and emotions.

But about half of his editorials were serious. He was glad to have a chance to write about music, to lecture readers on Beethoven's shortcomings, to point out that the national anthem was unsingable. He took Deems Taylor's place for a while as regular music critic, but quit when he realized his expertise failed to impress himself enough, although some compared him with the celebrated James Huneker. The Scopes trial in the summer of 1925 stuck Cain as a "clown's show," "an uproarious comedy," that did not warrant the attention Lippmann and Mencken gave it. On July 25, Cain gave it a single shot, bull's eye, attacking the same traits in the American religious and political character his *Mercury* essays satirized.

Having overheard the county commissioners, Cain thought readers of the *Mercury* ought to listen to the small town commissioners as they meet on the second floor of the Water Witch Fire Engine House to find a way to do right by a bogus hero in such a way as to satisfy all factions. Such key terms as "initiation," "password," "motto" and fraternal order "grip" pass from lip to lip. One man runs on "in the tempo of the intermezzo out of *Cavalleria Rusticana*," Cain indicates in a stage direction. With dubious logic derived from dubious ethics, they resolve their dilemma, confident they have placated all the warring fraternal orders. Cain mailed off his second dialogue.

In his essays, Cain had examined seven specimen American types. Now what about general traits in the American Character? Anti-altruistic, scornful of the reform element in American society, he would perform a pathology on the disease of Service, the most despised manifestation of which was Prohibition, now in its fifth year. Because he wanted the satisfaction of being in possession of the facts, always feeling the obligation *to know* from experts what he was talking about, he researched the subject of Progress and the specific cause of Service, and he would cite his sources. "I propose herein to isolate the bacillus of Service, the itch to make the world better." Service is peculiar to America. Only since 1900, twenty-five years, has it plagued us. "Critics accord it all the honors of a lucid idea. . . . I shall fall into no such error. I shall treat all these fine schemes as having no objective validity at all. I shall regard them as a social phantasmagoria, whirling clouds and specks in a national fever dream, and so doing, I shall try to discover what has brought them into being." Service is the business neither of superiors nor of boobs, but of the mediocre. "Factors must be found which operate in this particular place and this particular time."

"These factors, I think, like the factors which produce cancer, are two: there is a general agent and a specific one." "The general agent, I think, has its roots simply in the appetite for drama. That is, the Servist yearns to shine before his fellows and himself, to play a role which is heroic. Unconsciously, he seeks an escape from the meanness of his everyday existence." "It is my contention that this satisfaction is dramatic, that it has nothing to do with good and evil, pain or joy. . . ." He is "showing off," as in a parade, to "the despair and envy of those who line the sidewalks."

He was describing more clearly now a dominant strain in all his American portraits. In a long middle section, he gave them the historical, philosophical background, with doses of Darwin, Nietzsche, especially Spencer, using a musical metaphor. "Other nations have remained immune to the disease which is a plague among us." "America, I take it, needs more artificial bolstering up of personal roles than any nation on earth. . . . Since in America, all men are equal, all men must justify their existence, must get ahead." "But in the nature of things all men cannot attain success." The "great national adventure" ended in 1900. "The West was won, and the rest was faint perfume. Giving up that glamorous frontier was a wrench." "When we were brought up short by the Pacific Ocean, the spell of a destiny had become too strong to be cast off."

"Well, can anything be done about a cure?" We must strip service of its glory. "All that is necessary is to make it impossible for the Servist to derive a thrill from his work, and ridicule is the obvious way to do this." "I do not speak without clinical data." Invoke personal authority. Tell them how my old friend Hamilton Owens, editor of the *Sun*, opposed service of all kinds. "He ridicules it, mocks it, tweeks its nose and pulls its whiskers." "If we refuse not only to get in line, but jeer at him and withhold the admiration he so plainly desires, I do not see that he has received anything but his deserts. His plea that he works for God and morality is all bosh." "Actually, he works for his own aggrandizement. . . . Progress be damned! I am a fundamentalist." The piece exhibited all the merciless invective of Sinclair Lewis lacerating a go-getter. It went off to Mencken.

When Elina had to return to Finland on business, Cain spent one last night with her in the Willard Hotel in Washington, and vowed to be true while she was gone.

But one day, in front of the Pulitzer building, Cain ran into a girl from the editorial department. That she knew Cain loved Elina made no difference to her. Their strange relationship was purely sexual, though without the kind of physical communication that made Cain's attraction to Elina magical and profound.

In December 1925, Cain learned that Battling Siki, a very popular boxer out of Senegal, French West Africa, who had knocked out Georges Carpentier in Paris, and whose triumphs and dissipations made good copy, had been shot to death in Hell's Kitchen on the West Side by a mysterious assailant, provoked, it was conjectured, in a barroom brawl. When the *New Yorker* reprinted his editorial on Siki, Cain regarded it as the greatest moment in his life. The rumors that it almost got the Pulitzer Prize made him feel even better.

As the author of nine articles, Cain had become one of the *Mercury's* major contributors, and one of Mencken's inner circle of friends. They often had breakfast on the train from Baltimore to New York as Cain returned from a weekend with his folks and Mencken went up to work a few days on the *Mercury*. They drank together in Mencken's hotel room at the Algonquin (Mencken shunned the famous Round Table group) and Cain was the only out-of-town member of Mencken's Saturday Night

Club. Like Dreiser, Sinclair Lewis, and Willa Cather, Cain was marked for promotion by Mencken.

At the house of Woollcott's brother Willie, Mencken got Cain together with Philip Goodman, who had earlier expanded Mencken's horizons beyond Baltimore by publishing *In Defense of Women*. He regarded Goodman as an advertising genius. Goodman had been producer of *Poppy*, which had made a star of W. C. Fields in 1923. "Isn't that a silhouette for you?" asked Mencken, pointing to Goodman, who had an impressive paunch.

Having admired Cain's *Mercury* dialogues, Goodman wanted to persuade him to write a play. Remembering the West Virginia material of his failed novels, he told Goodman about the belief among coal miners in the imminent Second Coming of Christ. Goodman commented, "It's the measure of their despair. There's your play, Mr. Cain."

Goodman's enthusiasm inspired Cain to start immediately. And with Elina in Europe still, he had evenings and weekends free. He worked in a theatrical climate created in the past two years by Sidney Howard's *They Knew What They Wanted*, Maxwell Anderson's and Laurence Stallings's *What Price Glory?*, Eugene O'Neill's *Desire Under the Elms*, George Kelly's *Craig's Wife*, and John Howard Lawson's *Processional*.

The audience sees a coal-miner's wife, Linda Hicks, sitting at a window, watching for the Second Coming of The Savior. The miners are on strike. Her husband, Buzz, is not much count, her son Oakey was crippled in a mine accident, and their adopted daughter Sally Jewell shares their misery. The times are right for Jesus to come and Linda, a hysterical, superstitious fanatic, intends to be the first to see him. Sure enough, the Savior comes down the road, pretending to be Syd Gody, a charming, self-confident miner who also preaches fire and brimstone. Syd convinces her to make love to him, but she half-convinces him that he is the Savior and that he can work a miracle to prove it: He must heal her crippled son. Then the miners will follow their Savior to victory.

Those were the elements that appealed to Goodman, whose many talents evolved out of an understanding of what would appeal to an audience. What happens when Syd fails to heal Oakey? Oakey figures out what's going on with his mother and Syd and cusses Syd so stormily that

Syd confesses and offers him a gun to shoot him. But Oakey accidentally shoots himself and dies. The miners think Syd has murdered Oakey. They post Linda's husband Buzz as a guard and go for the sheriff. Cain imagined a double twist in which Sally Jewell comes into the tent, sees Oakey shot to death, and runs hysterically out of the tent, and Buzz Hicks, drunk, mistakes her for Syd, and shoots her. When the miners win their strike, Syd refuses to take credit, denies he is Jesus, and goes to work in the mines. Linda's faith remains strong, and she rejects her husband for Syd.

Goodman liked Cain's play and stuck on it the title *Crashing the Pearly Gates*, then changed it to *Crashing the Gates*, both of which Cain hated.

Crashing the Gates was tried out in Stamford, Connecticut, February 26, 1926, produced by Goodman, starring Charles Bickford who had argued for a new kid named James Cagney instead. At dress rehearsal, George S. Kaufman declared: "You've got a show. The next question is: Do they like it?" "Outrage" was the more accurate word for what "they" felt about the sacrilegious theme and the obscene language. Many walked out. That night, Cain took out the profanity, but in Worcester, Massachusetts, the audience reaction was only a little less hostile. When *Variety* called the last act "a mess," Cain tried to imagine changes but failed. The Worcester *Telegram* said the play was "truly heroic . . . brilliantly written." But it closed in two weeks, and Cain was plunged into the mood of failure he had felt when writing the West Virginia novels. It taught Cain a few things about writing, mainly that you should never jeopardize a big design by insisting on small imperfections, such as the profanity in Oakey's scene in which he attacks his mother and Syd. It had occurred to neither Cain nor Goodman that profanity in a play about a minefield Jesus would be objectionable to an audience. Until then, Cain had used profanity in his writing to the extent that men use it in speech, for cadence, not out of a compulsion to be realistic. Cain abruptly abandoned it almost entirely in revisions of this play.

One day Goodman introduced Cain to Vincent Lawrence, a tall, gaunt man who looked debonair, but who talked the art of playwriting like a cross between a Syd Gody evangelist and a Broadway wise guy. Goodman had produced Lawrence's *Love Among the Married*. George Jean Nathan called Lawrence "the greatest light comedy writer in the

United States." For about six months, Cain and Lawrence wrestled with the play, retitled *Jubilee*. It appealed to Lawrence's sense of melodrama, but one day, Lawrence exclaimed, "Goddamn it!" throwing up the window of Cain's apartment on East 19th Street in the Village, "Let's let some of this smoke out of here! Listen, Cain, I'm not paying five-fifty to see a play about a guy that tried to be Jesus but couldn't be. I'm capable of that myself. This guy has to be Jesus or someone must think he is." A dictum Cain knew he would never forget.

Cain rewrote it to suit Lawrence, and Goodman announced it, to star Louis Wolheim, who had played Captain Flagg in *What Price Glory?*, but when Wolheim took a Hollywood offer instead, Cain let it die, with some relief.

Goodman, like Lawrence, taught Cain a sense of what works in theater, but also, as a phenomenal advertising man, he taught him about newspapers, analyzing the *World*'s weaknesses and the reading habits of the public. Goodman's comments were based on insights into the heart of things rather than on cheap mercantilism. They helped shape Cain's awareness, as a fiction writer, of his readers. Goodman impressed Cain as being the wittiest man he had ever met. Goodman, along with Mencken, often expressed a kind of reverence for Cain's literary talent. At this time in his life, Cain needed encouragement from men he respected.

But how long, if Goodman was right, would he be a newspaperman? "The *World* is for sale," Goodman said, one evening in the spring of 1926. "Interesting, if true," Cain replied, one of his favorite qualifiers meant to defuse pompous certainty. Cain challenged Goodman to buy it. He tried, and failed, but Cain began to notice signs the *World* itself was failing as tensions grew among its leadership. The *World* offered Swope, whose life seemed a grand posture, a stage on which to perform his tough executive act, one that fascinated Cain. Lippmann lacked Cain's appreciation for shadow play, insisting on more substance. Watching tension develop between Lippmann and Arthur Krock, the two men he respected most on the *World*, was more excruciating. Krock moved to the *Times* in May 1927.

In the *Mercury*'s notes on contributors, Cain continued to bill himself as a newspaperman. But not until that fact was monumentalized in *Who's Who* would it count where it mattered. In 1926, he received the questionnaire from Marquis Publishers, and in the 1925–1927 edition, just above his father's own entry, he felt proud to see "James Mallahan Cain, newspaper man" appear for the first, he hoped, of many times.

> *CAIN, James Mallahan, newspaper man. b. Annapolis, Md., July 1, 1892. s. James William and Rose Cecilia (Mallahan) C.. A.B. Washington Coll., Chestertown, Md., 1910, A.M., 1917. m. Mary Rebekah Clough, of Church Hill, Md., Jan. 17, 1920. Mem. Staff Baltimore American, 1917-18, Baltimore Sun, 1918-23. prof. journalism, St. John's Coll., Annapolis, Md., 1923-24. editorial writer New York World since 1924. Served as pvt. (1st class) Hdqrs. Troop, 79th Div., U.S.A., with A. F. F., 1918-19. editor in chief Lorraine Cross, official newspaper 79th Div., 1919. Democrat, Contbr. to maga. Home: 11 Vannest Pl., New York, N. Y.*

Cain had an idea for a third dialogue, focusing on the sheriff of a small town. What if the ghost of a "nigger" returned to the spot when he had been hanged? A deputy and a constable tell the sheriff about seeing it there, howling, spinning around. The ghoul's friend was scheduled to hang soon. The two had tried to hang themselves at first. Or had it come looking for the sheriff, who was at the pool hall? "It wasn't when *we* hung him, no such. It was when *you* hung him," they tell the sheriff. "Just lay off this here *we* stuff." The sheriff said, "I been looking for him to come back." He had not been convinced that the two "niggers" were guilty, but folks around there were glad those two had rid the country of "that Bohunk." The constable reckoned anyway they were guilty of something else just by being "niggers." As they talked over the situation, Cain enjoyed making them say things like, "He kind of held his head on the side, like he had a crick in his neck," and other expressions using "neck," and one of his favorite dialect expressions, "I hope my die." Too bad, the constable observed, folks weren't in a lynching mood. Maybe he was not after "me nohow," says the sheriff. "Just looking for his friend." The solution then would be to get the friend hanged over at the penitentiary. "Why then we get both of them to hell outen this jail." Cain called it "Hemp," and imagined Mencken as his ideal reader.

As a writer who had yet to publish a short story, Cain was fascinated by the productivity of Burt L. Standish (William George "Gilbert" Patten) and the popular appeal of his 204 novels for boys. He admired Patten's professionalism, industry, and energy. In his Frank Merriwell series, Patten dealt with the basic sources of the American male's interest in masculine drama. Merriwell of Yale was a magnificent show-off, and Cain knew that in his own writing, he was, too. The *Saturday Evening Post* would be the appropriate slick magazine for a tribute to this one-man drama industry—about one book a week for ten years. Cain disliked doing interviews, but he had a long talk with Patten. He would open with a dramatic scene: the parents running home in the cold to see their sixteen-year-old son who had run away and returned—to shock them with his decision to become a writer. Patten sold the first stories he wrote. Now give them a straightforward history of the pulp fiction of Beadle & Smith and Street & Street. "It is now quite forgotten that the dime novel has an ancient and thoroughly honorable history." To Beadle, Patten's publisher, "the real romance of America, the great field for her literature, lay in the West . . . the land where supermen were rolling back a frontier on Indians and buffaloes. . . . the land that people wanted to read about." When he announced he would sell his short paperback books for 10 cents, he got laughter, but he got rich.

Now return to Patten ten years later, living in New York, loving the humbuggery, literary and other kinds, of the town. But with doubts now about the vitality of the western story. Street & Street offered him a series, centered on a character boys would identify with. Patten would "give the boys something they could believe in. Also, he would give them a hero they could really admire. And he would try to build the stories on character rather than on incident, and in that way make them live."

Get into Patten's thought processes as he starts the first Merriwell novel. "'Better start it off in style,' thought Patten, and this is what he wrote."

Chapter I,
Frank Makes A Foe.

"Get out!"
Thump. A shrill howl of pain.
"Stop it! That's my dog!"
"Oh, it is?"
"Then you ought to be kicked too! Take that for your impudence!"

Now let the last half be simply Patten talking, mostly about the writing of the series. Street complained once that the series had too much character, too little action. "Do the stories sell?" Patten asked. "Yes." Street let Patten "do his stories in his own fool way." As his own last word before he ended with Patten's, Cain told the reader, "Oddly enough, although he is easily the country's most prolific *literatus*, you will not find him in *Who's Who*."

As he wrote this article, Cain's imagination was working on a story Patten had told him, about two westerners who cut off their victim's head but were unnerved by the way it bounced around in their wagon. That Cain had found it hilarious had horrified Patten, who gave him permission to use it sometime.

Lindbergh's solo flight appealed to Cain's reverence for men who take risks, for achievement measured by what it costs the achiever. When the *Lone Eagle* landed in Paris, May 24, 1927, Cain called him, in the lead editorial, the ideal sports hero. When Lindbergh was received with a parade more impressive than the Doughboys had gotten, Cain in his second editorial let the comments of the spectators suggest what the event meant to Americans.

These climaxed a year of interesting editorials, among them a panegyric for another folk hero, Henry Ford, for his Model A, an attack on George Antheil's *Ballet Mécanique* score, and a campaign to demolish the Third Avenue Elevated Railway.

"You get more stuff into this paper than your God-given talent entitles you to," said Lippmann, one day. "I suppose you know that."

"Well, I don't. If so, why?"

"Because you know once I've read it for sense, that I can pitch it in that basket without having to spend the next hour translating flat-wheeled sentences into English."

At his desk under the golden dome, this man understood, as most scornful newspapermen would not, why Cain polished, often a dozen times, his editorials, as if they were Wilkinson Sword Blades. They shared an obsession with perfection in ways that were inseparable from a sheer love of words and language. In this revision process, Cain knew he was developing as a writer.

Socially, Cain enjoyed two separate worlds that seldom converged, for to Mencken, Lippmann was a snobbish social climber. In both worlds, Cain, aware that he looked ugly, especially with his severe case of acne, was shy, awkward, a little timid, though at the Goodmans' house he felt at ease breaking into song. Arthur Krock's talk in the *World* dining room was memorable, like his terse, understated prose. Cain was more attracted to this career newspaperman than to the many literary boys on the *World*. Cain and Laurence Stallings had a caustic relationship somewhat like that of Captain Flagg and Sergeant Quirt in *What Price Glory?*, with Stallings, a one-legged, embittered veteran, calling Cain "a phony tough guy" and Cain replying that Stallings's Georgia accent was overplayed. But Cain respected Stallings's intellect and his graceful style. Cain didn't like Morris Markey's Virginia accent any better, but Cain came to think of him as a kind of younger brother like Edward, whom he had lost during the war.

Cain endured the trauma of another illness that year. When his doctor diagnosed liver trouble, he put him on a diet and restricted him to table wine.

He got a letter from Elina. She was finally divorced and free to marry him. But Cain was still married. After a final request for reconciliation failed to move Cain, Mary filed for divorce in May 1927, in Centerville, Maryland, her hometown. The settlement reflected her bitterness toward Cain.

When Elina returned from Europe in June, Cain knew he was still very much in love with this slim woman who struck his friends as modest, humble, almost waif-like. They still had no language. She had two children, a boy and a girl, by the previous marriage. Cain asked Phil Goodman's advice about the marriage. "She's a nitwit," he told Cain. At City Hall in New York on July 2, 1927, the great love affair of his life moved into the realm of marriage.

Cain once caught Calvin Coolidge copying out of an encyclopedia material he later passed off as his own speech. He described that incident in an editorial, objectively, letting it speak for itself. It was often reprinted. Then potential for another dialogue struck him. The scene is the Towanda Chamber of Commerce conference room, just after the president has visited the town. The secretary of the Chamber of Commerce and the chairman of the County Republican Committee are elated. "He knew all about Towanda." The phrases "cooperative spirit," "old Loyalty spirit," "booster," "knocker," and "mossback element" get kicked around. But the high school principal reveals that the whole speech was lifted from an encyclopedia. He says he guesses he won't write the history of Towanda he had planned. Now show how they talk themselves, in true committee fashion, into a turnabout. "Suppose he was busy, and that secretary done it?" He hadn't liked that secretary anyway. "You know, maybe I will write that history after all." At the end, all three crow, "The main thing is: He's been here!"

Cain's style continued to intrigue Lippmann. "Do you realize that 40 percent of the allusions in your editorials are to *Alice in Wonderland*?" One day after lunch, Cain was chatting with some colleagues in the hall when Lippmann emerged from the elevator in a rage that undercut his image as a suave, elegant leader. "You, it would be you!" he snarled at Cain. "Well, obviously, I'm charged and I plead guilty at once, but just for laughs, I would like to know what I've done."

Lippmann quoted from one of the editorials Cain had written while Lippmann was out of town: "Writing, apparently, is not as easy as it looks." Lippmann pointed out that "so" goes after the negative.

Cain admitted his guilt in an editorial the next day, and his admiration for Lippmann was even greater because his outburst declared just how much he cared about language. But he cared in a very different way from Cain's father, who used to upbraid him relentlessly for grammatical errors in speech and writing, just for the sake of correctness. Lippmann's large head, his almost ghostly, breathy voice enhanced his air of authority. Cain's regard for him verged on hero-worship.

Going to lunch one day, they stopped at the curb in front of the Pulitzer building. "Jim, I think it's up to the few to keep civilization from being pulled down by the many—don't you?" Startled, Cain turned his head as he stepped off the curb. Lippmann's powerful grip lifted him out of the path of a taxi, saving his life.

Cain reached with delight for the issue of the *Saturday Evening Post*, one of the nation's oldest magazines, containing his Frank Merriwell article. That might be a good national forum for presenting his revised views of editorials. He would offer a balanced discussion of the positive and negative aspects of editorial writing in the United States, laced with anecdotes from his own two years of experience, gearing his style to a readership very different from the *Mercury*'s and the *Nation*'s. It would be a feat—to write interestingly (and for the third time) about ostensibly the most boring type of writings. "Are Editorials Worth Reading?" Lead off with a personal anecdote: the man who told Cain he never read editorials because they're too dry to wade through. With an "almost pathological fear of being bored … he was precisely the type of enlightened, hard-boiled American citizen for whom I had supposed that my own erudite compositions would have an almost irresistible appeal." He was of the kind of people "who demand that their reading matter be interesting on its own account. . . ." "Well, does it offer them anything? It does." A "dreadful handicap" is the "matter of its appearance. It is solemn, austere forbidding … filled with many a tedious whereas and windy wherefore." "The undertaker clothes are to some extent obligatory. The corporate awfulness of the paper speaks here. . . ." Now explain a little, "help clear up a number of misunderstandings." Cain described types of editorials. Now "put yourself in the position of a writer who must turn out pieces" on party politics, civic matters, schemes for public good, big-news editorials. "Try it. You will be amazed to discover how many banal phrases your brain can hatch in the course of an hour," when, as in the case of Lindbergh's flight, the only sensible thing to say may be "Hooray!" "Well, then, what does the editorial page offer that is interesting on its own account?" Four or five kinds of edits are good, especially those "born of the editor's hobby," "pieces that come from the heart," that "amuse as well as instruct." Give names of writers, their papers, their subjects. Cain's own favorite subject was prizefighters. But the climax focus belonged on this: "The men who write" for the editorial page "have time to write carefully."

43

The four *Mercury* dialogues had given Cain a good deal of notoriety. With Mencken, he had discussed the possibilities of a book. It would need a common theme, and more dialogues. So-called democratic government was a common subject, and a common premise was that wherever two or more yokels gather the God of satire attends. The formula called for the expressions of an attitude and the introduction of a catalyst that would produce a reverse attitude, both attitudes proving to be equally self-serving. The jury files in to decide the fate of Mr. Summers, who shot a Klansman as a bunch of them sang hymns on his steps. The Klan didn't like it that Summers didn't go to church. But it comes out that Summers didn't buy his supplies at the local store. He mail-ordered them. The jury sounds off against the Klan and its tactics. Then they learn that Mr. Moon, a rather dumb juror, is almost a member of the Klan. Now the jury praises the Klan, declares Summers ought to pay, manslaughter minimum. Although, ironically, Moon is afraid of them, the jurors take up a collection so he can join, buying his forgetfulness of their cracks against the Klan. "Trial by Jury" was his longest dialogue so far.

Cain wanted to dramatize the theme he had discussed in "The Pastor": the dramatic appeal and sexual excitement of fundamentalist religion. It might not fit on the same string with the other dialogues, but he wanted to try it. Mr. and Mrs. Nation and her brother sit on the porch of a Christian summer resort in Delaware. She has called her brother down to discuss Eva, now sixteen, who last year "was took," was revived, and vowed she'd been to Heaven. She recited the miracle many times in the parlor, picking her "banjer," jerking tears from flocks of listeners. But then she ran off with Reverend Day. Using reason, Mr. Nation asks, What could have happened when her heart stopped? She went to Heaven or Hell or stayed on earth or she was a ghost. He demolishes all arguments except Hell. Would a girl that had been to Heaven put her "vercher" in peril? The brother told them he knew a man who said nothing in the Bible prohibited a little cutting up before marriage, so they should invite this preacher and Eva to dinner and work it out. The parents agree to "what stands to reason." Cain called this one "Theological Interlude."

When and where had he started listening so keenly to dialect? Maybe back there when Ike Newton provided a base against which all other talk could be compared and contrasted. When President Cain decided to lay a brick walk down the campus, Ike Newton, a thickset man in his fifties, worked, putting the bricks in, gauging them with his eye, tapping them with a hammer that had a screwdriver in its handle, sitting on the ground among the bricks and sand, his legs spread open, while twelve-year-old Jamie listened to him talk, enthralled, not so much by his stories or his ideas, as by the language he couched them in. It was pure bucolic vulgate, so rich, so expressive, so full of color that he couldn't hear enough of him. It was pure enchantment. Repeating it at home got horrified reactions from his mother and his father, who knew exactly how people should talk. Ike didn't teach Cain how to write dialogue, but he felt a great debt to him for stirring in him a respect for his lingo and all that went with it, for exciting in him a feeling for simple speech, for the way people actually talk, for the country idiom as distinguished from the citified.

When the long agony of the Sacco-Vanzetti case exploded in the judge's final decision to order their execution, the *World* came out against that decision. From February 1927 to late spring 1928, editorials by Cain and Lippmann and columns by Heywood Broun and others had been on the attack. Several men on the *World*, including Cain, but Broun most of all, felt Lippmann's tone was too conciliatory, as if what was at stake was only an intellectual debate and not the lives of two men. Broun attacked the *World* in his own column and also in the *Nation*, an approach Cain and the *World* regarded as disloyal. When Broun continued to attack the *World*'s low-voltage liberalism even after Sacco-Vanzetti had been executed, August 23, 1927, and on other subjects, such as Cain's defense of the city's refusal to allow an exhibition on birth control in Grand Central Palace, Broun was fired in May 1928, and Cain wrote to the *Nation*'s editor an estimate of Broun's conduct as a journalist, "inept, stupid, and not remotely to be associated with courage," and euphemistically challenged him to a pugilistic form of argument.

With the dialogue sketches Cain contributed regularly to the Sunday paper, the editorial for the *Evening World*, and the essays for the *Mercury*, Cain made about $14,000 in 1928.

But was a newspaperman a writer? Certainly, in a vital sense. But as far as his aspiration to write fiction and plays went, he was still sitting on that park bench. It was not visible to the world that he was a writer, nor could he even tell himself he was. He lived in Greenwich Village—he moved among them, but was not of those who published little but persisted in declaring themselves writers. No, he was not really a writer. But he was definitely a journalist. He had put in the time, and established a reputation among other nationally recognized journalists: Mencken, Lippmann, Broun, Krock—he was of that company, if he was of any. Wash out all those interim jobs of his early twenties. Wash out even the creditable teaching he had done. What counted was that, even in the war—and he claimed, too, that he was a soldier—he had been and was and apparently would be a journalist. No, even though his many articles in magazines qualified him, "newspaperman" had a truer ring. Newspaper work had proved to be more than an interim job.

3

Our Government

THAT TALE WILLIAM PATTEN HAD TOLD CAIN WOULD MAKE AN EFFEC-
tive short story. He would shift the setting from the West to somewhere
in the Southeast. The kind of people he had made to speak in the dialogues. It'd work best in the first person. But who'd tell it? You couldn't
tell it without somehow dramatizing yourself as the teller. Then let one of
the two killers tell it out of a compulsion for self-dramatization, anchored
in his character—he often shows off, singing, reciting, claiming he was
once on the stage. But there's some of that in all of us. Let an unnamed
townsman retell it, hiding behind a community "we," so that it is implied
that dull people jealously thrive on the exploits of extroverts. A little like
Lardner's "Haircut," but without so much emphasis on the irony of the
narrator's revealing his own character through his manner of telling the
story. As in the dialogues, the reader would enjoy the dialect, but with
the important difference that they would listen to
a single voice (Cain heard Ike Newton's), in the
oral tradition of the southern storyteller, setting a
local legend in motion.

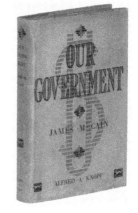

"Well, it looks like Burbie is going to get
hung. And if he does, what he can lay it on is, he
always figured he was so damn smart." Burbie
and Lida meet—"it was a natural." Lida is "just
about the same kind of a thing for a woman as
Burbie was for a man." Burbie wanders again.
Lida marries an old man. When Lida is about
due to have Burbie's baby, he comes back, and

they meet secretly. "So the way Burbie tells it, and he tells it plenty since he done got religion down to the jailhouse," he planned to kill the old man. Gets Hutch, a mean guy, to help, fools him into thinking the old man has money hidden. Hutch hit the old man with a wrench. When Hutch begins to suspect Burbie misled him, Burbie repeats, "Hope my die." They go to Whooping Nannie woods, the lair of a ghost. They bury the victim, but his head sticks up. Hutch makes Burbie hack it off with a shovel. "Here they come down the road, the horse a-running hell to split, and Hutch a-hollering, and Burbie a-shivering, and the head a-rolling around in the bottom of the wagon, and bouncing up in the air when they hit a bump, and Burbie damn near dying every time it hit his feet." Burbie heaved the head over the bridge. A pistol shot sound when it hits the ice on the river. Hutch drops into the bottom of the wagon. Burbie runs away. Next morning, folks find the head on ice, Hutch in a hole in the ice. He had tried to go after it. Burbie is in the clear. But Burbie loved to give a "spiel at a entertainment." Sounded like his "Face on the Floor," as he told it. Proud of hisself. Great performance. Now he and Lida are in jail. "And if he hadn't felt so smart, he would have been a free man yet."

"Only I reckon he done been holding it all so long he just had to spill it," which is what the narrator has just done.

What he had, he saw as he rewrote it and read it over, was a macabre story of torrid sex, greed, and murder, told in a gallows humor tone, with a neat structure, one action leading with mechanical precision to the next, entailing several ironic reversals. Nationally, in the *Mercury* and other magazines, and locally, in the *World*, Cain had set the scene for the appearance of his first short story. He would soon know from Mencken whether this little show would play.

The interest in Ernest Hemingway finally persuaded Cain in 1928 to read *Men Without Women*, which had made the author famous in 1927. Cain's interest in boxing attracted him to "Fifty Grand." Two other stories stuck to his ribs, "Undefeated" about a bullfighter, and "The Killers." Those stories proved that the acclaim was deserved. But the style he had already developed in his dialogues and in "Pastorale" was proof against influence.

When the *Mercury* came out and he held his first published short story in his hand, finally, Cain felt he had left that park bench in Washington behind him for good.

In 1928, in the absence of news stories or controversies to make demands on the talent he was developing, Cain routinely followed his own favorite interests in sports, music, and food. Many of his editorials dealt with the Yankees, Babe Ruth, and Lou Gehrig, and the World Series.

Cain's writing at polar extremes of style and genre gave anyone trying to *fix him* trouble. He would follow "Pastorale" with an urbane essay on the Solid South, written as if from inside the mental processes of the southern upper class male. "It is my purpose in this article to discuss certain twists in the Southern mind, the twist which leads it to vote dry and drink wet, and perhaps to hazard a few forecasts as to what the future may hold." He attempted to "clear up any misconceptions that may have arisen in your mind" about notions of lawlessness, intolerance, race relations, and the backwardness of the "bozarts" in the South. They weren't going to like the argument that the best people should have certain rights that the worst cannot handle. As for lawlessness, there are many fewer lynchings, "as you can see for yourself if you will consult the figures on it as given in the World Almanac." The South is not insanely anti-Catholic. As a Catholic growing up in Maryland, he had experienced no discrimination himself. "And while my personal charm is un-deniable, I don't think any exception was made in my case on account of it." The South is not culturally backward. The lack of large cities explains the cultural desert impression.

The typical southerner who runs the South is an "intelligent, reflective, and informed man." "It will help you a great deal, when you try to understand him, if you remember that . . . only make things a great deal harder for yourself" if you cleave to misconceptions. "The principles of democracy are merely so much bombast to the Southerner." "It has never occurred to him that they are actually to be put into practice. So far as he is concerned, all men are not created equal."

His point of view is inherited, and he reasons from the evidence of his own eyes daily. "The Negro in the South today offers conclusive evidence that the Declaration of Independence was a little previous with the things that it held to be self-evident. He is not the equal of the white man." Few Negroes in the South are "civilized in every sense of the word." "Laws must apply differently to different kinds of men ... It is not for these millions of irresponsible children who are not fit to govern at all, or even to exercise the 'rights' that are said to belong to them inalienably." "The Negro there has shown in pitiful fashion that there are certain rights that he cannot be entrusted with." Admittance to hotels and the right to vote are the only rights denied him. "And there are solid, substantial reasons" for denying those rights. When southern Negroes behave as well as Negroes in the North, the first right will come. As to the second, "it is a little hard to speak patiently." He has disenfranchised himself. No rough stuff was pulled on him. "Poll tax, literacy test, property test"—if he can pass all those, he can probably vote. Race prejudice is "a spontaneous physical thing"—anybody would feel it after two weeks in the South with the Negroes. "What the Negro race in the South needs is fewer organs of indignant opinion and more bathtubs." The southerner is "distinctly class-minded, and has every reason to be." "Element-minded" is the regional term. The southerner "has every intention of placing liquor beyond the reach of the farmhands and Negroes who were dangerous when they got hold of it." Real southerners abhor the Klan. It "is losing its poor witless members everywhere." The South needs to deal with whiskey, and when a sensible plan is devised "the South will be as hospitable to it as any other section." He sent "The Solid South" to the *Bookman*, in which he had not published before.

In September 1928, Cain wrote his first bylined column in the *World*'s Metropolitan section. He created a neighborhood called Bender Street, populated with typical New Yorkers. In one of the first of these dialogue sketches, a man talks to an old man upstairs about getting robbed. Finally, he accuses the old man himself. The cops know, but have no proof. Either the old man returns the stuff, or he'll sock him. His kids did it for a joke, the old man explains. "That's sure nice of you, Old Man. I bet there's a whole slew of them robberies done by kids just for a joke, don't you? I always did think so."

Cain was having lunch with Kenneth Littauer of *Collier's* when the editor said he was looking for a modern Cinderella story. That appealed to him somehow, as did many clichés that could be questioned or updated, but not enough to get him started.

Swope left the *World* in October, and although Cain felt it was a good move, it was another sign that the ship was lurching in stormy waters. Swope had been a good show to watch, but from several of the other men, Lippmann, Krock, Stallings, Markey, Charles Mertz, and Allan Nevins, he had learned respect for information, accuracy, and the sustaining power of character.

In December 1928, Cain corresponded with Knopf about the possibility of making a book out of his *World* sketches and the *Mercury* dialogues. He almost had enough, and was preparing more. The working title was *Government: An Absolutely Impartial Analysis*, and it would have an equally tongue in cheek preface.

To show the "Will of the People" at work in its state legislature, Cain let three representatives talk in committee at the state capitol on education bills. Hayes and Loman are ignorant, but Friend is so much worse, they criticize him as too stupid for the legislature. They want him to vote on a bill against teaching evolution, but he can't understand what it is. Loman attacks him all the way through, while Hayes tries to con him, placate him. "Why don't you go out there and talk to that tree?" asked Loman. "Because the tree ain't on the committee," says Hayes. Friend feels he was elected only to get a new school built, not for education but to provide jobs. Vote against evolution because of the Bible, they tell him, trying to simplify it for him. Then it comes out he's the one who's been propping up his still with a Bible and that the Klan is after him for it. Finally, when they tell him new textbooks would have to be purchased, he decides to vote against teaching evolution.

Cain's attempt to deliver a message at the front in World War I always struck him as a good story, but ten years after the event, his failure still made him feel humiliation. It would work best in first person, but he was temperamentally unable to tell his own story in his own voice even if he called it fiction. Putting it in the mouth of an illiterate southerner might create the distance he needed, and also enhance the humor that was in the episode. "I been ask did I get a D. S. C. in the late war, and the answer is no, but I might of got one if I had not run into some tough luck. And how that was is pretty mixed up, so I guess I better start at the beginning, so you can get it all straight and I will not have to do no backtracking." This narrator sounded like the narrator of "Pastorale," with the difference that he was telling his own story, not someone else's. In the end, the narrator of "The Taking of Montfaucon" felt as Cain himself still felt: "But I never done it, and it ain't no use blubbering over how things might be if only they was a little different." The feeling of having let people down still haunted him. Mencken accepted the story, it came out in June, and he was proud that the *Infantry Journal* was reprinting it.

The question of treason in a democracy continued to fascinate him. Remembering the treason trials of 1922, he imagined an ironic twist, compounded by the role of a drunken governor in a pardon hearing. Farce was the proper mode for this dialogue. Gathered in the governor's office are Farms, the petitioner, his lawyers, a witness for Farms, and a secretary. The lawyer informs the governor that Farms just went along with the miners out of curiosity, was arrested three months later, and sent to the penitentiary for ten years. A witness testifies that he and other firemen found Farms as a baby in a sewer. Nameless, he has no citizenship, therefore he cannot commit treason. Okay, his sentence is commuted to life, says the governor. But he only got ten in the first place! "Well, I'm a member of a volunteer fire department myself. Did you do it? he asks Farms. No, sir. Then you're free." They all leave, and the drunken governor falls asleep. "Citizenship" made seven *Mercury* dialogues, almost enough now for the book he had planned.

For his dialogue sketches for the Sunday *World*, he made a shift in locale from New York's Bender Street to Maryland's Eastern Shore. Luke and Herb Moore worked on a state road in the country, driving their father's teams, and the other men razzed them because their father was a tightwad. They decided to take the new horse and the new buggy to the station, go on a bender in Washington, and return the horse before daybreak, then brag on their bender to the boys. "So they done it." As they pass two men rolling the road at night so they could finish as per contract, the men blow the roller whistles to salute the boys' adventure. As they came back, the two rollers blocked the road. Nix on the detour. Too drunk to drive the rollers himself, Luke took the red lanterns and waved them, while Herb drove the little Buffalo roller off the road. But the Acme didn't work the same way and went forward instead of backward, crashing into the Buffalo and throwing Herb. "That roller, when it jumped frontward, had knocked Luke down and put out his red lights. And it had rolled him flatter than a German pancake." The father at the scene raved, "'Oh, God . . .Why did you send me a pair of worthless rascals like this when I asked you for sons?'" One of the regular roller drivers says, "'Well, if God made *you*, it ain't much else that I would put past him.'" The two men never razzed Herb again. Cain felt a little uneasy that his readers noticed the differences in his rendering of the same dialect in the *World* and in the *Mercury*. He could not restrain Mencken's inclination to edit in heavier, more ludicrous dialect.

Since 1925, Cain had met with Goodman and Mencken and Sinclair Lewis, famous for *Main Street*, *Babbitt*, and *Arrowsmith*, to eat, drink, talk literature, and satirize all the failings of the human race, and play pranks. But by 1928, married to Elina, who had proved to be a rather domineering wife, drinking with the boys was less frequent. Elina sensed the way Goodman felt about her. So Cain often went out without her, stayed late, saw other women. The little Finn had a strong arm. He told Goodman's daughter Ruth that "whenever Elina gets mad, she throws me around."

When Lewis came back from Europe in 1928, he was a married man, too. Dorothy Thompson, a journalist, had a calming effect on him. Cain had liked Lewis, had sensed his genius, but had observed that drunk, as he usually was, or sober, the man had a pathetic compulsion to impress people, as when in an attempt to "educate" Cain, he had forced on him a copy of Knut Hamsun's *The Growth of the Soil*, thus ensuring Cain's aversion to it.

When Elina had to return to Europe in 1929, Cain, though silent himself most of the time, enjoyed Goodman's dinners, the good talk of his wife, his daughter, Ruth, an aspiring playwright, and Lawrence and Mencken—much talk of the theater, for which Mencken had contempt. But it was always a fine feeling, knowing that these three men wanted to help Cain as a writer.

At one of his dinners, Goodman invited Cain to meet W. C. Fields. Goodman had produced *Poppy* in 1923, making Fields become famous as

Eustace McGargle, his first talking role on the stage. Goodman proposed that Cain would write, that he would produce, and Fields would star in a new play. The idea they came up with called for Fields to portray the proprietor of an Uncle Tom's Cabin theatrical company in the 1890s. Fields would fall in love with a teenage sexpot who plays the child Little Eva. The fact that Fields is much older and that the girl is in love with a man her own age would provide much of the conflict. Fields came to Cain's apartment for three months to work with him on the script, but unable to concentrate, Fields compulsively strewed gags and anecdotes around. Cain and Fields told Goodman they were making progress, Cain hoping that eventually they really would. When Fields accepted a Hollywood offer, Cain and Goodman dropped the project.

Cain wanted to produce a play himself, with Goodman. When Cain read a piece by John O'Hara in the *World* in 1927, he reprinted it on the Christmas page. Cain was convinced John O'Hara's dialogue was unusually effective, as others had said about himself. He invited O'Hara up to his East 19th Street apartment and urged him to write a play. O'Hara was surprised Cain liked the Christmas piece. He was a hard fellow to like, seeming indifferent to the idea of writing a play, and inattentive to what Cain was saying.

Cain was especially fond of the operetta form, but when Goodman asked his opinion of his production *The Rainbow*, by Laurence Stallings and Oscar Hammerstein, honesty required him to say, "I don't think an embittered Georgia intellectual could write a show for the Rialtos of the world. I don't think you have any affinity for the operetta. You're the king of Broadway comedy and you ought to stick at what you're good at. And you're telegraphing to these guys that you want them to steal *Show Boat* and they're getting the message." Goodman was offended, and his manner toward Cain cooled. *The Rainbow* failed. It seemed that only success attracted Mencken, so he dropped Goodman. On the day of the Crash, October 24, 1929, Goodman pulled what he had left out of the bank and said to Ruth, "Let's get out of this," and the Goodmans sailed to Europe.

"In the war I put in some time on an observation post, and it was in top of the tallest tree in France, and you climbed up by a ladder, and they had a little iron box up there what look like a coffin. . . ." For this Sunday

World piece, "It Breathed," Cain drew on another aspect of his war experience, alluded to in "Montfaucon." Two hours in, six off. Couldn't sleep good, so Foley "got a little wild," sick with fever, but they wouldn't come for him. Katz said, "You know this whole battle front is alive? Oh, my God, when that fog comes down and you can't hear a thing, and all of a sudden it turns over and breathes! And me up there all alone in that tree—." The narrator offered to switch shifts with him because Katz was "blotto" from lack of sleep. "A whole lot of people, they got the idea that on a battle front it's a hell of a lot of noise going on all the time. And most of the time it is, like shelling in the afternoon when the balloons is up, and the machine guns at night when they're sending up flares to spot raids, and all like of that. But from two o'clock in the morning on to dawn it ain't nothing so still as a battle front...." At 3:28 he was just about to make his 3:30 entry. "I felt my lips go numb and my heart began pounding like it would jump out of my throat.... I heared it, just like he said. Maybe you think I'm lying, but I tell you it give kind of a sigh and then went quiet again." Katz told him Foley died at 3:38.

One day, Claude Bowers, a writer for *World*, showed up with Houghton Mifflin editor Robert W. Linscott, who told Cain that his *World* and *Mercury* dialogues had convinced him he could write a novel. Cain said no, he'd tried and failed.

To fill the gap in the design he had imposed upon the dialogue collection for Knopf, Cain quoted directly from the *Congressional Record* to represent Congress. He wrote three new ones for the administration of justice, one on council, one on the judiciary, and another on the county school system. And to suggest something about the military forces of the United States, "The Taking of Montfaucon" ended the book.

While *Our Government* was in preparation, Cain played cavalier to Blanche Knopf who had taken the book on. She invited Cain to supper at her apartment. Mencken, Willa Cather, and Sir Thomas Beecham would be there. Even though he felt Mencken promoted Cather into a fame she may not have fully deserved, based on *My Antonia, The Song of the Lark*, and *Death Comes for the Archbishop*, Cain had great expectations of high literary discourse. What he got was the spectacle of Mencken ignoring Cather, as he held forth in his usual way. Cather said nothing and made no impression on Cain to overcome his earlier impression of her as the author of undistinguished magazine articles.

Knopf brought out *Our Government* in February 1930 in its *The American Scene* series, which had included Thomas Beer's *The Mauve Decade*, Herbert Asbury's *Up from Methodism* and *The Gangs of New York*, Ralph Barton's *God's Country*, and Joseph Hergesheimer's *Swords and Roses*, dealing with the mythic South. Cain dedicated it to Elina, and thanked Mencken, "who gave me many inspirational talks when my interest flagged," and his father, "whose manipulations of legislators for college appropriations formed the foundation of my political education." He also thanked Charles Mertz, Arthur Krock, Hamilton Owens, Herbert Bayard Swope, Walter Lippmann, Morris Markey, Gilbert Malcolm, and Philip Goodman—all of whom had made valuable suggestions.

Sensing that it might be received as a rather modest book, Cain surrendered to his habitual inclination to endow every project with absolute significance even though he wanted to mock the pomposity of prefaces. In a "solemncholy" (his father's word) preface, Cain declared that his "little book represents an effort to make a beginning" in the direction of a scientific examination "of our American government . . . There is no book, so far as I know, which sets out . . . to depict, without bias or comment, the machine which passes our laws, educates our children, and polices our streets. . . . It was to fill this hiatus that I set to work . . . for if the field proves attractive to scholarship, and others take up the work where I have left off, the United States will be unique among nations."

The organization of the book starts at the top, with the chief executive, "keen from the small town point of view, and goes down the governmental pyramid to the lowest local bedrock." To "achieve complete verisimilitude," his "method of approach," that had evolved from piece to piece, was to "select some typical problem of a particular branch of government, usually on the basis of newspaper clippings, and then reconstruct the manner in which it would be dealt with by the typical agents of that branch. . . . I was happily able to utilize an experience of my own, and give actual names, dates, and places."

At last, at thirty-seven, Cain held his first book in his hand, a somewhat unique combination of drama and fiction, serving nonfiction intentions. Expecting a stormy reception, he read the reviews eagerly. On January 4, Louis Sherwin, of the *New York Evening Post*, said Cain's "almost sadistic skill" had produced "a brutal portrait." Hamilton Owens, his friend at the Baltimore *Sun*, said some of the tales were too incredible, but that the underlying facts were correct. Cain was a master of rural dialogue. John Carter, in *Outlook*, said the book had "just that touch of Aristophanes which is necessary to act as a preservative and make it as readable" centuries later as now. The *Times* was not enthusiastic, said some achieved clever satire, but most were "mere takeoffs," shocking because "so sordidly photographic." Cain's scenes were stage worthy. He ought to write a play. Harry Hansen, of the New York *World*, said, "To Cain the processes of government mask a huge joke. These sketches are caricatures, ironic distortions that bring home the inefficiency, the hopelessness, the downright asininity of phases of popular government." The effect would have been stronger, he thought, purely as fiction than as a tract. Cain felt his first book had been well received. A modest case might then be made for his having become a writer.

In April 1930, Cain had heard that Scripps-Howard was discussing buying the *World*. When Cain suggested revamping the editorial page and Lippmann seemed inattentive, he sensed that the time for saving the paper had gone by. In March, Cain let Goodman inquire about a job for him writing columns for the *Nation* or the *New Republic*, but let that drop, when he realized, as he wrote Mencken, that first he had to decide whether he wanted to stay in journalism.

"Gold Letters Hand Painted" was another of several instances in which Cain drew directly on his own experiences for his *World* dialogues and sketches. "We boys," this one ran, "used to find ways to show we had reached manhood. Robert Plummer beat us all by buying a shaving mug and putting it on the shelf among others at Johnny Vandergriff's barbershop, whose chair was a palladium of masculinity. We planned a counter offensive by devising the Foggy club for smokers, knowing Plummer, as a minister's son couldn't join, so we invited him while he was being shaved. When he declined, with no sense of loss, we were defeated. Plummer tipped the barber, which made him seem even more of a man, until the barber declined it, saying, 'I've shaved you three times now and haven't clinked a whisker yet.' There was more, but on the whole I prefer to draw the veil at this point." Cain refused to risk humiliating his old friend Plummer in print.

In the summer of 1930, Cain sailed to Europe so he could come back with Elina in the fall. She had a delightful surprise for him, she said, in English, and that was the surprise. She had learned English.

Suddenly, September 27, 1930, Mencken married Sara Haardt. Cain had dated her himself a few times. She was something to look at. He knew Sara could see through people, and so was not surprised to learn that Mencken was breaking with his friends and was to watch his days of roistering dwindle.

What had Cain lost? Well, as he had loved listening to Ike, he had loved listening to Mencken just to hear the syntax and expressions, to marvel at his verbal dexterity, and feel the personal magnetism, as this egocentric man took center stage with his monologues. Anarchist, mocker, iconoclast, heaver of dead cats into the sanctuary, as he called himself, Mencken craved notoriety. To Cain, the nagging question became: What's he for? His defense of liberty meant only literary liberty. What affinities had they shared? Neither wanted children, especially not as a shortcut to immortality. They enjoyed music together. But Cain could not share Mencken's passionate Germanophilia.

Actually, Mencken struck him as neurotic. Like most clowns, Mencken's outward manner was a mask for moodiness and bitterness. Having seen Mencken turn, without warning, on his friends, Cain was wary when intimacy crept into their relationship. But now the drinking and the talking days were pretty much gone. Cain seldom agreed with his politics or his literary judgments. Shockingly, he'd never read Cain's own nomination for the world's greatest book, *Alice in Wonderland*. His thinking was shallow, a stew of thinkers from the 1880s and 1890s. "The man is bigger than his ideas," said Lippmann, another man whose talk held Cain spellbound, although his writing made less impact than Mencken's. The *Mercury* was a great magazine that had not realized its potential. Mencken was not a good editor. Unlike Lippmann, he dictated to his authors, and he edited so that everyone sounded like himself, a kind of ventriloquism. Take it or don't write for me was his attitude. Krock's attitude was I won't take it. But Cain knew that in his own essays, he was under the spell of Mencken's style and prejudices.

Cain's poem "Auld Lang Syne," satirizing the mawkish reunions of old college friends, ending with his realization that he had forgotten them all, appeared in the *New Yorker* a week before the *World*'s Christmas party, which turned into a premature wake.

By mid-February 1931, the sale was underway, and Cain wrote his last Sunday column. The staff tried but failed to buy the paper. The *World* would combine with the New York *Telegram* and some men would go there with it, but Cain's name did not appear on the list.

As Cain wrote two editorials for the last edition of the *World* on February 27—on Bertram Thomas's trek across seldom traveled Southern Arabia and on the travesty of Franz Lehar's announced intention of updating his music—he knew he was regarded as one of the most prolific and respected editorial writers ever to write for the *World*, a reputation based on over one thousand editorials and ninety bylined columns, from 1922 to the present, some pretty short, some long and serious, on such subjects as theater, literature, music, sports, and food—his favorites—and censorship, Lindbergh, Scopes, Sacco-Vanzetti, Beethoven, the presidency, male-female relationships, transportation, the Chesapeake Bay Bridge, the younger generation, civil liberties, and such light or human interest subjects as radio, the movies, holidays, the weather, pies, frogs, hog-calling, the man-eating tiger, and how to sing the national anthem.

If he had any talent to write good prose, Cain knew he had it from his mother. Her speech was terse, well-pronounced, and distinguished, rather different from his father's windy, elaborately grammatical and Yankeeish mode of utterance, and on paper, she was the model of prose composition—vivid, brief, and clear, with few adjectives.

Morris Markey, Cain's old friend from the *World* who had gone over to the *New Yorker* and helped forge the *New Yorker* style in his "Reporter at Large" column, recommended Cain to Harold Ross as his managing editor, or "26th Jesus," for each of his many predecessors had had to work miracles. Ogden Nash wanted out of that job. Cain had misgivings about his ability to adjust to the idea that a magazine sells entertainment instead of news or information, but he took the job, trusting the publisher Raoul

Fleischmann not to tell Ross what Cain had once said when Fleischmann asked him what he thought of the magazine. "Well, I read your ads in the *Times* and I feel I want to like the magazine. But when I buy it and snicker at its drawings, I then find nothing to stick to my ribs—it's fluff."

What Ross wanted out of Cain was suggested by his constant repetition of the line: "Cain, we got to get this place awganized." A cursory glimpse of the medieval setup convinced Cain that that was exactly what the *New Yorker* needed. As when he was instilling discipline in the boys preparatory dorm, Cain saw himself as the man who steps into a mess and sets things right. But he quickly learned that Ross was perversely opposed to Cain's simple solution: Fire the utterly incompetent secretaries Ross had hired at substandard wages because they were making it impossible for the editorial staff—E. B. and Katharine White, James Thurber, Wolcott Gibbs, and Robert Coates—to function, and replace them with top talent at competitive wages. As the man in charge of the budget, Cain knew that could be done. But Ross's response was first frosty, then icy. "Cain, we got to find new talent," Ross repeated. Cain's reply, that first they must make efficient use of the talent they had, made no impact. He went ahead and made the changes he thought imperative. But everywhere he turned, he encountered Ross's crankiness.

While he was adjusting in nervous anxiety to his new job, Cain felt a compulsion as an insider to explain to the nation what had gone wrong at the *World*. Lead off with Goodman telling Cain five years earlier that it was for sale. Because he'd analyzed what was wrong with it when nobody suspected anything was, and when "anybody could see that everything was wrong with it" a few months ago, it was the same things Goodman had cited. "What ails it?" Cain had asked back in 1926. "Nothing ever ails any newspaper but the man at the top." That meant Ralph Pulitzer. Ads were another. Not enough return on the *World*'s. "The *World* is bought, but it is not read." Different crowds buy it for different writers, Braun, Lippmann, Adams. "But I don't believe there is a single subscriber who buys the *World* to begin on page 1 and read it through. The stuff is simply not there. The *World* hasn't got news!" Nobody in the shop seems to know what the composite reader of the *World* looks like. "You've got an editorial page addressed to intellectuals, a sporting section addressed to the fans, a Sunday magazine addressed to morons, and twenty other things that don't seem to be addressed to anybody. Who can strike a common denominator among all these? I can't. . . . The *World* is not a newspaper. It is an agglomeration of twenty different newspapers, one or two of them good, most of them bad. And it's for sale. You wait, and you'll see!" The kind of newspaper Goodman described was pretty certain to fail.

Cain listed all the *World*'s writers. "I shall always believe that when this crew was hitting on all six, the *World* was probably the most interesting newspaper in the United States, and possibly anywhere." Joseph Pulitzer's ideals "had a lot to say about progress and reform, but they had nothing to say about bringing in the hottest news that a big staff could collect. . . . in his day the *World* was not only respected, but wholesomely feared." One of Ralph's handicaps was that he was a gentleman. Swope was of the old tradition, too. "Nobody knows better than he that the main product of a newspaper is smoke. Smoke was what he wanted, and smoke, as you can see by reading the . . . Ku-Klux expose, was what he got."

Lippmann was of the new tradition. "He is not fainted-hearted and he is not an editor." A clue as to why Lippmann was out of tune with the newspaper business was that he had a poet's aversion to the obvious. "Lippmann recoiled from the obvious as a cat recoils from water. And obviousness is almost indispensable to a newspaper." Illustrate with a talk Cain had with Lippmann over an attack someone made on him:

"You were worse in the Scopes trial."

"Why?"

"You were guilty of trying to make an editorial more than it can be, and usually achieving something less than it ought to be."

"What do you mean?"

"Well, if you ask me, the most that any newspaper should try to do is choose sides in a fight, and then fight as hard as it can, even when it secretly wishes the fight were going a little differently. But you are always trying to dredge up basic principles. In a newspaper, it won't work." Cain gave musical analogies. A bugle has only four notes. "Now if what you've got to blow is a bugle, there isn't any sense in camping yourself down in front of piano music." "You may be right. But God damn it, I'm not going to spend my life writing bugle-calls."

He wound up the piece with: "There I think you have the explanation of Lippmann, his strength, his weakness, his pride, his general attitude toward his work ... when he was aware of the combat, he was always trying to bring it to a gentlemanly level. He seemed to regard it as a sort of amateur's tennis tournament, as indicated by his invariable desire to shake hands afterward." He was so fair in the Sacco Vanzetti controversy, it looked as if it didn't really matter. But the sole excuse for a newspaper's activity is that it does matter. For my part, I esteem a certain churlishness in a newspaper. Being a gentleman is not a qualification for an editor.

"I shall reserve my salute for Mr. James W. Barrett, who headed the employees' movement to acquire the *World*. When Barrett stood up on front of the meeting at the Astor and stuck out his jaw, it was the most inspiring sight I think I ever saw while I was on the *World*. I felt that what he was attempting could not be done, and yet he tried to do it, and stuck out his jaw. Is there anything in the world so fine as a stuck-out jaw? It is the prelude to a bugle-call, and the older I get the more respect I have for it." End right there.

"The End of the World" appeared in the *New Freeman*, a left-wing revival of the *Freeman*, March 11, 1931. Several *World* veterans wrote obits, but the *New York Tribune* said Cain's was the best.

To get in the *New Yorker* spirit that preferred entertainment to information, Cain wrote a one-page anecdote about his run-in with the post office when it ceased providing sealing wax for registered letters. "Sealing Wax" added some humorous fluff to the May 2, 1931 issue.

In May, Elina made another journey to Europe to bring her children over to the States. Cain took up a third time with the girl in the editorial department. While Elina was gone, Cain made the disquieting discovery that he could live apart from her. Did that mean then that he should? In September, she returned with her children, Leo, fourteen, and Henrietta, a very lovely girl of twelve who charmed everyone, Cain most of all.

Ross scheduled a second poem by Cain, "Gridiron Soliloquies," for the November 21, 1931 issue. Cain thought Ross a fascinating man, and his relations with "talent" struck him as brilliant. He had an original mind, with enough naïveté about it to go questing for fundamentals that everyone takes for granted. But he wasn't for Cain. Feeling that his ten-month seminar with Ross was the most compromising to self-respect of any period in his life, Cain began to look around for an exit.

When Ross advanced money to John O'Hara without informing him, Cain urged his agent James Geller to secure a Hollywood offer. Within a few weeks, Cain's reputation, based on his dialogs in the *World* and the *Mercury*, spotlighted in *Our Government*, secured him a six-month contract at $400 a week, twice his *New Yorker* salary.

He was putting a continent between himself and an interim job that had turned into a profession he had listed with pride in *Who's Who*. In some ways, those seven years had been the most pleasant working years of his life, mostly because Lippmann was the most pleasant man Cain had ever worked under. He had learned a great deal from Mencken, Goodman, and Lawrence (who had already gone over to Hollywood). He had gotten a little magazine experience. He didn't consider himself a good reporter, but he knew a good editorial writer when he was one. He hoped in those years he had convinced his parents he had a potential that in some way commanded respect. The country was just into a new decade, a new era. A failed fiction writer whose sensibility had been shaped and whose craft had been forged on a newspaper in the grand American tradition of Twain, Bierce, Lardner, and Hemingway, Cain saw possibilities in the West for some sort of new life for himself, too.

THE POSTMAN ALWAYS RINGS TWICE

A NOVEL BY

JAMES M. CAIN

author of SERENADE

4

The Postman Always Rings Twice

Cain arrived in Los Angeles in May 1931, in a driving rainstorm. His first glimpse of the city included a man in a boat, rowing around under some palm trees. He checked into the Knickerbocker Hotel.

Next day, he was taken to the Paramount lot with little expectation of liking the work there. Shocked to discover that the story editor had read none of his writings, Cain could not understand how he expected to get good work out of his writers without reading their published stories.

As his first assignment, Cain was given the task of rewriting Cecil B. DeMille's *The Ten Commandments*. The original of 1923 was one of the biggest silent hits of all time. To Cain it stank, "it was a glaring monstrous piece of slimy, phony hokum." But nobody else seemed to notice. He went to work on "this masterpiece of hokum" with Sam Mintz, a remarkable fellow.

In a story conference, he told what was wrong with the DeMille script. "Jim, do you really like this story?"

"I liked the book," Cain said.

Mintz got out, but Cain stayed on. In the newspaper world, a difficult job was a challenge you eagerly accepted. But the key difference here was that he had little respect and a lot of scorn for pictures and for many of the hacks who wrote them.

After six months he had flopped.

Cain sat around for months, waiting to get assigned. When he got to the thumb-twiddling stage, Cain loved to drive his 1932 Ford roadster out into the country. At the gas station where he often stopped, a bosomy, commonplace, but sexy young woman filled his tank. When he read that a woman who ran a filling station had bumped off her husband, he imagined she was the one. When he drove by, the station was shut down. He inquired. Yes, it was she.

For months, in helpful conversations with Elina, he worked over the idea for a novel about a young tramp and a woman who murder her husband to get the station and the car.

Just as Mencken in Baltimore and Goodman in New York had introduced Cain to interesting people, Vincent Lawrence, who had come out to Hollywood a few years earlier and had made a name for himself, helped Cain and Elina ease into the social world there. Cain and Elina preferred small, improvised parties to the monotonously predictable large parties. At Lawrence's suggestion, Harold Lloyd invited Cain and a playwright Cain had admired in New York for his success with *Young Love*, Sampson "Rafe" Raphaelson, and his wife Dorshka, a former Ziegfeld Follies girl, to watch a screening of *Movie Crazy*, starring Lloyd, script by Lawrence.

Raphaelson then invited the Cains to his house, where Cain met Charles Laughton. He was so intrigued later by Laughton's "fag" portrayal of Nero in *The Sign of the Cross* that he researched it and asked Laughton where he got his conception of Nero. Laughton said he had invented it, and they became friends. Cain enjoyed having Laughton and his wife Elsa Lanchester over for dinner.

Lawrence brought Phil Goodman out and tried to get him a job in pictures but Goodman was too demoralized by his misfortunes to catch on, and out of a sort of self-destructive pride, he snubbed Cain, who always carried in his wallet a picture of Goodman, the best friend he had ever had. Lawrence himself was sometimes a little hard to take, with his heavy drinking, but through him, Cain got the feel of the movie world, while settling into the California way of life. He could count as friends and influences some of the best and highest-paid scriptwriters in the business, including Herman Mankiewicz, whom Cain had met when Goodman produced his play *Wild Man from Borneo*. Cain had made a few revision suggestions that Mankiewicz had used.

In April 1932, Cain was suddenly assigned to *Hot Saturday*, from a short novel by Harvey Fergusson about the events of a single day in a small western town. A naïve, romantic young girl wants a husband to fulfill a typical American dream of wealth and social splendor. Fergusson was the author of four nonfiction books and two novels set in the West and in Washington, DC.

Cain heard little of his efforts on this one, but after six months he was closed out, and then faced the reality of his impulsive switch to pictures. He had moved lock, stock, and barrel to California, with a wife and two teenage children to support. He had a liver ailment. He had no dependable income in the middle of the Depression, and no idea what to do next. Although looking back now, he felt he hadn't really liked newspaper work much anyhow. Newspaper editors had always praised his ability, his versatility. He hated to tell himself that he couldn't write pictures.

On October 31, 1932, he wrote to Mencken, "I now have time to do some decent writing." He'd like to start the novel about the woman in the filling station who conspires with her lover to kill her husband, but he hesitated to venture into a long work of fiction. His friendship with the chief attendant at Goebels Lion Farm resulted in an idea for a story set near there on the road to Ventura. In this one, too, a couple ran a gas station–cafe combination. The new elements were a baby in an icebox and a tiger.

The overwhelming reaction to his editorial asking, What does one do on meeting a man-eating tiger? suggested how fascinated people are by wild cats. Frank Stockton's famous short story "The Lady or the Tiger" capitalized on the fear of tigers. Balzac's most famous story "A Passion in the Desert" explored man's desire to tame and domesticate the tiger. Tigers fascinated Cain, too, but he was also fascinated by the various ways people respond to or deal with cats of all kinds. Part of a woman's appeal was her cat-like qualities and men tested their masculinity vicariously in the lion tamer's feats. Among other things, this story would be another in his studies of the American exhibitionist masculinity. His first story with a California setting. And for the first time his nameless, average-guy narrator would write his story, not tell it. That helped Cain cut down the dialect he was so used to writing.

"Of course there was plenty pieces in the paper about what happened out at the place last summer, but they got it all mixed up, so I will now put down how it really was, and 'specially the beginning of it, so you will see it is not no lies in it.

"Because when a guy and his wife begin to play leapfrog with a tiger, like you might say, and the papers put in about that part and not none of the stuff that started it off, and then one day say X marks the spot and next day say it wasn't really no murder but don't tell you what it was, why, I don't blame people if they figure there was something funny about it . . . a dirty rat getting it in the neck where he had it coming to him, as you will see when I get the first part explained right."

Cain imagined the nameless narrator telling him the rest of the story, some lines of which he might use. "I helped Duke take care of the filling station, while his wife Lura took care of the lunch room and tourist shacks. Then Duke brought in some wild cats to attract customers. One of them was dead. Lura had a way with cats, so she went into the cage among them, patted them, dragged the dead one out, but didn't tell Duke, knowing it would be an insult to his masculinity.

"Then Duke ups the voltage on the show with a mountain lion. How a wandering male lion got into the cage with it is a mystery, but I know Lura did it out of sympathy. Then Duke brings in an enormous tiger, Rajah. But he's too ferocious. Business falls off. Duke goes into the cage to tame him, with the human stare. Rajah gets between Duke and the door, tries to maul him, but I pulled him into the kennel. Lura didn't see all this, but she gives Duke a catlike look, as if she's Rajah's sister. Next, Duke says he's going out to trap some wild ones, but he's really going to tomcat with some woman down the road.

"Then into this set-up comes Wild Bill Smith, Texas Tornado, snake doctor, showman, fake. I was jealous of how he affected Lura. He came back, often. So one day Duke says, 'I'm going to be a father.' I let Lura know I knew what was what. Made her cry, and I hugged her. 'It's awful to have a pretty woman in your arms that's crying over somebody else.' She plays with Rajah the way lovers horse around.

"Next comes Duke's discovery of Wild Bill's snake ring. Lura tells him her story, alluding to his woman. I got this from Lura. 'So here is how it was': Duke pretended to leave, but he had starved the tiger, and he turned it loose in the house, but Lura stuck a burning stick in its face, hid the baby in the icebox, threw some meat through the screen to the tiger, shut it up to the bedroom.

"Duke returned, surprised to see her alive. She told him she knew what he was up to. He pulls a gun on her, but she beats him up, throws him out, and the gun after him. But he shoots her.

"What happened next I got from the state cops. Here's how they figured it out: Duke tried to make it look like suicide, called the cops, but the burning stick had set the room on fire, and the tiger jumped right through the wall. I passed the ambulance that was taking Lura away. I drove up. Duke and the tiger were screaming. They were found in the ruins, Duke with a tiger bite in his head. The baby was found in the icebox, okay. Lura was cleared, got an offer from the movies, and she and I ran the station. 'But one night I heard a rattle from a bum differential, and I never even bothered to show up for breakfast the next morning.'

"I often wish I had. Maybe she left me a note."

The structure was even more inevitable, and fast-paced, stroke-by-stroke, than "Pastorale." The plot was very complex, enough to carry a whole movie, with fifteen different developments or turning points. Never before had his imagination been so inventive, producing a somewhat improbable, wacky, but entertaining tall tale.

Cain needed the usual $250 he got from the *Mercury*, and he needed as usual Mencken's praise: it was one of his best works. In November, Knopf wrote to Cain to tell him Mencken had shown him the "The Baby in the Icebox" galleys, that it was one of the best stories he had read, and that he hoped Cain would try a novel. His response to Knopf, who held an option on his next two books, was: "Your note may turn out to be the push I needed."

He told Knopf he had in progress "a simple story," maybe a novellette, "laid in California, about a youth who commits the perfect murder with a girl, then has fortune kiss him on the brow, then gets so bored with her as she replays the murder of her former husband every night for the kick it injects into their carnal relations, that he is sunk. That is, he finds that the bond which put such a tingle in their doings in the beginning can also be a chain that he doesn't dare break. An accident gives him the trouble but he is hung for this one anyway. Sounds dull, I suppose, but I might pull it off."

Knopf asked Mencken for a reaction to Cain's ideas. "Cain ... not infrequently wanders across the boundary line of sense."

Cain got back to it, writing it in the third person, but it was going nowhere slowly.

When Cain's third short story, "The Baby in the Icebox," appeared in the January 1933 issue of the *Mercury*, the excitement it generated resulted in a sale by the William Morris agency to Paramount for $1,000, a give-away. The studio didn't want to rehire Cain to write the script. Everything in Hollywood seemed to be done on a lunatic basis.

Citizen reaction to Al Capone's conviction inspired Cain's first dialogue since *Our Government* appeared. Two citizens in suits coming into Chicago on the Twentieth Century Limited get to talking about what a dirty trick the US government played on Al Capone, getting him for income tax instead of murder. A fellow in the Department of Justice sitting nearby explains to them that that's the only way to get Capone, given the repeal of the beer act. "He gets out when they repeal the Income Tax Law. Is that it?" "That's it." They all laugh.

Cain felt his interest in the dialogue dwindling. He sent "Don't Monkey with Uncle Sam" to *Vanity Fair*, a chic monthly that appealed to a rather small circle, a magazine, as its editor Frank Crowninshield once said, that "covers things people talk about at parties—the arts, sports, humor and so forth." Since last year, it had recently added a little more substance, with pieces on labor, politics, and science. Among its contributors were Alexander Woollcott, Robert Benchley, Grantland Rice, Gertrude Stein, T. S. Eliot, Elinor Wylie, e e cummings, Ferenc Molnar, and Gilbert Seldes, their work graced by the look of Edward Steichen's and Cecil Beaton's photographs and reproductions of Picasso, Rouault, Matisse, and Gauguin. Cain enjoyed seeing his work in a variety of publications, affecting various kinds of audiences.

After more than two years, Cain would not feel he really belonged in the California paradise until he had mastered it by fixing its facts and features and his own ideas about them in persuasive prose. "I shall attempt, in this piece, an appraisal of the civilization of Southern California, but it occurs to me that before I begin I had better give you some idea what the place looks like. If you are like myself before I came here, you have formed . . . a somewhat false picture of it, and you will have to get rid of this before you can understand what I am trying to say." Enumerate the misconceptions, repeating this rhetorical phrase, "Wash that out. . . . Wash that out and keep it out." "You are now ready for the handiwork of man. I suggest that you put it in with water-color." Now repeat "put in" to lead off each item. "We are concerned here with appearances." "Now take your opus out in the noonday sun, tack it down on a board, and look at it." "You may suppose that . . . I exaggerate the effect which the sun has on things." Give evidence to bolster your position. For contrast, take Balboa, an oasis. Back to the typical. "There is no reward for aesthetic virtue here, no punishment for aesthetic crime. Nothing but a vast cosmic indifference, and that is the one thing the human imagination cannot stand. It withers, or else, frantic to make itself felt, goes off into feverish and idiotic excursions that have neither reason, rhyme, nor point, and that even fail in their one purpose, which is to attract notice."

Out of a sense of tough fairness, he would enumerate the good points. "In spite of the foregoing. . . . you have to admit that there is a great deal to be said for it." The English spoken here—"too articulate to seem plausible. . . . It is hard to believe that the common man can express himself coherently." "Well, I have listened to it for more than a year now, and I believe it. . . . The actual accent, to my ear, has a somewhat pansy cast to it. It produces on me the same effect as an English accent." But "there is a faint musical undertone in it. They 'sing' it. . . ." "Cleanliness and the sunshine . . . may be due for credit here. It is a sort of general disinfectant." Give it the personal angle. My two stepchildren in school here. Public education is excellent. "As to higher education, I can tell you nothing, as I have had no chance to study it." I love the roads, I like to drive. All Californians are very dependent on the automobile. "Even the cook comes to work in her car. Of course, she can't cook when she gets there, but anyhow she arrives in style." Curb-service food. "Of course, this gives me the colic, but it gives you an idea how far the thing goes." "For my part, what I take most delight in is the swimming pools."

"Now I come to the tough part of my piece." You may ask, why I don't praise it. "I wish I could, but I can't. The thing simply won't add up. When I take off the first shoe at night, and wonder what I have to show for the day, I usually know that I have nothing to show for it. . . . To me, life takes on a dreadful vacuity here." Admit the difficulty in writing this piece. "Frankly, I don't know exactly what it is that I miss. But if you will bear with me while I grope a little, I shall try to get it down on paper." "Let us take a fresh start." Look at Paris. "An unfair comparison is precisely what I want." "What I like is a jumble of the tangible and the intangible, of beauty and ugliness, that somehow sets me a-tingle: the sinister proximity of big things. . . . In other words, a perpetual invitation to explore, to linger, to enjoy." "This beckoning jumble . . . is the essence of the appeal which any place has for you, and that if it isn't there, you are going to be most unhappy about it, even if at first you don't know quite what ails you." California somehow "never manages to be delightful." I go to Goebel's Lion Farm, where my friend Bert Parks is chief attendant. "God in Heaven, a cat is something to look at!" Cain was eager to launch his attack on the food here. "Eat. That is the measure, alas, of the cookery of the region." "Brother, God hath laid a curse on this Pacific Ocean, and decreed that nothing that comes out of it shall be fit to eat." "I've got to be reliable and accurate about this thing" . . . He told a hostess, asking about the food. He knew he had devoted too much space to food. But maybe not.

"This gets us down pretty much to what we laughingly call my intellect. . . . I don't ask for talk about Proust . . . and I actually feel better when I am off it. But I do ask—what shall I say? Something that pricks my imagination a little, gives me some sort of lift, makes me feel that that day I heard something. And I am the sort that is as likely to get this from the common man as his more erudite cousin, the high-brow." "But what do I get? Nothing."

Finally, my main "squawk": "the piddling occupations to which the people dedicate their lives." Eastern workers "all take part in vast human dramas, and I find it impossible to disregard the stature which their occupations confer on them. . . . they share some of the electric importance of the stages they tread." "But they suffer from the cruel feebleness of the play which the economy of the region compels them to take part in." The play "cannot be evoked at will, and it cannot be faked. If the voltage cannot be felt, the whole piece falls flat." Cain sensed they might feel at this point that he was overstating. "You may think I overstate the case in a strained effort to be comical." Did he? "I assure you I do not." Every easterner says all that I am saying. "What I would like to see here, to make an end of my carping," is "economic vitality. The whole place would be pepped up . . ." with "things that appeal to the imagination."

Now, to the future. "I wish now to do a little speculating about the future of this place . . . favorable factors—check them over." If most "sections of the United States were first populated by failures," these here mostly have a pile to start with. As an admirer of know-how, he was glad to be able to say that the Chamber of Commerce is unique here: "addressing itself to the problem with a sobriety which I must confess impresses me." With integrity as a rock-like foundation, facts are power. "And there is something that I pay a great deal of attention to when I try to estimate a man's integrity, which is a healthy respect for fact. It amounts almost to a religion in this place. . . . I am a sucker for the man who is worried about the last decimal point." In most cities the C of C bears "about the same relation to the body politic as the Communist party does in Russia." Admit it. "I suppose I put that in out of pure malice." A city is big time if soap boxers damn the government, if there are parades with cracked heads. "Why I regard such things as cosmopolitan I don't know, but I do."

Feeling his reverence for history, Cain went on. "Some sort of destiny awaits the place. Of recent years, the implications of a destiny have bemused me greatly. And I believe that one of the troubles of the United States as a whole is that it no longer has one. In the beginning, its destiny was to reduce a continent, and that destiny as long as it lasted made everything hum. Transformed the most shiftless bacon-and-beaner into a pioneer, placed an epic frame around our wars, gave the most trivial episode the stature of history." Cain worked consciously in this piece as in his others to achieve a sense of control of his material, his techniques, and so, of his readers, and when he felt that control firmly, he felt the reader's presence intimately. "Now what? If you know, you are a wiser man than I am." "So when you come to a place that not only thinks it has a destiny, but knows it has a destiny, you cannot but be arrested. . . . In short, it is going to be a paradise on earth. . . . I, personally, even if the first act hasn't been so hot, am not going to walk out on the show. . . ."

"No, I stay. The climate suits me fine."

So far, he had failed in Paradise, but here he had also written a sensational story, a *Vanity Fair* piece, the beginning of a novel, and this essay, his longest, his most important, his best. Mencken wrote on December 21, 1932 that "Paradise" was "the first really good article on California that has ever been done."

Talking with Vincent Lawrence was like one endless seminar in writing. To him, every story was a love story. He talked repeatedly about a concept he called the love-rack. First comes the highly charged magical moment when the lovers meet, then they go on the love-rack when they work together to handle a problem that often separates them, but then they are happily reunited. Watching the lovers on the love-rack makes us care about them. That the reader or spectator must first care that the lovers are on the rack and sympathize with them struck Cain as a new idea.

During another session, Vincent got to talking about the famous Ruth Snyder--Judd Gray case. "I heard that when Ruth Snyder packed Gray off to Syracuse (where he was supposed to be staying at a hotel all this gruesome night), she gave him a bottle of wine, which he desperately wanted on the train. But he had no corkscrew with him, and dared not ask the porter for one, for fear it would be the one thing they'd remember him by. When the police lab analyzed it, they found enough arsenic to kill a regiment of men. Did you ever hear that Cain?"

He had not, but it clarified an idea about his filling station murder novel that he already vaguely had in mind. "Your idea of a love-rack interests me, and I would think a murder would be a terrific love-rack. The lovers wake up to discover that once they've pulled the perfect murder, no two people can share this terrible secret and live on the same earth. They turn against each other."

The reaction that concept got from Vincent encouraged Cain. He meditated on it for several weeks.

The sensation "The Baby in the Icebox" had created enabled the Morris agency to get Cain $200 a week at Columbia, which was just emerging under Harry Cohn from the "Poverty Row" of B studios.

Most of the other Columbia writers were new on the scene, too: Norman Krasna, Jo Swerling, Dorothy Parker, Sidney Kingsley, Sidney Buchman, Dore Schary. Cain felt more experienced than this new kid Billy

Wilder whose typewriter got hot first thing in the morning. "Take it easy until 11:45," Cain told him. "Harry Cohn never gets to his office until noon." One morning, he arrived at ten, broke the stony silence with curses upon all well-paid, poorly producing writers. Cain heard all typewriters instantly break out in song with his own, and that made Cohn scream, "Liars! Liars!"

Harry Cohn assigned Cain to fashion a script with James Kelvin McGuinness on the Chicago Insull scandal. That lined up with one of Cain's interests—high finance. Samuel Insull rose from Horatio Alger origins to build a Midwest utilities empire, one of the most impressive financial empires of the 1920s. It fell apart in June 1932. Insull, then seventy-two, was indicted on mail fraud and embezzlement, and million-dollar suits were filed by creditors. He went into exile in Paris and Greece. Out of their interest in writing, Cain fashioned a friendship with McGuinness, whom he had known on the *New Yorker*, but no script. Learning that he had been closed out prompted Cain to move from Hollywood to Burbank in the San Fernando Valley, where he tried to assess his situation. Maybe he would get back to that novel about the filling station murder.

On his last day in February 1933 on the Columbia lot, Cain was directed to report to Robert Riskin. Though Harry Cohn, tough-guy president of Columbia, had not liked Cain's work, Cain sensed that he had been impressed by Cain himself. So he had instructed Riskin to find out what made Cain tick, or whether he ticked. Riskin, one of the highest-paid screenwriters and most admired by other screenwriters, who worked usually with Frank Capra and who was just finishing a script called *It Happened One Night* for Clark Gable and Claudette Colbert, was five years younger than Cain, handsome, black-eyed, blessed with Fay Wray as his wife.

After a few hours of talk, Riskin said, "I don't think I ever met anyone with quite the slant that you have on story-writing. You have a very peculiar mind. You seem to think that embedded in any idea is the inevitable, perfect outline that will deliver the whole point—you make a sort of algebraic equation out of it, transforming your equations again and again and again, seeking this ultimate story. But it's not like that at all. It has to be *your* story, even if you're working for a picture company. There's no ultimate, inevitable, perfect 'move' that's going to give you an outline, determine your situation. It's not mathematics. It's a living thing. It's *you*." That gave Cain a laugh, but he knew Riskin was only expressing a characteristic of his mind that he had half realized himself, and so felt no resentment, but rather some sense of gratitude.

Thanks to Riskin, he made a sudden decision: to tell his story, regardless of how preposterous others might think it. Two or three days later, during the bank holiday, just after Franklin Roosevelt had become president, Cain sat down at the typewriter to begin *Bar-B-Que*.

Some of the basic elements emerged out of a pattern set in "Pastorale" and echoed in "The Baby in the Icebox": In "Pastorale," Burbie murders Lida's elderly husband. In "Baby," Lura and Duke run a filling station. All three of Cain's stories had violated the positive thrust of Lawrence's love-rack concept: the narrator of "Montfaucon" fails. The narrator of "Pastorale" doesn't do anything but talk. The narrator of "Baby" doesn't get Lida, the woman he loves. Those were negative actions. In a positive action, there must be a payoff, even if that action later ends in disaster. The characters would get what they wanted, each other, and money, but only for a while.

A major difference in technique from the three stories was that he would tell this one in the third person. Daily, as he wrote, he kept telling himself, "Fast means fast, Cain," but the pace was sluggish. Something was wrong. He traced most of the difficulties to the third person. The three first-person stories had been successful. But wouldn't an entire novel told in vernacular first person drive the reader up the wall? Who said Frank Chambers had to talk vernacular? He was from California. How do average roughneck young men here talk? He's been to school, he can spell, he uses fairly good grammar. So without vernacular, let Frank tell his and Cora's story.

"They threw me off the hay truck about noon. I had swung on the night before, down at the border, and as soon as I got up there under the canvas, I went to sleep. . . . I tried some comical stuff, but all I got was a dead pan, so that gag was out. They gave me a cigarette, though, and I hiked down the road to find something to eat.

"That was when I hit this Twin Oaks Tavern. It was nothing but a roadside sandwich joint, like a million others in California."

But then another thing bothered Cain. Frank kept leading into each speech with "I says" and "she says." That, too, could drive a reader up the wall. So he cut them all out, and it was clear without the lead-ins who was speaking.

So now, the novel, like the stories, was in first person, but with crucial differences besides style: Frank was not nameless and the story he told was not mainly about other love triangles but about his own. This story had more drive, a brisker pace, and the reader would care about Frank and Cora, despite their crimes.

But in draft after draft the story fell apart in the middle. While Cora was in jail, Cain had to invent something for Frank to do. That section ran to eighty thousand words. Cain turned to Vinnie Lawrence, who listened, walked it out a while, then said: "Cain, get her out of there. I don't care how you do it—get her out. Get her off. Because your story doesn't move till she's out and they both start up their lives again, so—get her off."

But how? Cain invented a crafty criminal lawyer who used the insurance angle to defeat the wily district attorney. That device got the story moving again. But Cain had to have verification from an expert, and he got it from Harrington of the insurance division of AAA, who told him: "If you think no district attorney has ever been left holding the bag like that, you're crazy, because I've done it!"

The algebra of this story was now much clearer. Frank Chambers, an easygoing young drifter, a spontaneous creature of action, not far removed in status or aspiration from the average male reader Cain anticipated, meets and immediately lusts for Cora Papadakis, whose husband, Nick, the proprietor of a California roadside restaurant, an obese, middle-aged Greek, offers Frank a job.

To make readers feel the impact of their encounter and its consequences, Cain had Frank and Cora meet on page 5, make love on 15, and decide to murder the Greek on 23. Sharing the dream of getting drunk and making love without hiding, they go on the love-rack. Frank's wish is to have Cora. Cora's wish is to have Frank, but the solution is not so simple as running away together. Their own dreams conflict: Frank wants

Cora on the open road. Cora wants Frank, but not without money and respectability. So Cora urges Frank to kill Nick. The restaurant will then be hers.

But there is terror in the wish come true. As soon as Frank and Cora believe that they have committed the perfect murder and have acquired money, property, and freedom, they turn on each other.

By concentrating only on the lovers and on the action that their wish produces, Cain felt he had created an immediately intense experience for the reader, as brief as a movie. A fable of love. This action kept in motion certain elements that almost guaranteed reader interest: illicit love, murder, tainted money, sexual violence that verged on the abnormal. He consciously played upon the universal wishes of the average American male.

And he had mastered stylistic and structural techniques for manipulating reader response. After the swift execution of the basic situation in the first twenty-three pages, each development, each scene was controlled with the same narrative compression. Inherent in each episode was the inevitability of the next. He kept strictly to the essentials. No conventional exposition. The characters existed only for the sake of the immediate action. Violence and sexual passion thrust forward along the spine of the action at a pace that would itself be part of the reader's felt experience. The swift rhythm of the dialogue contributed to the pace.

He had executed the ironies of action with an algebraic equation Riskin might come to admire. Frank cons Nick out of a free meal, but the con backfires in a way when Nick cons Frank into staying on to operate the service station—thus does Frank become involved in a situation that leaves all three of them dead. And after Nick recovers from what he took to be an accident in the bathtub, it is he who searches for Frank and persuades him to return to the roadside restaurant, thus helping to bring about his own death. Cleared of killing the Greek, Frank and Cora collect the insurance. Later, when she is waiting for a taxi to leave Frank, Cora sticks a note for him in the cash register. It refers to their having killed the Greek for his money. But Frank catches her. He insists he loves her. To test his love, Cora, who is now pregnant, swims so far out to sea that Frank must help her back. They become reconciled. But driving back from the beach, Frank swerves to miss a truck, the car wrecks, and Cora is killed. The police find Cora's note in the cash register and deduce that Frank has engineered the wreck so he can have all the money. He can't be tried twice for killing Nick, so they will execute him for murdering Cora.

"Here they come. Father McConnell says prayers help." Let him speak directly to the reader: "If you've got this far, send up one for me, and Cora, and make it that we're together, wherever it is."

Finished in June 1933, Cain realized with a shock that he had only 159 pages, but he sent *Bar-B-Que* to Knopf.

Remembering his promise to Lippmann, while showing him the sights in his car several months before, to show him the novel, Cain sent him a carbon. Knopf's response was negative. The novel, he said, was below the standard Cain had set in his work for Mencken. He would publish it without an advance, but only if Cain would revise. That hurt Cain, then made him furious. Lippman wired praising the novel and asking permission, as consultant to Macmillan, to offer it there. Cain gave him the go-ahead and wrote to tell Knopf he was offering it elsewhere. Mencken read it and tried to infect Knopf with enthusiasm. Macmillan hesitated. Blanche Knopf read it and declared to her husband, "We'd better buy that book." Lippmann wired that Macmillan was too squeamish and that Knopf was willing to take the book without revision and on revised terms. The badly needed $500 advance and the other terms were acceptable to Cain. And the dedication was to read: "To Vincent Lawrence."

Cain had many arguments with Knopf over the title *Bar-B-Que*, and over alternatives, *Black Puma* and *The Devil's Checkbook*. One day, Vincent was telling Cain about having mailed his first play to a producer. "I almost went nuts. I'd sit and watch for the postman, and then I'd think, 'You got to cut this out,' and then when I left the window I'd be listening for his ring. How I'd know it was the postman was that he'd always ring twice."

"Vincent," Cain cut in, "I think you've given me a title for that book."

"What's that?"

"*The Postman Always Rings Twice.*"

"Say, he rang twice for Chambers, didn't he?"

"That's the idea."

"And on the second ring, Chambers had to answer, didn't he? Couldn't hide out in the backyard any more."

"His number was up, I'd say."

"I like it."

"Then that's it."

But Knopf didn't like Cain's new title. He urged *For Love or Money*. Cain refused that one, offered a few more: *Western Story*, *Malice Afore-thought*, *The Queen Commands*. Finally, Knopf accepted *The Postman Always Rings Twice*.

Noticing the way Malibu captured the popular imagination aroused Cain's compulsion to be the man who would tell them its history, give people the inside story, while offering a witty, cynical interpretation of the significance of its image. It was a packaged paradise within a paradise.

"Whatever else may be said of Malibu, the place where the movie queens grow their sunburn, there is one thing that you have to hand it: it is probably the finest beach ever created by God." Watch the swells, the surf. "Then the sea stirs again, there is another swell, and the perfor-mance is repeated. Each swell gives a strictly solo number, with entrance, build-up, punch line, and tag all complete. While it is on, no other swells appear to crab its act." "It is dazzling, a little wearisome, and more than a little unreal: it has that quality, whatever it is, that marks off the Pacific Ocean from all other oceans. . . ." Certain other creatures "here visible pretty much as God made them. . . . blend in with the seascape, being in much the same key. They too are dazzling, a little wearisome, and more than a little unreal. They too have that quality, that suggestion of having stepped out of somebody's fever dream, that goes with the Pacific Ocean and no other ocean." Now "ring down the curtain on this exercise in rhap-sodical prose."

In a long middle section, provide a history of the intricate financial deals. "Whether Mr. Jones takes a commission from the builder he desig-nates, I must confess I don't know." When the offer was made, the super-visor on a movie lot reasoned, "If they gave you the sand, it couldn't be any good. But when they charge $12,000 for it, it must have production value. It is the shrewd business sense of the supervisors which has put the movies where they are today."

"Thus the history of this Elysian spot, but we still have to ascertain what the residents get out of it, now that they are there." Follow a lovely film star. This is what she sees at the parties: no dancing, no necking, no gayety, no jumping in the ocean at 1:00 a.m. "There will be nothing but dice, drinks, and conversations" about making movie bucks. "As to where she goes to bed, it would perhaps be indelicate to inquire." She does everything but enjoy her beach. Out of a hundred houses, Cain had never seen more than three people on it. Wind it up this way: "It is the most deserted beach this side of Paradise. The only living creature that seems really to enjoy it is a chow dog. He stands there and barks at the waves to go back. Mr. Jones motions to them to roll in. And they roll."

Feeling the piece had a certain charm, Cain called it "The Widow's Mite, or Queen of the Rancho," and sent it off to a Mr. Brokaw at *Vanity Fair*, who turned out to be a woman named Clare Booth Brokaw. For some reason, he couldn't seem to shake off the embarrassment of that gaffe.

Having mastered California in "Paradise" and a piece of it, Malibu and Hollywood, in "Widow's Mite," Cain wanted to explain to himself why he had failed at pictures, and to explain to the nation, in an objective analysis, the nature and process of the medium, especially as it involved the writer, and to get off some of his own attitudes and convictions. Maybe it was too soon to take all that on, but maybe the sooner the better.

Cain had often recalled his first exposure to movies. He had attended the nickelodeon with a boyhood friend in Chestertown in 1906. The comic John Bunny was repellent and the *Great Train Robbery* was simple-minded. As two young intellectuals who knew what was good, they left the theater with a scorn for movies that for Cain had not diminished.

"Of the 300 or so writers actually employed in Hollywood, I suppose I know fifty, and I don't know one who doesn't dislike movie work.... This is a singular state of affairs, among the other people engaged in the business the feeling is the other way around." The writers with no other accomplishments in writing, who see movies as their big chance for "a whiff of stardust here," are the bitterest. "No matter what kind of a cheap hack he may be, to all signs and appearances, there comes a time in his day when he has to be a writer.... to do his best." He claims that the movies won't let him. How he takes it "is what I want to probe into here. I have to warn you that I am a disappointed movie writer myself, so you can take my remarks at a proper discount. I have had two flops." Bad judgment, not ineptitude. "I worked as hard as I knew how, but both times I flopped flat." But failure here hurts far less than when I look back through old magazines at earlier articles and decide they're no good. I'm upset all day, if it was especially bad, "and have to pound the typewriter furiously to shake it out of my mind. The movies had no such power to punish me."

His worst mental anguish came with the realization that he was being paid for something he didn't deliver, "a new sensation to me, and a disagreeable one. I was in a scramble of personal emotions, for on both lots there were men who had treated me very decently, whom I had got to like, and whom I had let down."

"But all that involved what you might call my social conscience. My artistic conscience barely stirred." "That is what I want to get at here: Why is it that the movies seem unable to afford the writer the requital that he finds so quickly elsewhere. Burning shame for work badly done, glowing pride in work that hits the mark? If I do get at it, I ought to be able to shed light on" this question: "Is this really destined to be one of the major arts, worthy of serious critical attention?"

Give your own practical perspective on writing for the screen and on cinematic "art" in general. Cain felt obliged to be fair to both sides, to the writer and the producer, and to disabuse the reader of certain preconceptions about both. He must "clear the deck of some of these before going on." Outsiders and writers themselves charge that the studios want only the worst a writer can do. That the studios are run by barbarians is not true. "Wash out all stories about the ghastliness of life on a movie lot." Producers are full of self-educated information. "When they get it they have it." "They have one bad fault. They are prone to condone bad work that makes money, and overlook good work if the picture flops." To describe writers' attitudes use the "No doubt" rhetorical refrain, ending with: "No doubt they pity themselves handsomely, but I'll tell you why their effort was turned down. It was no goddamn good, and that was the beginning of it and the end of it." Producers want good stories. "By good they mean just what you mean by good. That is, they mean what you mean when you have paid your money and want something to show for it. . . . They have learned that good means good. It means what you paid for: that kick, that excitement, that emotion, which takes you out of the seat you are sitting in, transports you to where things are going on, and holds you there in hot suspense to see how it all comes out."

The word "pictures," their word, "states the essence of the business . . . a series of photographed pictures." That these move and talk is incidental. Because of the nature of the "art" of "pictures," the writer can never really achieve satisfaction in his work. The movie writer, unlike the stage writer, must write first of all for the actor, the model. One difference between stage and screen is that a play has a literary script that is separable from the actor, but a movie has no real, accessible script.

Look at portraiture. In a painting, you feel the painter. In a photograph, you respond to the subject. "Sargent's imagination speaks to your imagination, says something that transcends all models, however eminent. . . . But the photographer imagines nothing, communicates nothing . . . from one imagination to another imagination." "What goes on the plate is the model, and that is all that goes on the plate. . . ." "If the model is interesting, the picture will be interesting, and that's all."

"Mickey Mouse is the one outstanding accomplishment of the talking picture to date . . . it is one imagination speaking to another imagination. A script may say "section of crowd." The director can make that the big scene, but there's "nothing in the script to show it. If you want this story, you have to get it from that film: for the first time in the history of such things, imagination and performance go together," and you can't part them.

The "very nature of this movie business compels" the writer "to write for an action," for his special asset. "Imagination is free or it is not free, and here it is not free. It serves the medium, instead of the medium serving it, and once that is felt, that is the end of pride, of joy in getting things down on paper, of having them appear in front of your eyes." "If the camera has a defective capacity for conveying what somebody imagined, it has a positive genius for conveying what nobody imagined." When an alligator accidentally intruded upon a scene and Charles Bickford beat it with a paddle, that became the picture's greatest moment. "But who imagined it? Not the authors. Not the director. Not Bickford, for he wasn't imagining about that time." "When a beauty like that is caught on a negative, story, and all such things must make way for it." All other artists work in media "absolutely under their control." In film, the writer "obeys the medium, the medium doesn't obey him." The serious critic, "posterity's bookmaker," refuses to make book on anything so mechanical as pictures. Art "pays off on wings, on that imaginative vitality which can fly down the cruelly long distance through the years." "Thus the critic is concerned with what, in telegraphy, is known as the phantom circuit . . . the imagination." "Critics can never be quite sure that a crash of cymbals which he especially admires is not, in reality, the sound of the conductor falling off the podium."

The writer shouldn't aspire "to functions which simply are not there." The high-minded writer will always be disappointed with the movies because he can never be sure *whose* imagination has made a particular film good. "Well, there are worse trades than confecting entertainment, and if you realize clearly that you *are* at work on entertainment, something that lives tonight and tomorrow is forgotten, then the suspicion that you are a prostitute of the arts loses much of its sting." "There is good entertainment and bad, and a chance for plenty of honest resourcefulness." "For my part, when I go to a movie, I am entertained best if it is unabashedly a movie, and not a piece of dull hoke, posing as something else." In this conclusion, he had expressed his own attitude as a fiction writer.

Having analyzed the nature of his own failure in "Camera Obscura," which he sent off to Mencken, Cain now felt a compulsion to analyze the paradoxical nature of success as it impressed him profoundly when he was a boy in the example of a Washington College football hero who had a "yellow streak." Start with the memory of first impressions of Chestertown, upon coming over the bay from Annapolis. The balance sheet: first what was good, then hit them with what was bad about Chestertown and the college. "But when all this had been duly inventoried and marked on the pleasant side of the ledger, there were other entries in red which gave us great uneasiness, and which stuck at parts of our natures. . . ." Swimming: the river "was all bottom." "I hated it. I was annoyed, too, at the way they swam . . . showed that they had no idea how the thing should be done." Many insults to the intelligence and palpable phoneyness. "These people, although they held their noses when they dived, and said 'H'y,' and raced home from the steamboat to tell who had been to the city that day, and in other ways exhibited the familiar symptoms of yokelry, all prided themselves on their fine Southern blood. If there was one thing my father detested it was fine Southern blood. I do, myself. It gives me the pip."

"At heart we weren't Catholics at all." After the impressive ceremonies in Annapolis, church was a farce, so we pulled out. One day a woman panicked, when the organ introduced a song she had not learned. "My mother picked up the music, adjusted her glasses, and sang it at sight.

"It was the first time it dawned on me that she must be good. I knew she had a voice, an enormous thing that could trill and do acrobatics that other ladies apparently couldn't do, and I knew that for years she had been a professional singer. These, though, were facts I had grown up with and never thought much about. But when she stood up there that time, and put on a show, that to me was black magic, I knew she must have something. What got me wasn't that she could do it, but that she knew she could do it."

He had contempt for the other woman, who "couldn't do anything right." "This, place, then made us uncomfortable. It violated all our ideas of how things ought to be done. . . ." It "still is a hick place. My father . . . never wanted anybody around that wouldn't take a drink."

The football team was "a dreadful shock." "This outfit had no gear, and God knows it had no snap." "And if I was hard to fool," his father, who had played at Yale, coached at St. John's, then at military school, "was impossible to fool." "I take exception to many of my father's notions, for example his notion that he can make a speech." But he knows football, and "when he spoke, God was talking."

Then he learned about Mr. James Garfield Moore. "He had none of the big, raw-boned look that I associated with football. He was compactly made, with the neat, precise movements of a tightrope walker. . . . Even in his football clothes there was a touch of fastidiousness about his get-up. His manner was one of bored fretfulness, and altogether he seemed as uncompromising a candidate for fullback as I had ever seen." His father pointed out that Moore plays hard. "He's got that quick, nervous energy that a player has to have . . . he keeps his mouth shut."

When Cain watched Moore in the first game, "It seemed amazing that such a sleek little pate could command an act of such electric ferocity." Cain felt "a surge of gratitude, of exultation, of downright worship. Here was a guy who could do it so it lifted you, gave you that incomparable ecstasy, made you feel that man after all was a god." Moore doesn't like football, he is a "voluntary," but not a coward, Cain's father told him.

But before the final game, Cain saw Moore seized by fear. "It wasn't his face. It wasn't the way he leaned. It wasn't what he said. It was the spit. That awful foam around his lips told its own story. It made me sick." Cain watched his father tell Moore to quit slobbering like a baby and make up his mind.

"I'll show him," snarled Moore.

"All authority on that field . . . had dissolved into his authority." "Such leadership is not based on inspiration, or on any of the gaudy things that the layman always imagines. It is based on trust, that simple, childlike faith which knows it is not going to be let down." "He was a true line plunger, a very rare breed. . . . He did it, my father said, by his unerring instinct for the hole, that place between two struggling players which could be struck, and if properly struck, would yield." Moore finally folded. "The power, the cunning, the skill for offensive play might be gone, but the spirit was there." "So ended the first chapter of my life at Chestertown." "But more importantly, a great man had come through, had proved he was really great. Did you ever have that happen to you? It is like nothing else in this world, it can happen only when you are young, for when you get older there are no more great men. Yet if it does happen to you, it stays with you through life, and warms you when you think of it. To me now, football is of as little consequence as anything I can imagine. Just the same, I lay this wreath at his feet unashamed, as he still seems great to me."

In a P.S. Cain called on the man who had bet his mother a box of candy that Moore would fail, to send it, twenty-eight years later, and gave her address. "It will greatly improve your standing in certain quarters." This "Tribute to a Hero" had ended up paying tribute to his mother and father as well.

Cain was also proud to be able to hold in his hand a book his father had written, *Financial History of the United States.*

The failed scriptwriter could now look back on the most productive period, the latter part of 1932 and 1933, of his life.

And B. A. Bergman, Cain's choice as his successor on the *New Yorker*, offered him another showcase, another source of income: $85 a week to write three columns a week for the op-ed page of Hearst's *New York American* that Bergman edited and that offered pieces by Aldous Huxley, Emil Ludwig, Frank Sullivan, and G. K. Chesterton.

In his first column, "Wanted: A Western Story," November 11, 1933, Cain discussed his inability to read Hemingway's *A Farewell to Arms*, Faulkner's *Sanctuary*, Nathanael West's *Miss Lonelyhearts*, Lewis's *Ann Vickers*, and Hervey Allen's *Anthony Adverse*. Compared with the old Beadle dime western novels, some of which he knew to have been written by Twain, Bret Harte, Ambrose Bierce, Jack London, Frank Norris, O. Henry, and Willa Cather, those novels gave no sense of going anywhere. The older writers told the kind of story that "fires writers and sets readers atingle, one that transcends plot, characters, and writing as writing," to deal with a big subject that was going somewhere: The West.

He continued his observations on modern literature over several columns. Writers ought to describe the times we live in, avoid the fashionable lure of fantasy. "These times are going to bulk larger in history than most other times, and it is important, for historical reasons, if for no other, that they be recorded, vividly and imaginatively, as only the novelists can do it, before their flavor is lost forever."

But most of his other subjects came out of the various human-interest categories he had developed on the *World*.

Cain felt the writing in his signed columns was weak. He didn't know why until he got back into the routine of it and an unexpected revelation came to him: As an editorial writer pretending it to be somebody else, that is, speaking for the "corporate awfulness" of the newspaper, he knew what he was doing, he had a sure, light touch, and a definite style. Writing now under his own byline, he began to detect a self-consciousness in what he said, a lack of naturalness, that surprised him. He had made a similar discovery in writing short stories: when the character told it in the first person, it moved, it lived, and had point, as *The Postman Always*

Rings Twice had. When he spoke in the third person, as himself, his story bogged down in self-consciousness, awkwardness.

When "Tribute to a Hero" came out in the November 1933 issue of the *Mercury*, it drew some very good comments, but Chestertown vocally resented it, and Moore failed to acknowledge Cain's gift of a copy.

Cain knew that his favorite magazine was in dire financial straits and the tension between Mencken and Knopf over the polarity of their interests—Knopf's in Hitler's rise, Mencken's still in exposing Babbitt's buffooneries—exploded. Cain heard that Mencken was leaving the only magazine that offered him that "curious excitement" of seeing his writings in print. Mencken wrote October 24, 1933, "I tell you the literal fact when I say that they were among the best things I printed, if not actually better than any other." Knopf brought in Henry Hazlitt, a conservative literary critic, whom Cain considered "never anything but dull in person or on paper." But Mencken's attitude on leaving made Cain feel that "I thought more of the magazine than he did."

As he read galleys for *Postman*, another idea took possession of him. In his essay on Frank Merriwell, Cain had commented on The West as a concept affecting private and national destinies. Having moved west, he witnessed firsthand and described in "Paradise" the effect of the concept. Now, he was so under the spell of it himself through research, personal experience, and having written a novel in its argot, that he wanted to write a new history of the United States in terms not of government but of the progress across the continent of economic forces of conquest. "As a publishing venture," he told Knopf, "it will be worth a dozen novels." His feeling of lack of direction had, with this history project, passed. Knopf told him to go ahead.

Cain was riding to lunch one day from the Columbia lot with James Kelvin McGuinness, his producer, and they were at the eternal job of talking stories, when McGuinness said, "Of course, there's one story that has never missed yet, and that's *the woman who uses the man to gain her ends.*" Cain rejected the femme fatale blueprint as repulsively obvious, but the challenging idea came of an American housewife, a grass widow with two children to support, who was not conscious of using men.

The Postman Always Rings Twice went into first and second printings before publication date, February 19, and had a third within a month.

A distributor gave it a four-star rating: "If this one doesn't smash, we're going to look for another job." Arthur Krock's blurb linked Cain to Zola and Tolstoy. "He has the most accurate ear for the speech of common Americans of anyone I know." Wanting a reaction from a hit screenwriter, Cain lent Louis Weitzenkorn a carbon. His reader's report was, "I think when that book comes out you're going to wake up famous."

At last, at forty-two, six years after having published his first short story, "Pastorale," Cain was a first novelist reading his reviews: the *New York Times Book Review*, "Six Minute Egg," Harold Stearns: "Cain is an old newspaper man who learned his reporting well, so well that he makes Hemingway look like a lexicographer and Caldwell like a sob sister at her first eviction ... its success is due entirely to one quality: Cain can get down to the primary impulses of greed and sex in fewer words than any writer we know of."

Franklin P. Adams, Cain's colleague on the old *World*, in the *New York Herald Tribune*: "Mr. Cain has written the most engrossing, unlaydownable book that I have any memory of.... So continuously exciting that if you can put it down before you've finished it, you are not the reader I think you are.... To my mind, its style, which some will compare with Hemingway's, is better than most of Hemingway's.... It is as tightly written, and as vernacularly dictaphonic as Lardner.... I can't detect a stylistic flaw in the book."

Charles Angoff, the *Mercury*: "He makes the art of Hemingway look like the befuddled and stuttering thing it is."

The *Nation*, which had published his second article: "the reader cannot catch his breath from the first page to the last ... what is technically termed a 'Wow.'"

Gilbert Seldes, *New York Journal*: "It is a long time since I have heard so many people of so many different tastes say that a book is 'great.'" Seldes himself thought it good, not great.

Edith Riley, *Houston Post*: "if you would see life stripped bare," read this book.

Hershel Brickell, syndicated column: "It has vigour and economy of method ... but its artistic merit won't keep it from giving the sensitive nightmares."

Lewis Gannett, *New York Herald Tribune*: "I hate the book! Ever since I read it two weeks ago, it has been sticking in the back of my mind and I can't stop talking about it."

Hal Borland, *Philadelphia Ledger*: "The next time anyone tries to tell you that newspaper work spoils a writer for serious or artistic work tell him to read *The Postman Always Rings Twice*." Its achievement and its influence would in time prove comparable to Hemingway's *The Sun Also Rises*.

William Rose Benét, the poet, in the *Saturday Review*: "You read about such people as those in this novel almost every day in the newspapers. . . . This novel derives from the sensationalism of America fostered by the daily press." Cain has learned compact writing and many other things in the city room. May become as good as Frank Norris of *McTeague*. He makes "his exciting and disagreeable novel carry conviction . . . His style is like the metal of an automatic. You can't lay his story down, for all its brutality and ugliness. . . . In the hard-boiled school of today here is a new student of considerable promise."

London, *Sunday Times*: "Brutal and shocking."

James Agate, *London Daily Express*: "a major work. Unheralded, it takes the reviewer's breath away . . . shakes the mind a little, as the mind is shaken by *MacBeth*."

Birmingham Post: the word "nausea" stuck out.

James Hilton, *London Telegraph*: "nearly perfect American conte, bare of every ornament and as ruthless as the kind of life it portrays."

He waited for praise from his father and mother who had said he was born to be a writer. What came was a query as to where he learned such awful language. Cain tried to find the awful language and failed.

Vincent was disappointed with the way Cain had handled his love-rack concept. Samson Raphaelson raved about it. Back east, Laurence Stallings and Morris Markey were violently enthusiastic, and hoped he was in the money. When Cain invited Dorothy Parker over to dinner, she set everybody straight: "Well, there's all sorts of stuff being written about what kind of novel it is—it seems to baffle these critics as they keep trying to label it. But to me it's a love story and that's all it is."

He was glad the Baltimore library had a waiting list. His alma mater, Washington College, bought no copies. Readers wrote to him. One charged him with corrupting people's morals. Cain shot back: "If you read the book without having your morals corrupted, why do you assume that others will be less fortunate than you?" *Postman* was banned in Canada. Hailed for his frankness and condemned for his preoccupation with sex, he still remembered his sense of fright at the teenage girl, "a cheap, brassy little trollop," who displayed her breasts in the sixth grade.

By
The Author of
The Postman Always Rings Twice
SERENADE
JAMES M. CAIN

5

Double Indemnity and *Serenade*

PRAISE OF *THE POSTMAN ALWAYS RINGS TWICE* FROM REVIEWERS AND friends for its literary quality surprised and delighted Cain, but what made its success fully authentic was its place on the bestseller lists and its sale for $25,000 to MGM. During the year in which he wrote the novel, he had made a measly $3,000.

Now publishers were leaving doors open for him in case he left Knopf. His New York agent, Edith Haggard, begged him not to "go in for articles at this point. Editors are crying for short stories by you and the field is wide open." She had already sold "Come-Back" to *Redbook*.

With Geller, his Hollywood agent, he talked over a slew of movie ideas. Planning to do a script called *Aida* for Mae West, he arranged to meet her, found her "preposterous and for some reason rather appallingly decent," and never finished that one.

Treason continued to fascinate him, so he worked on *The Traitor*, which dealt with the love affair between Benedict Arnold's wife and one of his co-conspirators, Major John Andre, but Geller could not sell it.

He became so famous that by spring when the movie version of his second published short story "The Baby in the Icebox" reached the screen as *She Made Her Bed*, most reviews praised Cain as a writer while blaming Paramount, the director, Casey Robinson and Frank Adams, the writers, and Richard Arlen and Sally Eilers, the stars, for throwing together a bad movie.

When Geller told Cain he had gotten him a job at MGM writing a script for Clark Gable and Jeannette MacDonald for $10,000, Cain knew the power of fame was real. Called *The Duchess of Delmonico*, the story was set in Goldfield, Nevada. Cain went out there looking for background, but an old miner's comment, "Gold is where you find it," was the only nugget he could dig up, a good refrain for a song, but he lost interest in the story.

It was not in him to keep money for work not done, so he returned the $3,333 advance, but MGM's accounting system had made no provision for such a unique event. Friends and columnists took sides as to whether he should have kept or returned the money.

Mencken needed money, too, and he came west where it was big, but when Geller got him a job at Cain's request, he backed out and returned to Baltimore. Cain had given some of his *Postman* money to his divorced sister Rosalie who had a son to support. What he wanted to buy for himself was freedom from Mary with a final settlement. To watch the progress of spring, he took the southern rail route to Maryland. After three years in the West, he found everything eastern dull, dead, hopeless. He visited Mencken, but fled Baltimore. New York City was no longer "Baghdad." He disliked New Yorkers and the way they talked, remembering how phony he sounded when he tried to write their lingo. To get a fair settlement, he needed Elina's tough business sense. She flew out, got what she wanted, and Cain was totally free of Mary.

Cain was so happy to be back in California, he knew he had finally found a place where he could feel he belonged.

Geller told him that MGM, which owned the stage as well as the film rights, had assigned a writer to adapt *Postman* to the stage, hoping for a hit that would impress the Hays office. Cain liked the writer well enough, but the thought of someone else doing a play based on a story he had imagined horrified him. He didn't want to write it himself, but wanting success as a playwright even more than as a screenwriter, he asked Geller to get him the job. He conceived the play somewhat in the impressionistic style of Clifford Odets's famous one-act strike play, "Waiting for Lefty."

While working on the *Postman* play, Cain continued to get sustenance from his talks about drama with Vincent and Rafe. As he wrote, he kept thinking of Rafe's reaction to a bad play they had seen together in late July. "A bad play is an awful thing, isn't it?" Rafe had asked. Bad plays terrified him, made him sick. Cain had the satisfaction of knowing that he had helped the man whom he had admired for *Young Love* in 1928 improve the comedy he had been working on in 1933, *Accent on Youth*. Having said the first act was terrible, Cain had analyzed each of a series of love scenes, and shown Rafe what was wrong, and he'd always been grateful.

Driving very slowly over the Southern California landscape, with Elina and her children, Leo and Henrietta, or with friends, Cain could conjure stories and plan his work for the next day.

Engrossed though he was in the play, Cain maintained his habit of corresponding at a great rate with all his friends. He reported to Lippmann that he disagreed with the thesis of his new book, *The Method of Freedom*. When Wolcott Gibbs wrote to Cain, asking him to submit something to the *New Yorker*, Cain, recalling the magazine's Byzantine editorial process, replied, "On the whole I'd rather be dead."

He asked editors and agents to urge Sally Benson, whose writing he had liked when he was at the *New Yorker*, to do more short stories. To Sally herself, he said, "For God's sake, can those little *New Yorker* pieces and spread out." The *New Yorker* was got out by a bunch of precious but gifted amateurs. "What they pay their money for is a yarn—excitement, the only thing that can light up your characterization so that it really glows, makes the reader feel it."

Working on the play all summer, he came up with a two-act drama, powerful in the scene in which Cora persuades Frank to murder Nick, a little weak, he was afraid, in the middle of the second act. He sent it to the Theater Guild.

He resented the fact that MGM would get one-third and that Knopf would get one-fourth of the stage royalties. But money came in for the second serial rights when the *New York Daily Mirror* and *Boston Daily Record* bought them, and he liked knowing millions of newspaper readers would be following the story. His Hearst columns continued to add to his income, although he had heard that Hearst himself disliked them.

Seeing the image of himself as a tough guy slowly harden into concrete, Cain asked Knopf to cut that element out of his ads. "I protested to the New York critics about their labeling me as hard-boiled, for being tough or hard-boiled is the last thing in the world that I think about. . . .

I am shooting for something different, and plugging me as one of the tough young men merely muddles things up." Knopf gleefully predicted that "every other review of every other hard-boiled book that may be published in the next three years will drag you and *The Postman* into it."

Writing "light pieces" for some western newspapers got him off on a string of articles on food, a frequent subject of his editorials. How about a series on food for magazines? Edith Haggard's response was, "You have made me an old woman, my lad. With the magazine world at your feet . . . pleading with you for short stories, you want to write food articles." She'd do her damnedest, but "for the little widow, do a story." Cain went to work like "a wild-man" on the food pieces.

"How to Carve that Bird." Cain's attitude toward the reader was, I know how and you don't, so pay attention. He saw it as a class act, center stage. "Friends, if you want the cook to take the bows after that turkey dinner, list and learn somewhere else, for there is a mighty literature on how to get this bird ready for the table. But if you want to take the bows yourselves, you will do what I tell you." Speed is important, or "You will have piled up a fiasco on yourself that will haunt you to the last day of your life." Do it "this way," he told his reader before each step. "We are still, remember, on the subject of speed." "You can now stand up, for I wouldn't attempt the bravura of carving while sitting down. The gag you stand up on is up to you, but the best gag is none at all. Let others do the gagging, for not all your wit can save you now, unless you deliver some turkey with it, and deliver pretty quickly at that."

Now take up the knife. "And when you sink it, sink it. Don't half do it, so the turkey is skating all over the platter, like a gun loose at sea." "Step on it, brother, and keep stepping: you are out in the middle, they are all looking at you, their cruel gaping jaws want turkey, and turkey is the only thing that will satisfy them. . . ." Cut the leg quickly. "If you can't do it gracefully, get if off anyhow, even if it makes a loud crack: a laugh is better than a stage wait, and the show doesn't go on until that leg is off." "Whet your knife. You have been cutting joints with it, and if you don't put it on the steel, you are not going to slice, you are going to mangle." "Don't try to slice vertically. . . ." "Now let us have a second look at the geography of your platter. If you have done it as I told you to do it, you have, northeast, a wing . . . ," etc. "Very well then, cut the strings." "It's no cinch, but if you insist on doing it, this is the way it will work, and no other way. Oh, and one more thing." Tell them what wine to drink. "Well, God bless you, and don't say I didn't warn you."

In "Them Ducks," he told his reader, "The first thing you must get through your head, if you are plotting a wild duck dinner, is that there is something silly about the whole rite." It's not a family affair. "You try that, and you are in for a flop." "Bow your head, then, to reality. Banish dressing. Banish politeness. Banish women. In other words, keep your eye on this central principle. . . ." This has to be a stag affair. Trust men to "confer an agreeable air of importance on the show." They know instinctively that "Saying everything is lousy doesn't get them anywhere. It is a theme, somehow, that doesn't orchestrate. It brings the curtain down with a bang. . . ."

"So much then for the general approach: we shall take up the thing itself." No champagne. "Too much of a good thing. . . ." "Now, then, for the ducks. The whole trick, here, is in timing. . . . This is the way the thing goes." List the separate acts of the show. "I said nine, not one second more, not one second less" to bake. "All right, then, we are back again, now, at the table. . . ." "If you have invited the right mob, it will be quiet, restrained, and interested. . . . These boys will carry you through: they know what you are feeling. Shoot the maid out into the kitchen as fast as she can go and make her get those ducks." "Now all your life you have heard a lot of talk about how these ducks are carved, and most of it is hooey." "You are supposed to do it with a fair show of speed," but that "somehow evokes a wrong picture, and you had better get the right picture, for if you don't, you are in trouble." Take the reader step by step to the end. "That is your wild duck dinner."

For "Oh, les crêpes Suzette!," the third in the series, a little sex would make the difference. "Brother, it's none of my business why you want to make *crêpes Suzette*, but you can't blame me for having my suspicions about it." "It is heresy to say so, and no doubt hurts the elegant tone of the article, but at a certain stage of the proceedings a *crêpe Suzette* is indistinguishable from a flapjack, except that it is a peculiarly troublesome flapjack . . . if you attempt quantity production with them, you are sunk and will wish you hadn't." "I warn you," no cook, don't trust her with it. "I advise you to practice it quite a bit in secret, so you can do it with an air, before you attempt it before a witness." "*Crêpes Suzettes*, as you know and I know and we all know, are for the feminine gender, and there is no use in your trying to hand me any applesauce about it." "This leaves you, as well as I can make out, at the hour of midnight, with a member of the feminine gender sitting not far away, the fire stoked up and the lights stoked down, and *crêpes suzette* on your mind. As I say, what she is doing in your apartment in the first place, what gave you this idea of *crêpes suzette*, what your intentions are after she has gobbled the dish—these things are none of my business. They hire me to tell you how to make the cakes, not to make dirty cracks about your conduct. . . . I shall make everything clear, don't worry about that. Indeed, the whole thing is so clear by now that I am beginning to wonder whether it ought to be printed at all." "If you have followed these pieces, you should have the proper chafing dish by now. . . ."

In preparing the sauce, "I suggest you peer at it closely, and mutter to yourself over it, as though it were a brew of inordinate complexity. This won't make it better, but it will make it seem better." "It is part of her nature, at the end, to steal your act and begin talking about *our crêpes suzette*. For my part, I find this annoying and I think she should be made to keep her place." "Rapt concentration is the proper note in the kitchen, the attitude of a maestro. . . ." "As to when it is done, I can't tell you very clearly. You will have to learn by experience." "Have her go ahead and open doors for you: this will keep her from sticking her finger in the sauce, although she has probably done this already." "Now then, pour on a good generous jigger of cognac and cut your room lights." "Such is her nature that she likes to 'blow out the fire' on her plate, so you had better have a little on it for her to blow out." "Make one or two technical criticisms. Be evasive as to where you learned the art. Sit back. Look at her. Forget to turn on the lights. Estimate your chances. If you have done it right, you ought to rate an even break."

Cain had come to like Hollywood better than any place he had ever lived. He wanted to be closer to the studios and to the social life, although his own participation was low-keyed. There was a house he'd wanted to buy on Belden Drive in Hollywood Hills near the "Hollywood" sign, sedate in front, spectacular out back.

Needing fast money for that and other expenses, he tried to come up with a concept for a serial. "All the big crime mysteries in this country are locked up in insurance company files," he remembered the AAA insurance men telling him, when they had given him the green light on certain details in *Postman*. "You ought to write more stuff along that line." Cain wanted to, but he needed something to set the algebra clicking.

A memorable anecdote Arthur Krock had told him at lunch while they were at the *World* sparked the equation. One night when he was managing editor of the *Louisville Courier Journal*, Arthur learned that the paper was selling down on the street for $1. What had made the edition so rare was an ad for ladies underwear: "If these panties are too big, take a fuck in them." At first the terrified printer had no explanation, but Krock suspected it had not been an accident, so he caught him by surprise a day or so later and blackjacked the truth out of him. "Mr. Krock," the printer said, "you do nothing, your whole life, but watch to head it off, something like that happening. And then, *and then*, Mr. Krock, you catch yourself watching for chances."

So now what if an insurance agent spent his whole life on guard against people who try to swindle the company, and then found himself looking for chances? There's the wish. A striking Glendale widow Cain knew about came to mind. Suppose she had a wish, too? To kill her husband for the insurance money. So when the agent, Walter Huff, meets the woman, Phyllis Nirdlinger, another wish—to make love to her—triggers the wish for money. They go on the love-rack, and their adventure is the murder of the husband, which they set up to look as if he fell off a train, enabling her to claim double indemnity. When the wish comes true for both, they double cross each other. Huff realizes that he had only lusted for Phyllis, and he falls in love with her stepdaughter, Lola. Phyllis, it turns out, lusts not only for sex and money, but murder as well. End it with a suicide pact between Phyllis and Huff. A neat equation.

Even before they moved into the new house, Cain set to work at high speed, confident his own background selling accident insurance in Baltimore back in 1914 and the knowledge he had gained of intrigues at the top of the business from his father's fifteen years as a vice president of an insurance company would enable him to write a story at the details of which no insurance man would laugh.

"I drove out to Glendale to put three new truck drivers on a brewery company bond, and then I remembered this renewal over in Hollywood-land. I decided to run over there. That was how I came to this House of Death, that you've been reading about in the papers." Phyllis enters a few pages later.

Just when he'd about decided the Theater Guild would, after its long silence, reject *Postman*, Theresa Helburn wrote to say she was interested in the play, but that it needed revision. Cain asked for specifics, indicating his own doubts. Miss Helburn didn't think it was weak where Cain did, but she saw five places in act two that needed work. Cain did it, stuck the revisions in the mail December 19 and, leaving Elina and the kids in the new house with an amiable ghost, set out by train for New York City.

Rafe's play *Accent on Youth*, that Cain had helped him straighten out, was due to open Christmas night. He was standing on the sidewalk when Rafe came out during the act break, astonished that Cain had come all the way from California without telling him. The play was a hit, and Cain was glad he had been present for the launching.

He worked out a contract with the Guild, had lunch with Lippmann, met Charles Angoff of the *Mercury*, and with a case of the flu went down to Baltimore to his parent's house, where he stayed two weeks convalescing.

They were still writing about the novel. Here was the popular novelist Gertrude Atherton in the *New York American*, saying, "There are several disgusting scenes and the characters are scum, but that book is a work of art. So beautifully is it built, so superb is its economy of word and inci-dent, so authentic its characters and so exquisite the irony of its finish, it is a joy to any writer who respects his art."

Paramount wants you, Geller told Cain when he got back, to work on *Dr. Socrates*, about a small-town doctor who unwittingly becomes a mob doctor. W. R. Burnett, who had written *Little Caesar*, had failed to make it work. Apprehensive about returning to the studio where he had first failed himself, Cain plunged into the work, got approval of the changes he outlined, and started incorporating the story editor's suggestions.

One night at a party, a man came up to Cain, declared, "I know you. You're the guy that wrote all those beautiful editorials for the *World*."

"How the hell did you know?" asked Cain.

The man was a very successful screenwriter, John Lee Mahin, with credits for *Scarface*, *Red Dust*, *Bombshell*, *Treasure Island*, and most recently *Naughty Marietta*, so the admiration was mutual and they became friends.

When Warner Brothers bought *Dr. Socrates*, Geller was unable to get Cain assigned to finish it there.

During the six weeks he was at Paramount, the image of Charles Bickford whacking away at that intrusive alligator kept coming back to him as emblematic of Hollywood madness. There was a good story in it somewhere. Everybody's nuts for animals and Hollywood glamour. The two combined, and with the right twist, would be surefire. How about an Irish star cast as Kowgli the Wolf Man who rides a hippo on the Ganges River? Agents, producers, and lovers double-crossing each other, with the lovers making up for a Hollywood finish? A light romance. Just right for *Redbook*.

How to tell it? Let an observer tell it to a friend to untangle events he's read about. He dictated this one. "This stuff the papers had about what happened up to Lake Sherwood, they didn't get the half of it. Then what they did get, they balled it all up." "So here is the low-down on it, once and for all." The editor didn't like the ending of "Hip, Hip, the Hippo," so he spent a long time rewriting it, telling Edith Haggard at last, "I never had such a hell of a time with a story in my life."

When he wasn't talking playwriting with his friend Henry Meyers, they were talking music, especially opera. They decided to start a small singing group in Cain's home. When it got so large it interfered with their work, they had to scrap it, but Cain felt so good about what he had experienced and learned, he wanted to pass it on to the readers of the *Mercury*. "You are familiar, no doubt, with the lament that people don't make music anymore. We would actually try to make some music, and see what happened." "We found out a few things about music and some of them may interest you." How does music homemade stand up? "It is rather hard, perhaps, if you have never taken part in such a rite, to understand the excitement that takes hold of you when you do good music, the sense of accomplishment that you get when you have mastered it, the feeling that comes to you after a whole evening of it, of having stood in the shadows of great edifices, of having identified yourself with something that was pointed at the stars.... It is comparable ... with eating a good dinner ... drinking with it a great wine ... there is a sense of becoming a part of positive beauty, something beyond words, something that can be felt alongside the most commonplace cerebration, and the most casual talk."

As opposed to only listening, singing yourself eliminates certain factors—the "entertainment coefficient," for example. You discover that Pagliacci doesn't work. "In your home, you see, entertainment doesn't entertain." "Music, in your home, must win as music, and as nothing else." It brings into the open certain factors you never notice if you only listened to music. If singers "don't feel it is worth it, they won't take any care at all.... It is the chance to observe this factor at work, I think, that is one of the main values of home music, and that eventually will cause you to revise many of your previous estimates of music." Sullivan, for instance. "We were grievously disappointed." Singing Sullivan requires hard work, but "after you put that much work on it you are pretty clearly aware of what you've got. Well, what have you got? ... a most pretentiously designed cream-puff." We "couldn't make ourselves take pains with it ... we didn't feel it was worth it ... overrated.... He simply doesn't stick to your ribs...." Cain had loved light opera, and was impatient with snobs who were against it, "merely because it was light." But I was wrong. "I got cured." I don't know what went wrong, but "It is like those short stories that seem so sensational when they come out, illustrated, in some maga-zine: reprinted, between covers, they are absurd ..."

"If music of this kind doesn't repay your efforts, then what music does? What are their anticipations?" "I am sorry to disappoint you if you have been hoping for some recondite titles that nobody has thought of before, but I am afraid I shall have to. The music that stands up, when you are spending your own sweat on it, is that same music you have heard about all your life, and somehow forgotten." Standard classic composers. "They still rule the roost.... If light opera, on rendition, turns out to be molasses, grand opera turns out to be molasses and sulfur, a most unpleas-ant dose." Puccini flops: "subtract the tenors, the violins, the lights, the paint, and the tears, and there is nothing left." "Our great discovery was Rossini: Friends, there's a man." Try the *Stabat Mater*. "Where Sullivan wrote the obvious with a hocus-pocus of originality, Rossini wrote the original with a hocus-pocus of obviousness."

Rossini's "idiom is clear, natural, and simple." Most people, as mere listeners to music, have become connoisseurs of novelties rather than appraisers of value." "Modern music is written for the audience, pure and simple." The idea that one could enjoy them while playing them is absurd. "They pay off, in this art as in all others, on what reaches the emotions, and stirs them." Music in its golden age was a community affair. It was "utile," "religious," and had, as movie people say, "vitality."

Now in the last part, give them, as in the food articles, some specific, practical advice. "Before I finish I think I had better pass some tips about the home chorus, for you may be thinking about one yourself, and I can save you a lot of grief. Be advised, then, that . . ." and so on. "And there must be somebody to take charge of things and see that they get somewhere. . . ." "Your good leader must have a passion for 'effects' . . . something more than a set of notes correctly executed." As long as they are good, it doesn't matter who you invite, for "on this lyric spot they will meet as equals." This is where I get back at ASCAP, for charging me for those eight lines: "As for what happens to popular music, I don't care." It's a bore. If radio kills it, more power to radio. "Well, I have achieved the feat of writing a piece which says exactly what any musician could have told me, and in point of fact, what every musician *has* told me. But this much you have to admit. I tell it a lot better than they do." "Close Harmony" was just right for the *Mercury*. He sent it to Paul Palmer, the new editor.

Cain got back to work on the revisions of the *Postman* play. It didn't have his undivided attention because he was still cranking out columns for the Hearst papers. He continued to be attracted to a wide range of subjects, and enjoyed taking them on. He liked seeing a different angle to somebody else's vision, as when Edgar Lee Masters called for a "spiritual history" of America, Cain argued for an "aesthetic history," prompting Leonard Schuster, the publisher, to propose it to Masters, who declined.

Cain enjoyed the controversy he had stirred up with his claim that Kipling's *Jungle Book* notwithstanding, there was no such thing as a panther. But the routine was debilitating and B. A. Bergman seemed to share Hearst's misgivings about Cain's columns. When Bergman wrote to end their arrangement, Cain didn't like losing the money and facing another failure, but he was a little relieved.

The magazine serial about the insurance agent was coming along, and Cain told Knopf that he was planning a tale about a famous singer who would commit a crime, probably murder, escape, and then not be able to sing for fear of giving himself away. The conversations he had had with Dr. Townsend at Washington College about the story he had continued to have with himself for twenty years. But as years went by, it seemed more workable that a girl should commit the crime and that it would be for her sake that the man mustn't sing again. Then while listening to opera concerts in New York he had become aware of the effect of a singer's "sex co-efficient" and the way his voice sounded. A homosexual's voice had a peculiar, disagreeable quality. Then here in Hollywood, he had met a singer who confided that his voice was affected by feelings of guilt over his affection for a man. That got into the evolution of the tale, except that the singer would not at first be conscious of the cause of the change in his voice. A psychiatrist would know, but that solution smelled of formaldehyde.

Trips to Tia Juana and Agua Caliente inspired the idea that a Mexican whore, with her knowledge of men and their offbeat problems, would be able to detect the cause. So the washed-up singer would drift down to Mexico, meet this whore, escape a violent storm by taking refuge in a church, where they would make love, the singer would get the "toro" back into his voice, and the whore would tell him why. He would meet his lover again, lose his voice again, and the whore would kill her rival, the lovers would return to Mexico, and for her sake he would not sing again.

But he had put off writing it all these years, suspecting that it would prove clinically ludicrous. Singers male and female had given it the go-ahead, and Rafe and other writer friends had encouraged him, but what he needed was confirmation from a man in the know. One night at Rafe's house he met Dr. Samuel Hirshfeld, a prominent Los Angeles physician. When he told him the story, the doctor asked him why he didn't write it, and Cain replied, "I just don't care to write a book a doctor would laugh at."

"Well, *I'm* not laughing," said the doctor. He found the idea one of the most interesting he had ever heard.

The Paramount picture he had failed to write, *Dr. Socrates*, came out October 19, directed by William Dieterle, starring Paul Muni and Ann Dvorak. *The Duchess from Delmonico* had never reached the screen. Instead, Gable and MacDonald had done *San Francisco*, a hit.

Nostalgia for his Annapolis childhood impelled him to write a short story about a boy whose moral shiftiness gets him caught in a quandary with a girl. Masculine self-dramatization clashing with feminine competition in the male realm. A little Tarkington-like, and a departure from what he had been writing. The boy's age, about eleven, forced him into the third person. "He bounced the tennis ball against the garage with persistence, but no enthusiasm. He would have gone swimming, but Red would be there, and he owed Red ten cents. Red drove the ice-cream truck evenings, and so swam in midafternoon. Debtors, therefore, used the creek mornings, late afternoons, and, if there was a moon, nights. Between times they passed away the hours bouncing tennis balls against garages."

Marjorie's mother invites Burwell to Marjorie's birthday party, but he doesn't want to go. He slips off to swim. Resists going in naked. "The water felt queer, and all his tricks seemed shriveled: He kept opening his mouth to yell, 'Hey, look at this one,' but there was nobody to look." He had a local reputation, he felt, for a feat he invented himself. "Treading water, about to try again, he felt a tingle in his back: somebody, he knew, was watching him. . . . Where he came up . . . he breathed through his nose to conceal the puffing, and to show that, staggering though the performance might be, it had been done with ease." "Marjorie was on the boat landing." He tried to terrify her with noise and water blowing. She is not fazed. He deals out all his tricks for her astonishment.

She pins her shirt into a swimsuit for herself. Scared to go in? "If you're scared, you've got to dive in," he told her. She climbs on the piling, dives. He'd never had the nerve to do that. Nobody told him girls could do *anything* better than boys. "She had done it. And not only done it, but done it, apparently, without even knowing that it was hard." "She threw back her head, gripped the pile with her toes, stiffened, sprang. But he didn't see her swash into the water. The pilings shuddered so sickeningly from her leap that he had to clutch them tight with his fingers." Next, she did a back dive. As he climbed back down, he was enraged. He told her about her surprise party. She knows it, but he's mean to tell her, ice cream she says. He can't go. Got to work for Red on the ice cream truck. He brags about his duties, including driving. She's very impressed. "Yet admiration even now, was not quite enough. He craved definite superiority." Imply that she lets him win. "From now on she must be his creature, to worship him without question, to look on from a distance while he dazzled her with tricks. It was short-lived." He tripped on his bathing suit. She kissed him on the mouth. When he opened his eyes, she was gone.

At home, he doesn't want to eat, nor go to the party. But he does eat. His father says he must go. How could he explain to her his not working with Red? "What he craved now was humility, the sweet sacrifice of love: the sensation of being unselfish, and noble, and wan about the eyes." He would tell her he worked two weeks just for this present. "She would be aware at last of his lofty nature."

He looked through the window, sees her about to cut the cake secretly. "Then he felt creepy at the enormity of the thing she was about to do. He was numb with shocked astonishment. . . ." She cut a piece and hurried from the room. The reader, like the boy, will think she's going to chase after the ice cream truck. To eat it. No, she waited by the street for the ice cream truck. "Then shame, panic, fear, and love shot through him in one terrible stab. . . . He slipped the present under the rail. He ran blindly to the street, into the night. From the distance, up the street, came the bell of the ice cream truck."

He sent "The Birthday Party" to Edith Haggard, who observed that this was a new Cain, but what happened to the other guy?

After *Redbook* sent back *Double Indemnity*, Edith Haggard sold it to *Liberty* for $5,000. Had his contract with the Theater Guild not put him on call for revisions of *Postman*, he would have used the money to go to Mexico and Guatemala to research his homosexual singer tale. In late October, the Guild dropped the play.

One day, Charles Laughton interrupted Cain's work at home to tell him how clever he had been in avoiding the part of Micawber in *David Copperfield*. Poor W. C. Fields had to play it.

Then he wondered whether Cain would like to watch his latest picture, *Ruggles of Red Gap*, with him. After the picture, Cain made one of his astute observations about Laughton's performances: "It's an autobiography, isn't it?" That prompted Laughton to go maudlin. In Laughton's apartment in The Garden of Allah hotel, his mood slipped into a cold little smile, and a stare. Cain realized Laughton had deeply regretted revealing himself, and he knew then that the odd relationship they had created was "shattered," as Laughton would have said.

The image of the young hobo, silhouetted against the twilight sky, on top of a moving boxcar, among men who seemed already dead, haunted Cain. This sense of *looking at* the figure of the young man led to the third person. "He felt the train check, knew what it meant. In a moment, from up toward the engine, came the chant of the railroad detective: 'Rise and shine, boys, rise and shine.' The hobos began dropping off. . . ." Then the detective went down the line, brushing them off, like caterpillars from a twig. In two minutes, they would all be ditched, a crowd of bitter men in a lonely spot. But they always cursed, always seemed surprised. "He crouched in the gondola and waited." He was nineteen, named "Lucky" in the pool hall at home, not long on the road, didn't like to mix, admit he was one of them, had a notion he was sharper than they—a lone hand. How could he trick and defeat the railroad dick: "and thus, even at this ignoble trade, give him a sense of accomplishment, of being good at it." Lucky kills him with a spike. He wanders into a dark building, not knowing it is in a zoo. An elephant wakes him. He imagines being interrogated. "*That* was where he had spent the night. 'In the elephant house at Lincoln Park.'" He must get rid of the clothes. Applies for a job at a filling station, cons the man in the clothing store into letting him have a uniform until he gets paid. Burns the old clothes. He's turned down for the station job.

Then the newspaper says the dick was killed by accident. His head was cut off by a train. That's why they call him Lucky. But up ahead, he sees a police station. "A queer feeling began to stir inside him. . . . He recognized the feeling now. It was the old Sunday-night feeling that he used to have back home, when the bells would ring and he would have to stop playing hide in the twilight, go to church, and hear about the necessity for being saved. It shot through his mind, the time he had played hookey from church, and hid in the livery stable. And how lonely he had felt, because there was nobody to play hide with. And how he had sneaked into church, and stood in the rear to listen to the necessity for being saved." He goes into the station to confess. What's your name, kid? "Lucky, like in good luck."

Edith Haggard, who had wanted him to get tough, now thought the grim ending of "Dead Man" too depressing for the magazines. He rewrote for those readers, and they read it.

In Thurber's *The Middle-Aged Man on the Flying Trapeze* Cain found his former colleague on the *New Yorker* parodying *Postman* in "Hell Only Breaks Loose Once." "They kicked me out of college when I was about twenty-seven. I went up to see the Dean and tried to hand him a couple of laughs but it was no good.

"Then she came in the room. . . . She wasn't much to look at but she was something to think about. . . . She leaned over the chair where I was sitting and bit me in the ear. I let her have it right under the heart."

Driving, hard work on a new play, "about an out-of-work musician in Paris, who finds a rich sucker who makes the greatest conductor in Europe out of him," went smash when Joe Pasternak, a producer whose musical knowledge Cain respected, told him it had already been done.

He promised Paul Palmer at the *Mercury* an important essay proving that colleges are run not for students but for the colleges. He had researched the facts and had his father's and his own experiences to draw on. "Stirring up a stink is the fondest thing I'm of, and the mostest I have talent at." But work on it was endless.

In November, the news that Jack Curtis had bought his *Postman* play and was going into production as fast as possible was so exciting he dropped the education essay to go east. His fortunes had changed so much for the better, he wanted to give Elina something he knew she wanted: a chinchilla coat. But Jaekel's wanted $25,000 for it, and Cain postponed the gesture.

Cain went east to spend Christmas 1935 with his seriously ailing father and his mother, to visit Mencken, whose wife had died during the summer, and to revise the play version of *Postman*. This was to be Richard Barthelmess's return to the stage and he was scared to death, but had plenty of advice for Cain, who had little respect for him as an actor. But the director, Robert Sinclair, as they reworked the play and rewrote the scene many times, worked miracles.

Cain arranged a meeting with his old army buddy, Gilbert Malcolm, in Philadelphia, but although Malcolm taught at Dickinson College, he struck Cain as a man marking time with the years, and he, like Mencken, only depressed him.

The play opened in Philadelphia with a massive set designed by Jo Mielziner. Two sets outdoors with real cars, and there were ten scene changes. During Cain's favorite scene, the audience got a severe tickle in its throat, but it applauded the much-reworked scene. Cain felt the action was too slow. It lacked bounce, and the audience was not sitting on the edge of its seat, holding its breath.

He saw *Liberty* on the newsstand in Times Square carrying his first serial, *Double Indemnity*, the title Geller had suggested. It would be a little like theater, with the curtain coming down after each climactic installment over eight weeks. Even the time it would take you to read each episode was given under the illustration.

The Postman Always Rings Twice opened in the Lyceum Theater on February 25, 1936, and the audience liked it. Reading reviews within hours after the curtain fell was certainly not the same as reading book reviews. The critics liked Barthelmess and Mary Phillips but not the characters they played. Brooks Atkinson's crucial review in the *Times* would, Cain expected, shorten lines at the box office: "these are loathsome people when their crime is offered in the realistic style of footlights display." The love-rack collapses if one thousand breathing spectators dislike the lovers. But Richard Lockridge's objection in the *New York Sun* was that the play made "us sympathize with Cora and Frank and forget about poor Nick." Some reviews cited miscasting as a problem. But the approval of the *Brooklyn Eagle*, the *New York Times Tribune*, and *Women's Wear Daily* may have motivated some people to see it.

Cain and Sinclair thought the play would be more effective in three acts, so they restructured it, and the *Hollywood Reporter* agreed that the change made a difference.

While Cain was working on the play one day, he got a call from Paul Palmer at the *Mercury*. He had accepted "Dead Man" but thought the sappy ending unlike Cain. So Cain reinstated the old ending, and sent it over by messenger.

He waited for magazine reviews of the play, which might give attendance a boost. In the *New Yorker*, Robert Benchley was not thrilled, but he recommended the play. *Time* said the novel was a masterpiece and the play exciting. The *Literary Digest* reported that most critics had found the play "a skilled, forceful melodrama ... written with gravel on sheets of flint." Meanwhile Cain saw all sorts of people standing in line at newsstands to grab up the next episode of *Double Indemnity*. Edith J. R. Isaacs in the April *Theater Arts* was happy to see less of the novel's "foulness" on the stage. Still, Frank and Cora were "part of the lower order of humanity. . . . But at least a portion of the audience found a degree of sympathy, rather than revulsion, for their exhibition of human baseness."

In March, Cain returned to Hollywood broke, so Geller got him a job with another studio, but that didn't last long enough to rejuvenate his financial situation, and he seriously considered moving to Mexico, where he could live cheaply, freelancing for a living.

Maybe part of his income might come from a syndicated newspaper column he very much wanted to write called "Bright Gold." To avoid the problem he had writing in his own voice, he'd use the editorial "we." He prepared some samples, but Geller wasn't able to sell the column idea.

When the revised, enlarged edition of Mencken's massive study of *The American Language* appeared in April, Cain was proud to see himself cited as an expert. "To the common people everything English, whether an article of dress, a social custom or a word or phrase has what James M. Cain has called 'a somewhat pansy cast.'" That was from his essay "Paradise." Cain shared Mencken's obsession with words, especially clichés, but he marveled that any man could learn so much about a single topic.

When he got hold of a copy of the *Ladies' Home Journal*'s May issue with his story "The Birthday Party" in it, the headnote caught his attention: "*Marjorie was cutting the cake that was to be the surprise of the evening. Burwell was numb with shock.*" So was Cain. Why in hell had they given away the surprise and point of the story?

In June, after seventy-three performances, *The Postman Always Rings Twice* closed down. His "intellectual parent" had proven to be right. Vincent had given him a long analysis of the play's difficulties, all traceable to the fact that he should not have adapted the novel at all.

The sensation *Double Indemnity* had created, raising sales of *Liberty* rather startlingly, he heard, motivated editors to press Edith Haggard for another serial. The irony of a man saving a man's life in the morning and then killing him in the afternoon appealed to Cain. He set "Brush Fire" in California, and again, he used the third person. "He banged sparks with his shovel, coughed smoke, cursed the impulse that had led him to heed that rumor down in the railroad yards that CCC money was to be had by all who wanted to fight this fire, the papers were full of, up in the hills . . . he thought he would go, frantic if he didn't get a whiff of air." "The shovel became the symbol of their torture." Larkin will kill with it later. He saves Ike from the fire. It's Sunday, visiting day. Women come. Larkin is twenty-two and this is the first money he has ever earned. Ran away from home—"dreadful career of riding freights, bumming meals, and sleeping in flophouses." Newspaper reporters make a hero of Larkin. A girl teases him. He buys her ice cream, takes her off to show her the fire. But he doesn't. They are isolated. They kiss. They part. She was the "sweetest human being he had ever met in his life."

He goes to a BBQ shack. Coming back, he senses something ominous. Ike is threatening the girl—his wife. Larkin hears that Ike doesn't live with her. She didn't know he was here—came to see her uncle. She can't get her car started. Ike goes at her with a knife. Ike knifes Larkin, who hits him with the shovel. A newspaperman says, "I tell you! Guy saves a man's life this morning, kills him tonight! It's a hell of a story!"

He stoked up the fires and kept going with another story, set in the mines of West Virginia, about a nineteen-year-old miner and a sixteen-year-old girl briefly trapped in a haunted mine, a sex situation that appealed to him. He was getting away now from the first person, trying to control the third. "From up the entry came a whir, the blackness was hot with blue sparks, a cluster of lights appeared and approached. Lonnie opened the trap and the motor passed through. He closed the trap, sat down, and wished he was a motorman."

Explain about the mines. "Of course, *you* might not have found it pleasant to be alone in a tunnel so dark its coal walls sparkled by comparison, with only a carbide lamp to see by and nothing whatever to keep you company. But *he* minded neither the dark nor the solitude: he was so used to both that he hardly noticed them." "As for the tunnel, it had its points." "He was just as at home in it as you are in your world, and found it just as familiar, just as real, just as satisfying to the soul." Was he over-explaining? He discovers a girl in a torn dress who had slipped in to peep. She was traveling with her father. "You see, it's bad luck for a woman to enter a mine. . . ." The miners will beat her, and him, and he can't work in any of the mines if she's caught.

Men come. Explain how Lonnie knows who it is by the light. One miner has just been crushed by a car. They must blow out the mine. Lonnie hangs back. He and the girl go out by an abandoned entry. His lamp goes out. They took a wrong turn. This is the haunted entry. "But fear is a peculiar emotion: it cannot be sustained indefinitely at the same high pitch. In spite of his horror of the ghost . . . there was something distinctly pleasurable about this: lying in the dark with this girl in his arms, shuddering in unison with her, mingling his breath with hers . . . an almost exquisite agony. . . ."

She says no, that's not a ghost miner, but water we hear. It is. He lights the lamp so they can get out. He doesn't want to leave her. Wants to marry her. He'll have a better job now, having discovered that the haunted mine can now be worked. End on a ghostly note: "An astral miner picked up an astral bucket and sadly prepared to join the great army of unemployed."

He thought those three tales ought to satisfy Miss Haggard, but he was still nostalgic for Annapolis in the summer, and so to satisfy himself, he wrote a variant on "The Birthday Party" story, showing how a little boy's boasting about his swimming prowess gets him into trouble and how a girl rescues him from the scorn of his peers. How boys back then viewed masculinity, girls, and honor. "It would be idle to deny that when

Edwin Hope moved from Annapolis to Fullerton he definitely promoted himself. Around Annapolis he had been in no way unusual. But when his father got the big estate to manage, and decided to transfer his legal practice to Fullerton, and then moved the whole family there, Edwin's status underwent a rapid and altogether startling change."

"It started innocently enough." "But by the end of the week the temptation became almost irresistible to cheat a little. To share, in some reflected degree, the glories he recounted" about Annapolis and the Naval Academy. There were two factions: Roger and the scoffers. Phyllis and the true believers. "It was from the females that Edwin got real support." "His first lapse from truth came as a slip." "He boasted that he had ridden in a shell and dived from a schooner." Wally, his pal back in Annapolis, visits, and forms "a hot treasonable friendship with Roger, and betrayed the stark and bitter truth." "Only Phyllis, lovely Phyllis, remained staunch." School opens. Wally stays. Edwin wears his "work suit," much admired. Wally wears his, coming into the drug store. They fight. Phyllis says let's go swimming. "In view of his boasts and claims, about the last thing he should do was go swimming." Wally and Roger say they're not going. Okay, I *will* go.

But when he gets there, there they are. "The reckoning had come, and he knew it. He left the water with a fine show of contempt, and headed for the wharf." He dares them to make him jump from the schooner. They climb up there. Wally gets caught. Roger slips, falls into the water. Wally falls on top of him. Edwin falls, hits Wally, but Roger is drowning. Edwin rescues both. All three end up in the hospital. Phyllis comes. Did Edwin dive? they ask her. Of course he did. "I saw it. It was a beautiful dive." "Phyllis beamed. 'Oh, *my*, Edwin! Don't you feel *grand?*'"

"Edwin indeed felt grand. Such is the faith of ten that he believed every word of it. His soul was at peace."

Edith Haggard sold this one, like the two before it, to *Liberty*.

Writing articles based on research gave him a sense of control. Perhaps other people would be as startled as he had been to learn just how much a chinchilla coat costs, and why. In his ignorance, he had tried in 1935, when he'd had what he'd assumed was enough money, to buy one for Elina, who was especially fond of that fur. Cain researched the chinchilla raising industry in the United States and found it quite interesting. "Fit for a Queen, Worth a King's Ransom" was amusing, he thought, and ought to appeal to a magazine like *McCall's*.

The first week in December, *Liberty* published the first of the three, "Brush Fire." *"The Author of Double Indemnity (Remember?) Gives You Another Stark and Powerful Story*. Reading Time: 15 min., 58 seconds." That was one way to look at pace in fiction.

He was delighted to see that "Dead Man" had made the *O. Henry Prize Stories* for 1936.

He got some pressure from Knopf to produce another novel, but Cain told him that, knowing in advance that any hardcover book he wrote was foredoomed to be censorable and thus not suitable for pictures, he was having trouble getting started. "God knows what twist there is in my mind that makes it run in these directions, but even when I try to write a serial, before I get done with it, it gets a very censorable cast to it, and if it doesn't, goes feeble on me."

Knopf wrote back. "You can't write fiction with one eye on the movies." Knopf offered, as he had before, a substantial advance, but the thought of accepting it and being unable to deliver so horrified Cain, he stuck to his policy.

He focused in on an idea he had had for a serial that had no censorable elements, and so might sell to pictures. What if a successful woman, a buyer in a major department store, had one of those nice guys who can't make a success of anything for a husband, but she doesn't throw it up to him, she loves him, and all her friends are impressed by her decency, but then by accident, the husband discovers he has a great singing voice? The wife then discovers she can't endure being upstaged. That approach somehow did not work. Why not make it the woman who tries for a singing career, but her home life prevents her? He started to work on that angle, but she finally struck him as a 100 percent ninny.

Having written too much, in too many different media, in too short a time, he felt burnt out. Another source of tension was his growing awareness that something important was missing from his marriage, despite the fact that he had a wonderful intellectual relationship with Elina, whose advice about his writing was usually excellent.

All that aggravated his health problems, centered on his gall bladder for a while, then on a stomach ulcer, causing his health status to fluctuate, and his writing to suffer.

When he went east again for Christmas, he found most of his family ill, and Mencken hospitalized. As New Year's Eve 1937 approached, he saw himself as a sick, discouraged, forty-four-year-old famous writer, who was nevertheless unemployed in Hollywood, unable to write, unable to keep his marriage together, unable to fix on a permanent career.

On New Year's Day, at his desk in Hollywood, he heard Lippmann's voice repeating some advice: When you can't write, write anything. "How you write 'em," Cain told himself, "is write 'em."

Why not make her a bitch? The story of the woman who wants to be a singer would work much better that way, and he could combine it with his earlier idea of having the husband pursue an operatic career in conflict with hers. An aspiring opera singer who is a bitch upstaged by a husband in the contracting business. But make it his story and let him tell it. "All this, that I'm going to tell you, started several years ago. You may have forgotten how things were then, but I won't forget it so soon, and sometimes I think I'll never forget it. I'm a contractor," and business was bad. "I want you to remember that, because if I made a fool of myself, I was wide open for that, with nothing to do and nobody to do it with. When you get a little fed up with me, just remember. . . ."

So Leonard Borland's wish is to live with Doris without the disruptive effect of her wish to become a famous opera singer. He is alone on the love-rack. But then a lovely, famous opera singer, Cecil Carver, helps him make his wish come true. By becoming a sensational singer himself, he upstages his wife, and finally convinces her that her own talent is minimal.

Working on *Two Can Sing*, Cain realized that for much of his writing he had drawn on the background from those years when he held so many interim jobs. If he had proved he lacked qualifications to build roads, for instance, he wanted the reader to have no doubt about the qualifications of his hero, nor about his own capacity, based on his early experience and later research, to be persuasive about it. He felt indebted to John R. Monroe, his voice teacher, for the background for his fiction that deals directly with music.

Although it contributed to her social popularity, Cain's mother did very little professional singing in Annapolis and Chestertown. In his childhood, he had heard her sing many times. But her voice had made no impression on him, though her capacity to read music and to conduct choirs and orchestras fascinated him. But at fourteen, when he heard her sing the "Inflammatus" from Rossini's *Stabat Mater*, a fiendishly difficult thing for solo soprano, he had suddenly realized how good both she and the music were. Such a performance, such a spectacle, he now realized, had appeared repeatedly, in one form or another, in his fiction. It wasn't so much that she could do it that interested him, but that she knew she could do it, and never even got excited about it, or nervous, or worried. Then and now all that struck him as black magic. Had his novels, about singers subconsciously, been votive offerings to her?

He gave *Two Can Sing* a happy ending: "We sang it together, and it was terrible, and it was the sweetest duet I ever heard. That's all."

He had written it in record time, twenty-eight days, and in less time than that, *Liberty*, which had begged him for a story, rejected it, and Geller sold picture rights to Twentieth Century Fox for $8,000.

With the *Two Can Sing* picture money, Cain could afford a two-week trip with Elina to Mexico and Guatemala to get "dope" for his other, very different tale of an opera singer. He hoped to find a Mexican prostitute to have in mind as he wrote. And there she was in a bar in Guatemala City. If she was to take refuge with the hero in a church during a storm, he had to know whether Mexico had such storms. A Mexican weather expert put him on to Acapulco as the most likely setting.

He rented a car and drove over there, mainly to find the church he needed and to fix an image of the inside of an Indian hut. With Elina's help, he got what he needed for confidence, but Mexico gave him a dismal feeling and struck him as a tragically backward country.

Back in Hollywood, he began, "I was in Tupinamba, having a *bizcocho* and coffee when this girl came in. Everything about her said Indian," getting the lovers more quickly on the love-rack than he ever had before. *Sombra y Sol* was obviously going to be controversial and censorable, with little chance of picture money. Vincent urged him not write a book about "a goddamn fairy," but his lesser mentor, Rafe, encouraged him. Stranded in Mexico City, his singing voice having failed as a psychological expression of his fear of responding to the homosexual advances of his conductor, Winston Hawes, John Howard Sharp meets Juana, this whore, and his wish is to enjoy her magnificent body. After sex with Juana in the church helps him to get the "toro" back into his voice, he pursues another wish—of regaining his fame as an opera singer.

When Hawes re-enters his life, he poses a threat to both those wishes. To save John again, Juana impales Hawes on a bullfighter's sword. In exile in Guatamala, Juana and John eventually turn on each other, he sings in public, and as Burbie exposed himself in "Pastorale," Sharp exposes her as the killer in the well-publicized murder. A policeman kills her, and Sharp gives up singing.

The writing of this one, too, came fast, and left him exhausted every day. But it was a great relief to sneak off and be with Kate Cummings, whom he had met recently at Rafe's. He was no longer worried about the clinical foundation of his main idea, that sex and singing tone are related, but he suspected the nature of fiction had forced him into the somewhat silly proposition that a whore could bring the toro back into his voice. He also hoped no guitarist would challenge the virtuosity on the guitar that he had attributed to his hero.

By early July the novel, with its new title, *Serenade*, was in the mail to the Knopfs. The title *Serenade* lacked punch, but *Sun and Shadow* wasn't better. Still, Blanche wired: "Superb." Alfred wired: "I am proud that my name is going to be with yours on this book, and he rushed it into production for Christmas trade."

Mencken wrote: "I hear from Knopf that your new book is not only good, but a masterpiece." He spoke of his intention to read Lippmann's new book, *The Good Society*. Cain was reading it himself, glad he could write to tell Lippmann that he agreed with him this time. Lippmann wrote back to say that since the *World* days, "what you thought about what I did mattered very much to me. I have somehow always thought you had a subtle nose and a delicate palate." Replying to Mencken, Cain said that while he was writing the homosexual story, he had hated it.

Now he could return to a play he had mapped out while the play version of *Postman* was still in revision. If a Broadway producer with Jed

Harris's record thought the conception full of promise, as he had, listening to Cain tell about it on the train a few years ago, it ought to be worth the time and financial risk. A movie director is murdered in a 52nd Street restaurant, and if people think of "21" that's fine. A temperamental movie actress and a writer are involved. *7-11* was a winning title. A producer showed interest in it, but he wanted revisions. Cain said okay, and word got out that it would open in late winter, starring Lupe Vélez, the Mexican Spitfire, and Robert Benchley.

The magazines had been rejecting *Two Can Sing*, but *American* finally came across with $5,000, and MGM wanted him to work on *That Was No Hero* for $1,000 a week. The man who had been down was now very much up—a sequence he had experienced often before and often forgot.

One day, a collegiate-looking man knocked on his door and said he was F. Scott Fitzgerald and just wanted to welcome him to the lot. Cain thanked him, and he faded away. F. Scott Fitzgerald deserved better treatment, so Cain went down to his office and invited him to lunch. Off they went. When he realized Fitzgerald was not going to say anything, Cain said it was good seeing him, and faded away himself, feeling that he had never spent such an uncomfortable hour in his life.

When the *Mercury* put out *Postman* in a 25-cent paperback edition, Cain, who had written with respect of the old dime novels, enjoyed the thrill of holding his first paperback, a vehicle for putting his novels, like his serials and stories, into the hands of the millions.

He went to New York once again to rewrite a play. Richard Aldrich, Peter Arno, and Richard Meyers would produce *7-11* with Lupe Vélez and Fred Keating, to open January 18, 1937.

As Cain worked on the revisions, reviews of *Serenade* started coming in, beginning with J. Donald Adams's in the *New York Times Sunday Book Review*, December 5. "If you read for excitement, 'Serenade' is built to your order. And for the musically inclined there is a lot of interesting byplay around what is evidently one of Mr. Cain's major interests."

Lewis Gannett, *Herald Tribune*: "The bare outlines of Mr. Cain's plot are constantly revolting," but "he manages to invest his most sordid details with glimpses of the human subconsciousness which give them much dignity."

Pittsburgh Post Gazette: "the sensationalism of its subject matter is more than matched by the brilliance of its execution ... literature of a high order."

Out in the sticks, the *Springfield Republican* was telling them: "James M. Cain overdoes the 'rough-neck' style of narration in 'Serenade,' very much as Mr. Hemingway overdoes it in 'To Have and Have Not.' He has nevertheless, a better story to tell, and he reveals a gift of story-telling which should stand by itself, unsupported by profanity and occasional crude indelicacy."

Ralph Thompson, "Books of the Times" column in the *Times*: "James M. Cain's new novel is an amazing performance, a piece of great story-telling. It carried me away as few other books have ever done."

William Soskin, *Herald Tribune*: *Serenade* has "a gaudy, rhapsodic, Lisztian quality, a magical concoction of complex suspense and recurring climax that leaves the reader silted and hugely entertained."

And here was Heywood Broun in the *Atlantic Journal*: "Many years ago, Jim Cain was nothing but a newspaper editorial writer. They didn't even assign him to any of the serious subjects. He wrote the short light pieces on Santa Claus and southern cooking and the New Haven Railroad. Two hundred words was the most he was permitted to do at one sitting." How come he'd never gotten around to punching that guy in the jaw?

Dawn Powell, one of the *New Yorker* gang, a kind of tough girl novelist herself, told *New Republic* readers: "Mr. Cain's secret lies ... in a brilliant manipulation of story and a dexterous staggering of terror effects ... the story grows in memory. Its minor implications will roam through your dreams for days to come. There is nightmare material here for a whole winter."

The *New Yorker* noted: "beautifully contrived hokum, guaranteed to thrill."

William Rose Benét once again in *Saturday Review of Literature* nailed down Cain's essential qualities: "In the theatre they call it 'pace.'" "Mr. Cain has phenomenal pace.... I once heard Joe Hergesheimer [one of Mencken's pals] say that he would like to write a novel as compact and deadly as an automatic. He never brought it off. But Mr. Cain has—twice. . . . Mr. Cain has an intense sense of the dramatic . . . a real writer who can construct and tell an exciting story with dazzling swiftness—one of our hard-boiled novelists whose work has a fast rhythm that is art. You may not like 'Serenade,' but I defy you to lay it down!"

Cain felt that whether they liked his novel or not, these reviewers seemed to write *to* readers and *about* the effects he had tried to have on readers. And they wrote as readers themselves.

It was very gratifying to hear that *Serenade* was prescribed reading in psychiatry courses all over the country. "You," said Dr. James M. Neilson, a Los Angeles psychiatrist, "found one Krafft-Ebing missed, that's all. That's why the book has kicked up such excitement."

Homosexuals showed up at his door, expecting brotherhood. Cain made it clear he thought homosexual love was abnormal.

He was sorry to learn that the Catholic Church had denounced *Serenade*. Libraries had problems with it. Sales leveled off at about twenty-five thousand, not bad, but not the sensation it had started out to be. Maybe, as a friend said, the story took hold, then when readers learned that the narrator had a possible homosexual problem, they were repulsed. Then, as some scriptwriter friends pointed out, the action lagged after Sharp and Juana went to Guatemala.

The studios weren't touching it, but they wanted Cain himself, the author of the much talked about *Serenade*, the still controversial *Double Indemnity*, and the very popular *Two Can Sing*.

Universal offered $1,000 a week for work on *Algiers*, an adaptation of a French film called *Pepe Le Moko*. Walter Wanger expected Charles Boyer to make it as popular in America as Jean Gabin had in Europe. And in *Algiers*, Wanger would debut a young Austrian actress. When Cain met Hedy Lamarr, he was not prepared to look upon the most beautiful creature he had ever seen. But after four weeks, Cain had failed again, and they brought in John Howard Lawson, who had written a celebrated social drama, *Processional*, in 1925. Because they retained Cain's dialogue in the first twenty minutes, he got his first screenwriting credit.

Albert Benjamin at *American* begged Cain for another story, giving him the welcome news that *Two Can Sing* had proven to be the "most popular short novel we have ever published." Well, he had dreamed up something about a man who becomes a conductor of a symphony by some sort of fluke, or he might finally draw on his newspaper experience to tell a story that would depict newspaper work as it really was, washing out all the cliché misconceptions. Or maybe there was more immediate potential in the modern Cinderella concept. He had run into Kenneth Littauer of *Collier's* again recently, and had jokingly recalled their conversation years ago in New York, when Littauer had said: "Let me put it this way: We want a Cinderella story with a modern twist." Pondering that slightly blood-curdling formula he had had an impulse, he told Littauer, expecting a laugh, to write a tale that would tell what really would happen in the modern world to a Cinderella who married her prince, but that he had luckily repressed that impulse.

Littauer sucked his pipe, said: "You know, I think that's a damned good story idea." Then okay, he would do that one. A waitress marries a rich Harvard graduate. And then what?

A call from MGM to write a script that would get Robert Taylor out of pretty-boy roles and into he-man epics delayed the answer. A script in which railroad pioneer Taylor could battle stubborn stage-driver Wallace Beery: *Stand Up and Fight*, based on a novel by Forbes Parkhill, an epic historical spectacle set in 1850 in Cain's home state Maryland—a sort of western, set on the Cumberland frontier.

Laurence Stallings came out and worked with him for a while, but when Cain finished after nine weeks, the credits were Harvey Fergusson, Jane Murfin, and Cain. This one was very absorbing, and he came out of it feeling he had learned a great deal from another writer at MGM, Jack Rubin, whose lingo and slam-bang story-conference delivery was a little like Vincent's, about the technical questions involved in writing an effective script. And he racked up a second credit.

He was eager to see that lovely Hedy Lamarr in *Algiers*. The audience was far more animated in its response to the first twenty minutes of well-paced dialogue, his own, than to Lawson's remaining sixty minutes.

A few days after the end of the MGM seminar, Cain had to go to Baltimore in August to be with his seventy-seven-year-old father, who, his mother feared, was gravely ill. Elina flew with him.

Seeing that his mother and his sister, Rosalie, had everything under control, Cain and Elina flew up to Cohasset on Cape Cod for the opening of the out-of-town tryout of *7-11*. Cain was delighted to see Sinclair Lewis on stage in a production of *It Can't Happen Here*, held over. Alexander Dean directed both plays. When Lewis was no longer center stage, he attacked Dean, and when he failed to fall in with his complaints, Cain felt a chill from Lewis. Success for *7-11* looked possible, although he had to make revisions before the Broadway opening.

He worked on those until October while keeping vigil in Baltimore as his father's illness worsened daily. Word came from Hollywood that Henrietta was sick, so Elina returned.

7-11 would open in the winter. Meanwhile, as the long, grim wait continued he could take up *The Modern Cinderella*. He called in a secretary and dictated it, turning Carrie, the heroine, loose to write it in her own way, which, although she was a waitress, was as grammatically correct as his mother's way of writing. "I want to tell my story, partly because it is my story, and partly to correct false impressions. Yes, I am Carrie Selden, the Modern Cinderella, but if a girl emerges who is different from the girl the newspapers pictured, then all I can say is that the newspapers printed a great many surprising things, and if they are shown up it is no more than they deserve. My story really begins, of course, with the appearance of Grant, but perhaps I should give some of my background, for it is not true that I was raised in an orphan asylum, and was scrubbing pots in the Karb kitchen at the time I met him."

This was the first time he had ever dictated a story, and he felt a little self-conscious talking as if he were a young woman to a female secretary.

As a contrast to the momma's-boy Prince character, that Cain had trouble liking, he created a labor union boss, a tough Welshman who went after Carrie aggressively. Just as Borland in *Two Can Sing* suddenly proves to have a talent for singing, Carrie proves a quick-study as a stock manipulator, using information she gets from her labor leader suitor. Cain got fascinated by that part of the story, running the serial a little longer than he'd intended.

Elina wanted to rejoin him in the East, but he told her he had to concentrate on the serial and the plays, that he had to tell himself: This is it, and stick to it. If only he could make a living writing serials, instead of writing pictures, which meant nothing to him. Writing a play that would become a hit on Broadway did mean a great deal to him, he wrote Elina.

Then in early October his father died. With the father dead, only his mother now stood between himself and death.

When he realized that his mother was expecting a great crowd, he tried to prepare her for only a few people. But twelve hundred showed up. To her, "a great man had died—something she had known all along, but it helped that others thought so."

He wrote to tell Elina that near the end he and the family felt closer to his father as his mood changed to a dignified resignation, and that he could look back on his father's several careers and years of public service with respect and admiration.

Among his father's writings, he found a definition of tragedy that corresponded to his conception of *Postman*: "the force of circumstances driving the protagonist to the commission of a dreadful act." He hadn't known of it when he wrote the novel.

But he had to admit to himself that he had never felt close to his father, as he had to his mother. There had always been some hostility between them, for he had always known that his father had rejected him as a child and young man, and disapproved of him even after he had become a successful writer anyone could look up in *Who's Who*.

Facing crises in his own life—illnesses, divorce, loss of jobs—Cain had had the will to go on, owing much of his spirit to his father's example. To see, in late middle age, everything he stood for plucked from his hand, and then to turn around, and without any self-pity, to make a new life for himself, find a new sphere of usefulness, and do it so successfully that when he died in 1938 he was the lead story of both the afternoon and morning papers, and a tremendous throng gathered at this graveside, a measure of community respect—this struck Cain as something.

Cain wanted to finish *The Modern Cinderella* before returning to Hollywood, so he stayed on in Baltimore. Then the Morris agency informed him that Jed Harris, the producer of *7-11*, "calls the plot confusing. He says the characters are not established. They're plunged into the midst of situations . . . the action plan troubles him. He can't visualize the set ... the action piles on without breathing spells for the audience." He met with Jed Harris and they parted with greater confidence in *7-11*'s chances.

Despite distracting work on *7-11*, he finished the serial November 2, sent it off to *Collier's*, with a copy to Geller for immediate submission to the studios. Then he concentrated on the *7-11* revisions.

When *Collier's* turned down *The Modern Cinderella*, his disappointment was distracting but that bad news was a little offset by Geller's report that he had sold it to Universal for $17,500. He kept at the play revisions until they were done.

Geller got him a job with producer Gene Markey. So, having delivered *7-11* to Jed Harris, he returned to Hollywood. But working for Markey, he quickly discovered that having written two novels in 1937, *Two Can Sing* and *Serenade*, and a play and a novel in 1938, he was utterly written out, and so he quit Markey and took time off to go to Europe. He told Knopf that when he got back he would start a novel he had wanted to do for a long time, set in West Virginia. He and Elina drove their new Buick across country and sailed from New York on the *Normandy* the day after Christmas.

To help him trace his Irish ancestry, Cain looked up Sean O'Faolain in Dublin. When Cain gave his name, O'Faolain asked, "You wouldn't be the postman?"

Cain wondered why, being totally Irish, the Irish gave him a pain in the neck. He found no satisfactory answer in Ireland. But Knopf had been telling the truth when he'd reported that Cain was famous and admired abroad.

When they returned to Baltimore in early February, Cain's stomach trouble put him in the hospital briefly, then he and Elina set out in their car for Hollywood, passing through West Virginia so Cain could revisit the coalfields and dig up some "dope" for *The Butterfly*, his novel about incest.

In Sharples, where he had worked in the mines, he was sad to learn that Colonel Wiley and his wife had died. Time had passed, individuals had grown old, and some had died, but the language and the people were as fascinating as before.

In Hollywood, *The Butterfly* wouldn't come out of its conceptual cocoon.

Cain learned that while he was taking the hairpin curves in West Virginia, Twentieth Century Fox had previewed *Wife, Husband and Friend,* made from *Two Can Sing,* at Grauman's Chinese Theatre on February 9, screenplay by Nunnally Johnson and Dwight Taylor, produced by John Stahl, directed by Gregory Ratoff, starring Warner Baxter and Loretta Young, with Binnie Barnes, Cesar Romero, Eugene Pallette, and J. Edward Bromberg. Frank Nugent in the *New York Times* advised moviegoers that it was "the pleasantest show of the week . . . good fun all the way." It was very well received all around, making Cain hot again at the studios, and knowing just how hot he was worldwide, he felt at ease telling one presumptuous producer, "I'm world famous without doing one of your goddamn B pictures."

It was known that John Stahl and Dwight Taylor were fashioning a script for Irene Dunne and Charles Boyer with some resemblance to *The Modern Cinderella.*

An assignment at Universal for $1,000 a week doing an original comedy set on a ship struck him as just right. In four weeks, he submitted *The Victoria Docks at 8* and was fired. This time, he knew the script was good, others agreed, and he refused to accept failure as the reason for his dismissal.

But the money and attention buoyed his spirits, as the lack of them had often plunged him into sour rejection of this Wonderland. Wanting to share the loot with friends, he urged Wolcott Gibbs and Sean O'Faolain to cash in. "It's not art, but it's money, and the older I get the more I wonder whether the two are not the same thing."

He also kept working the *Liberty* lode.

He was still fascinated by the figure of the young hobo. When he's riding the rails, what does he most wish for? A pretty girl and food in an isolated place, like the Mexican church, or the coal mine. How about a half-finished house in a violent storm, surrounded by a flood? Set in California, like the other two hobo tales. He was getting more comfortable in the third person. "He woke up suddenly, feeling that ice had touched him, but it was an interval before his mind caught up with what he saw.

Through the open door of the boxcar it was pouring rain.... When he scrambled to his feet and looked out, the breath left his body in a wailing moan. For as far as he could see no land was visible, nothing but brown, swirling water full of trees, bushes, and what might have been houses, moving in the direction of the bridge, off to his right. It was already lapping at the door of the boxcar." He ventures out, sees a chain grocery store, a half-finished house that has a fireplace.

At the door, he sees a car come, flounder in the water. He helps a woman in a raincoat out of it. She has matches. He doesn't see her strip, put her stuff on sawhorses to dry, put the raincoat back on. She's not very pretty, but she wasn't "bawling at her plight." He tells her he rides the freights. She says she was over at her uncle's, trying to get home. He feels ashamed of his clothes. He drapes them beside hers. She works in a drive-in. He tells her there's food in the store. Just take it? she asks. He goes. She joins him. "If you've got the nerve, I have." Well, he's been in jail before, he says. He "didn't see her look at him queerly, he hesitated, and start to leave before deciding to follow him." "If you don't help yourself, nobody'll do it for you."

He can't find his carpenter's trimming knife. "They ate like a pair of animals, sometimes stopping to gasp for breath." They sit, his arm around her. "For the first time in his short battered life he was happy." He kisses her. He feels the knife. She has betrayed him. She says she didn't know what he might do. "Once more he felt cold, forlorn, and bitter, the way he felt on the road.... He ... sat down on the floor, drove his feet into the cold clammy shoes. Savagely he knotted the stiff laces. Then, without a word to her, he went slogging out into the night."

He sent "The Girl in the Storm" to Miss Haggard. If *Liberty* took it, that would make four short stories published there.

Maybe they would take another serial. In February 1937, a friend from his *Baltimore Sun* days, Claude Fitzpatrick, who had gone to work for the same insurance company his father had worked for, had sent for comment a study he had written called "1001 Embezzlers." That gave him an idea for a serial.

Dave Bennett, bank executive, is on the love-rack with Sheila Brent. Their wish is to have each other, but hers is also to clear her husband of the crime of embezzlement to save her children's name. Sheila persuades Bennett to help her doctor the records and replace the money. Her husband is killed in a gun battle with police, and their wish comes true. As for *Double Indemnity*, he made the setting Glendale. "I first met her when she came over to the house one night, after calling me on the telephone and asking if she could see me on a matter of business. I had no idea what she wanted but supposed it was something about the bank. . . ." He gave this one, like *Two Can Sing*, a happy ending: They are married, living in Honolulu.

Liberty paid $4,000 for *Money and the Woman*.

When the Morris agency reported that ten major magazines had rejected *The Modern Cinderella*, Cain started revising it. But he refused to cut the long sections dealing with labor, which Elina argued was killing the sale.

The old stomach problems put Cain back in the hospital briefly and when he came out he got a look at what Stahl and Taylor had done with, or to, *The Modern Cinderella*, which they called *When Tomorrow Comes*. To fit Boyer, the hero was now an international concert pianist and Irene Dunne was changed to a waitress who aspired to become a torch singer. But when he saw they had pirated from *Serenade* the lovers-take-refuge-from-a-storm-in-a-church scene, he explored the possibility of a plagiarism suit, but finally considered it too difficult to prove.

A copy of Merle Armitage's book, *Fit for a King*, published by Longman Green, including Cain's piece "Spaghetti," came in the mail one day. He was glad to see another of his food articles in print.

He heard the French had released an unauthorized picture version of *Postman* called *Le Dernier Tournant*. That might help sell the French edition of the book, but he'd like to see some money from the studio.

In January 1940, Warner Brothers bought "*Money and the Woman*" for $3,500. Several hospital stays had drained his account, and he needed the fast money, so when Geller got him the job of adapting his novel at $1,000 a week, he signed on. They wanted drastic changes, but Cain held out, with help from directors on the lot, for the original storyline. It was agreed, but to do that, they felt they had to fire Cain, so it was Robert Presnell who turned out a script and it was true to Cain's original story.

But Cain walked away with $10,000 and another example of Hollywood madness to ponder.

The decks were clear now for concentrated work on *The Butterfly*, but it still wouldn't come. An invitation to have cocktails with Thornton Wilder, whom he had met in New Haven in 1929, the year *The Bridge of San Luis Rey* appeared, and his sister, Isabel, came while he was struggling with problems posed by the incest element in the novel. He and Elina liked Wilder very much, and Cain was grateful for his insight into the incest problem. He gave the example of the nineteenth-century novelists, who dealt indirectly with incest. "They get the quality of incest," said Wilder, "but not quite the slimy thing itself." That, in some form, Cain decided, would be the solution.

But hunting and pecking at the typewriter, he could not find a way to do it.

6

Mildred Pierce and *Love's Lovely Counterfeit*

So HE TOOK ANOTHER SHOT AT A NOVEL HE HAD STARTED SEVERAL DIF-
ferent ways over the past seven years since Jim McGuinness gave him
the idea when they were at Columbia Pictures in 1933, about the great
American institution that never gets mentioned on the Fourth of July,
a grass widow with two small children to support, and who becomes
a woman who uses men to gain her ends. He liked the name Mildred
Pierce for her.

On the first try, he made her an airline stewardess, then a beauty
contest winner on the make. No go. When he asked himself what kind of
woman and what ends and how these answers interacted, she became an
ordinary housewife with shapely legs who throws her unemployed phi-
landering husband out and has to support her two daughters by selling
pies, waitressing, then running her own chain of chicken restaurants. He
sort of had in mind Elina's mother, who had a weak husband and had
successfully run a hotel in Helsinki. And the very resourceful Kate Cummings who was separated and had two children.

"It is a different kind of book from any I have ever attempted," he
wrote Blanche Knopf. "It is nothing but a straight novel, but it is new for
me." Several of his recent stories had gone well in the third person and
the third person seemed most appropriate for his first serious long novel,
twice as long as any of the others. Carrie Selden had written *The Modern
Cinderella* in the first person, but that was a romantic magazine serial and
serials don't count as genuine novels. He wanted to be able to comment
on Mildred's motives and behavior in his own voice as a conventional

Mildred Pierce

A New Novel by

JAMES M. CAIN

omniscient author. By starting with her husband in the foreground, he could make her act of throwing him out more effective:

"In the spring of 1931, on a lawn in Glendale, California, a man was bracing trees. It was a tedious job, for he had first to prune dead twigs, then wrap canvas buffers around weak branches, then wind rope slings over the buffers and tie them to the trunks, to hold the weight of the avocados that would ripen in the fall. Yet, although it was a hot afternoon, he took his time about it, and was conscientiously thorough, and whistled. He was a smallish man in his middle thirties, but in spite of the stains on his trousers, he wore them with an air."

Elina had talked him through a lot of projects, but who helped him through *Mildred Pierce* was Kate, as a sort of model for Mildred. He was seeing her regularly now. There was great sagacity in many of her suggestions, so he used them.

In June, Edmund Wilson asked Blanche for some dope on him for a piece he was doing for the *New Republic*. *Mildred* was going slowly, but he stopped to get up a long memorandum for him. Then Wilson wrote asking him to describe the influence Hollywood had had on him, John O'Hara, William Saroyan, and Horace McCoy. "My own belief is that pictures needn't hurt a writer, but they probably will." That they could teach you a lot about concision and other matters: but that the big easy money overrides other considerations. "I work for them now and then, rather cynically, I am afraid, and not any too successfully," but they did send for him. "My taste is to live simply, and see the few friends that I care about, and call that a life." That he had complete respect for men like Nunnally Johnson who know their talent is limited to pictures as they really are and who enjoy the writing, the money, and the Hollywood way of life. And he told him about *Mildred*. "I am telling it 'straight,' in the third person, that is, and am having plenty of trouble with it." The problems he had in 1922 stuck with him. "Probably I am not really a novelist. If I can pretend it is somebody else's story, be a sort of secretary to the yarn, I do all right. But when I try to step out on the stage myself, I get red behind the ears and boot it."

In August, Warner Brothers released *Money and the Woman*, the script by Robert Presnell, the direction by William K. Howard, starring Jeffrey

Lynn and Brenda Marshall. The first three movies based on his fiction had offered good, solid, glittery commercial entertainment, but this one was a "B" that the *Times* called a modest melodrama, and dull.

Then Twentieth Century Fox sent for him and he worked on *Lucky Baldwin*, set in the Gold Rush era in Virginia City, Nevada. He'd never been there, so he drove over on a weekend to soak up some atmosphere and research some background. The place stimulated his imagination and he knew he'd set a novel there someday. He did the synopsis for *Lucky Baldwin*, but once again he was closed out, after seven weeks.

By November, *Mildred* was over half finished. But on page 254, it fell apart right in front of his eyes. Mildred's wish is for money so she can raise her children. At various points he had tried clever devices for advancing the plot, but it always failed. But when he remembered his original premise and devised a trick for Mildred to use, such as stealing Bert's car key, to advance herself one more step, she seemed alive and the plot moved. But he was stuck on page 254. He sensed it had something to do with the way Veda, the snobbish, bitchy oldest daughter, was taking over Mildred's life, and his own.

When Edmund Wilson's article appeared November 11, 1940 in the *New Republic*, he discovered that he was one of "The Boys in the Back Room." Back there with him was Horace McCoy, of *They Shoot Horses, Don't They?*, Richard Hallas (Eric Knight) of *You Play the Black and the Red Comes Up*, John O'Hara of *Hope of Heaven*, William Saroyan of *The Daring Young Man on the Flying Trapeze*, John Steinbeck of *The Grapes of Wrath*, and Hans Otto Storm, of *Pity the Tyrant*, all influenced, Wilson claimed, by the Hemingway vernacular, all writing about or out of California. Cain had a school, according to Wilson, consisting of novelists who derived from him. He slotted Cain with mystery writer Dashiell Hammett. He didn't write crime stories, goddamn it, he wrote fables of love. The lovers commit crimes, sometimes. There's violence, sex, but also music, food, etc. He wrote love adventures. Cain's typical "heroes are capable of extraordinary exploits, but they are always treading the edge of a precipice. And they are doomed" to "falloff the precipice," which they carry with them, "like Pascal." "His fate is thus forecast from the beginning. But in the meantime he has fabulous adventures." But Cain's plots too often are chips off "the wooden old conventions of Hollywood." The echo in the murder scene in *Postman* is "a Hollywood gag." *Serenade* rings false with "the punctual Hollywood coincidence," and "reversal of fortune." *Serenade* has its "trashy aspect, its movie foreshortenings and its too-well oiled action. But it establishes a surer illusion," than *Postman*. "Yet even there brilliant moments of insight redeemed the unconscious burlesque. And there is enough of the real poet in Cain—both in writing and in imagination—to make one hope for something better than either."

Wilson went on to say that Cain, "the âme damnée of Hollywood," was a studio writer who wrote novels in his off time. "They are a kind of Devil's parody of the movies." The reverse was, of course, the case—he wrote movies so he could write novels. All the taboos that offend Catholic censorship Cain turns "loose in these stories with a gusto as of pent-up ferocity that the reader cannot but share. What a pity that it is impossible for such a writer to create and produce his own pictures." The article was a cliffhanger, the second part to appear next week. "The men and women of the Cain-O'Hara novels are doomed: they are undone by their own characters or by circumstances. But ... the socialist diagnosis and the socialist hope begin to appear in the picture ... the tradition of radical writing out of California, as in Storm and Steinbeck, from Norris, Jack London, and Upton Sinclair." Was he actually then a proletarian writer?

By March 1941, he was doing his third revision of *Mildred* and needed money for surgery, so he offered Blanche *Money and the Woman*, retitled *The Embezzler*, to fulfill the two-book option in his 1933 contract. She offered a $1,250 advance, and like Alfred with *Postman*, tried to slip the noose around his neck by saying it wouldn't count as the last book in the option. He told her he wasn't just asking for money, to consider the book on its own merits. "It will be much better all around if you make this a business matter, rather than a personal one." If she didn't like it, she could reject it, and he could offer it elsewhere. "Please don't get big-hearted about this. I'll come out of it all right provided I know where I'm at." Knopf took it under the old contract, and that released *Mildred*, so it could be offered to the highest bidder.

On the fourth revision, he stopped cold again at page 254, as if on cue. He reminded himself that the original premise was not of a mother's obsessive devotion to an unloving daughter, but of a woman who uses men to gain her ends. Going back to middle C helped him get it going again. But then he wrote himself into a climax he couldn't keep. Finding Veda in bed with Monty Beragon, a filthy-rich playboy, Mildred's husband, she throttles Veda, destroying what she most loved, that beautiful voice. But the author had come to love that imaginary voice, too. In fact, Veda was more real and alive to him than any of his other characters. So he made Veda so clever she only faked, to further her own designs, the loss of her voice. Except for that contrivance, he felt he had gotten off a really fine novel.

He asked Geller to shoot for $5,000 and he got it, from Knopf of all people, the best deal he'd gotten so far.

That removed one source of tension that was aggravating his ulcer. When the doctor told him he was killing himself with smoking, he squashed his cigarette out in his office ashtray, and knew it would be his last. That helped.

But in May, he got work with Arnold Pressburger Productions, doing a script for *Shanghai Gesture*, based on an exotic play. Walter Huston discovers his daughter, Gene Tierney, in an Oriental gambling scheme. Stuff like that.

One day he was in the Brown Derby and Dwight Taylor came up to him and was eager to confess that when he was writing the script for *The Modern Cinderella*, he had reluctantly, out of economic necessity, conspired with John Stahl, the producer, to steal the church scene from *Serenade* and loop it into *When Tomorrow Comes*, the movie title. He hated lawsuits, and he liked Taylor, but as a matter of self-respect and as a duty to the whole writing profession, he felt he had to go after them, or no copyright was safe. So the wellspring of the worst tension was having that lawsuit looming in the future—slated for June of the next year.

The new spinal anesthesia enabled him to survive the excision of the lower part of his stomach, which produces most of the acids, and the removal of two gallstones. Then he could eat anything he wanted and drink with no after-effects at all, not even a hangover.

Elina's mother was living with them now, and to escape the kind of tension she produced daily, he fled east, to recuperate at Mama's house in Baltimore.

He had liked E. B. and Katherine White when he worked at the *New Yorker*, so when she asked him for a story, he did his best, but it was lousy. "I never did have any skill with the kind of thing the *New Yorker* publishes, and I haven't the faintest idea why." But he told her she could expect him to propose some "Profile" pieces later on. She told him she and E. B. had edited *A Subtreasury of American Humor*, that it was coming out soon, and that she had included "The Governor," one of the dialogues in *Our Government*. That meant more to him than he cared to admit, for it was one of the few pieces he had a real affection for.

The reviews of *Mildred Pierce* started coming.

Robert van Gelder, *New York Times*: "It is a bath in sensation. . . . The details of living that fill his story are fresh and interesting."

Ralph Thompson, *New York Times*: Veda was an "incredible, preposterous child."

Stanley Walker, *Books*: "One of the most uncompromising observers of our more swinish countrymen, has written a story in which there is not a single admirable main character . . . glimpses of fine, brave dreams. . . . It is probable that this novel will add little to Mr. Cain's excellent, if peculiar, reputation . . . stretches of Cain at his mordant best." May disappoint some of his faithful readers but "will bore very few."

The Retail Bookseller: "The ultra-conservatives are likely to condemn it because of Cain's reputation for sensationalism. Whereas the true James Cain fans are likely to find it decidedly mild and tame."

Time: "drugstore-library sensationalism" but "one of the most readable storytellers in the U.S." "With a cruel anthologist's tenacity," he "wrings his subject matter dry."

Nation: Cain has "wrapped his iron fist in a silk stocking to knock together the sexy, highly sensational and sometimes outright sentimental odyssey of a grass widow. . . ." He has softened.

Stanley Edgar Hyman, the *New Republic*, pairing Cain's *Mildred* with Farrell's *Ellen Rogers*. "Veda is an utterly incredible little girl. . . . The novel has about three books' worth of plot . . . six punchy trick endings one after another. Yet it has many good things. Cain makes no pretensions whatsoever to being a social novelist, but the scenes of Mildred looking for a job, Mildred waiting on table, and Mildred talking to the rich mother of the boy who got Veda into Farrell's favorite condition, are bitter, incisive and unquestionably authentic. Cain's talent here is the hare to Farrell's tortoise. He is a slick accomplished writer, with a genius for effective, sparse dialogue and tight, neat plots with trick endings . . . unlike Farrell he has now become readable." But "Cain deals with ciphers, picturesque cardboard characters whom he cuts into attractive designs. He has certain specified knowledges that he draws on in all of his novels. . . . He has a few favorite themes: fate, the relationship of art and sex, and particularly the relationship of sex and violence. All his books give the sense of having been pieced together skillfully out of these shiny bits of glass, having no organic existence or internal necessity. The blurb speaks of Cain as a 'first-rate story-teller,' which is so unconsciously fair and exact an estimate of his ability as well as his limitations. . . ."

As Cain told Knopf, "None of these critics seemed to have read the book I wrote."

Clifton Fadiman in the *New Yorker* insisted on yoking *Mildred* with Farrell's *Ellen*, too, for no very impressive reason. He noted the Cain "trademarks: his slightly brutal contempt for his own characters . . . violent extremes of conduct . . . mastery of cinema-plot tricks, his non-tragic handling of tragedy. . . . Mr. Cain knows how to pin you to your chair till you have turned the last page. . . . I wouldn't miss a new Cain novel any more than the Major would miss a fire. . . ." "His novels transfix you as you read them. . . . Veda . . . as nasty a bitchling as has ever been committed to paper. The situation resolves itself into a whirl of melodrama truth, beauty, goodness, faith, hope, and charity coming in for no notice whatsoever. . . . You feel ashamed to find yourself following the fortunes of these dismal characters with breathless interest, but shame or no shame, you follow them. . . . it is a first-rate example of the sort of tricky, cynical realism that the superior Hollywood writer likes to turn out in his more conscientious moods." Farrell's *Ellen*, said Fadiman, is less interesting.

He happened to be in Geller's office with Jim Farrell when someone called their attention to a piece in the *Times* called "Topics of the Times." It said "People are not as much in the mood for that kind of heroine," referring to *Mildred* and *Ellen*.

Then came late magazine reviews in December. Phil Stong, a former *World* colleague, said in the *Saturday Review of Literature*: "Veda is a great creation ... a miserable poseur and ruthless opportunist." "No one has ever stopped in the middle of one of Jim Cain's books."

Robert Littell, *Yale Review*: *Postman* kept us awake, but this is "a flabby, slowish, and unrealized story."

Wilson Library Bulletin did a profile with a photograph, taking as the lead angle Wilson's essay: "Just how many of the 'back-room' boys will be remembered by the literary historian of 1991 is always meat for an argument." This Alsterlund fellow had misread Wilson as saying that he was a writer "to whom the novel represents merely an escape from the repressions of his background."

Now that it was totally out of his hands and in the hands of reviewers and readers, he began to get his novel in sharper focus: Mildred's wish is to have her daughter Veda's love and respect. This wish spawns another—for money and respectability so that she can win her daughter from competing forces, manifested in music and in Monty Beragon, whom she unknowingly shares with Veda. When her wish for money comes true, she suffers the greatest pain on the love-rack as she loses Veda. And he saw now that the third person had been a mistake. Well, he was proud of Veda, anyway.

Many of his friends liked it, and it especially mattered that Rafe said, "It marks a definitive development in you as a writer," although he thought he'd just missed making it great. Knopf made a full-page ad out of Fadiman's review.

The book caused the same kind of library, magazine, and reader controversy as the first two had. But it made the bestseller list, although it sold about ten thousand fewer copies than *Serenade*'s twenty-five thousand.

The Hays office once again seemed to be in the business of putting Cain out of business. So he still had hospital bills and he was unable to take assignments. He had a few notes on a novel set in New Orleans, and hoped to go there soon, but the immediate task was money making and that meant another serial, one that would have instant movie potential as well.

What if an ex–professional football player, now working for a crime syndicate in Los Angeles, got it into his head to become a big-time operator instead of a chiseler? To fulfill his wish, Ben Grace *uses* June Lyon, a political secretary. Makes love to her. But gives her money to help her get her sister Dorothy out of trouble. When Ben meets Dorothy, his wishes for money and sex come true. But his fortunes immediately change—Dorothy shoots Ben's former hoodlum boss. Later, a cop shoots Ben. On his deathbed, Ben marries Dorothy. For this lurid tale, the title *Love's Lovely Counterfeit* was just right. But he wasn't up to doing the research necessary to expose corruption in Los Angeles politics, and with the threat of war hanging over the nation, he somehow didn't feel right attacking a real city, anyway, so he moved the locale to a fictitious midwestern city, and by early December the thing was finished and off.

Sunday morning, Henrietta came upstairs to tell him that "The Japanese have attacked us." The shock to his own system, personally and professionally, and to all systems in the United States as he observed them made him useless at the typewriter for some time.

But early in 1942, he forced himself to keep writing, adapting his play *7-11* to a serial called *The Galloping Domino*, shifting the setting from New York to Reno. Sylvia Shoreham, famous movie star, wants to divorce her husband Baron Adlerkreutz, who has connived with her producer, Dimmy Spiro, to tie her up in a contract that forces her to do a string of lousy movies. She discovers that her husband is about to marry her sister, Hazel, who is rather unstable. At this point, someone murders her husband, and Sylvia becomes involved with Sheriff Lucas, one of her greatest fans. The possibility of double indemnity insurance payment to Sylvia brings in George M. Layton, an investigator.

A light, rather complicated romantic comedy mystery tale with a happy ending. To handle its elements most effectively, he had to use the third person again, enabling him to move back and forth among the characters in different places and times.

In that one he seemed to have struck the wrong note for the wartime mood. This rotten war had stood him on his head. It had scorched everything he had cooking. Magazines and movie studios had gotten oriented to the demands of war propaganda, but although he did his part as a very conscientious air raid warden, teaming up with Cecil B. DeMille in Hollywood Hills, and writing letters to the editor on British imperialism, and Elina was working in an aircraft factory, and Leo was serving in the air force, all these changes left him disoriented in his life and his profession. And he was drinking and eating, because he could now, after twenty years, and watching himself disappear into fat.

Out of a need to understand his life in this new unsettling context, he started his memoirs. From every angle, neither he nor the nation was headed anywhere. His function as a writer in the past didn't look right to him. "With a great many of us, a virtuously cultivated aestheticism has taken the place of the social consciousness that is the food of intellects in other parts of the world. Indeed, we have been prone to regard a concert hall as somehow superior to a husting, and attendance at a political meeting as a gross social error." His own crowd, that is. He was stranded on some beach he couldn't place.

The way it looked to him, the major action would converge on Alaska, and he wanted to be the *New York Times* Alaskan correspondent. But he never wrote to them.

A bunch headed up by Clifton Fadiman and Rex Stout asked him to sign a letter to Roosevelt asking that Elmer Davis be authorized to coordinate America's "word-men" in "word-warfare." He was appalled. "The very phrase 'word-warfare' is enough to bring the whole writing profession into public derision for years to come." Because after the war, there would, of course, be "years to come."

Meanwhile, the magazines were saying no to *Love's Lovely Counterfeit*, and the studios were buying neither it nor *Mildred Pierce*.

So he went back in time to just after his own war for a story he cared a great deal about. His tale would counteract the Hollywood burlesque version of the newspaper routine. Some of his best creations had been women, and this one was dear to him, a tiny woman who couldn't face the real world, who hid, ironically, in the morgue of a great New York newspaper. Her husband was killed covering World War I for the Washington Bureau of the paper and she went to New York for the unveiling of a plaque in his honor. The widow takes a job they offer her in the library of the paper in a cold building on Park Row, and she meets a man who is working there. Both are dreamers who get a romantic excitement out of working together among their clippings to provide the paper with information that produces headlines. Her son had also been given a job, and in time he takes over the paper and persuades her to quit her job and stay cooped up in an apartment on Fifth Avenue. The son's policies wreck the paper, it is sold, and the widow goes to work with her old friend in the library of the newspaper. Let them try to find in this one the same old Cain ingredients. He told Knopf he ought to finish it by mid-July.

But he didn't.

He got to thinking of a boy during the Depression who flees a bad home life and wanders the country on boxcars, something he had gotten started in different ways in "Dead Man," "Brush Fire," and "The Girl in the Storm." But he needed money and access again to the studios, so he dropped that one too and tried to adapt *Serenade* for pictures. By writing the script himself, he ensured Knopf wouldn't get 50 percent of the movie rights. But he never could get it right.

When Geller went to work for Warner Brothers in June, Cain was forced to reconsider his thirteen-year-old relationship with the Morris Agency, where Geller had made some deals for which he was forever grateful, others he knew he would resent the rest of his life, especially the give-away deal for *Postman*. Kate urged him to meet with H. N. Swanson.

Meanwhile, Knopf wanted to publish *Double Indemnity*, *The Embezzler* (no longer called *Money and the Woman*), and *Career in C Major*, a revised, much longer version of *Two Can Sing*, in a single volume called *Three of a Kind*. As usual, Knopf haggled over the advance, which he wanted to handle as a loan, but Cain didn't take loans, so he threatened to go across the street, and Knopf gave in.

Several days later, Knopf also made a deal for *Love's Lovely Counterfeit*, also with a $1,500 advance.

But as he told Morris Markey, he couldn't get down anything new that would work. "I can't imagine anything with less point to it than this endless fictioneering I seem condemned to." And added a swipe at Lippmann for his Anglophile attitude toward imperialism. "Walter, I think, is on the other side of the river from his clothes."

Cain was writing letters at that time to the *L.A. Times* calling into question our policy of helping the imperial nations maintain their stranglehold on their empires. "We do not fight for four freedoms, but for four empires." The editors dismissed him as a writer of "snappy fiction."

Tension in the house lessened when he set Elina's violent mother up in her own apartment. But he was seeing Kate Cummings as often as possible. Elina had a procession of hand-kissers, led by Gene Gary, who hung around the house, for a while, and made a habit of tagging along when Elina and Cain went out, or maybe it was Cain who tagged along, but it was Gary who wrecked Cain's car.

Julian Street wrote to him in August, wanting him to write a promo for the Treasury Department, and he agreed, adding that the United States could inflation Germany to death, if the Treasury Department would rain phony marks down on the people. They didn't do it. The stuff he wrote for Street was to go on the backs of the jackets of his two forthcoming books. "A Word to You from James M. Cain," urging the multitudes to buy bonds. He warns, predicts, sternly advises, and promises: "To us, who are primarily makers of things, the chance to start afresh, with all molds broken and no hampering link with the preconceptions of the past, and supply a world that must have the progeny of our skill, is indeed an exciting prospect." Another, more practical, appeal. "Unless this investment pays, all other investments collapse."

In August, he wrote to the Morris Agency, cutting off their relationship with reluctance and regret, explaining that "I am in a spin, and if I don't pull the stick I am going to crash." He was, among other tribulations, $4,000 in debt. Then he went over to Swanson, or "Swannie" as everyone called him, who had some big names on his list.

Two days later, on a Sunday, he quietly, sadly walked out on Elina, and moved into the Knickerbocker Hotel with his typewriter. He would miss her beautiful mind—sardonic, ironic, sometimes almost savage in its comprehension of basic things. It had helped with the kind of writing he did. He had written seven novels during the period of his marriage, from 1927 to 1942, fifteen years, through much of the newspaper and Hollywood careers.

In August, Cain felt a great urge to make another assessment of his situation as a writer, this time in public, and over the objections of Knopf, sat down with the reader to explain himself in a preface to *Three of a Kind*.

"These novels, though written fairly recently, really belong to the Depression, rather than the War, and make interesting footnotes to an era. They also make, to anybody who finds me interesting, an interesting commentary on my own development as a novelist, and as I am probably the most mis-read, mis-reviewed, and mis-understood novelist now writing, this may be a good place to say a word about myself, my literary ideals, and my method of composition. I have had, since I began writing, the greatest difficulties with technique, or at any rate fictive technique." Tell of early writings. "For ten years I resigned myself to the conviction that I couldn't write a novel. I tried plays with no success, and short stories with very little success, but with a curious discovery. What had made the novel so hopeless was that I didn't have the least idea where I was going with it, or even which paragraph should follow which. But my short stories, which were put into the mouth of some character, marched right along, for if I in the third person faltered and stumbled, my characters in the first person knew perfectly well what they had to say. Yet they were very homely characters, and spoke a gnarled and grotesque jargon that didn't seem quite adapted to long fiction. It seemed to me that after fifty pages of ain'ts, brungs, and fittens, the reader would want to throw the book at me. But then I moved to California and heard the Western roughnecks: the boy who is just as elemental inside as his Eastern colleague, but who has been to high school, completes his sentences, and uses reasonably good grammar. Once my ear had put this on wax, so that I had it, I began to wonder if that wouldn't be the medium I could use to write novels. This is the origin of the style that is usually associated with me, and that will be found, in a somewhat modified form, in this book. No writer would be telling the truth if he said he didn't think about style, for his style is the very pattern and weave and dye of his work. Yet I confess I usually read comments on this style with some surprise, for I make no conscious effort to be tough, or hard-boiled, or grim, or any of the things I am usually called. I merely try to write as the character would write, and I never forget that the average man, from the fields, the streets, the bars, the offices, and even the gutters of his country, has acquired a vividness of speech that goes beyond anything I could invent, and that if I stick to this heritage, this logos of the American countryside, I shall attain a maximum of effectiveness with very little effort. In general my style is rural rather than urban. My ear seems to like fields better than streets. I am glad of this, for I think language loses a bit of its bounce the moment its heels touch concrete.

"About the time I was having these meditations on style, I fell under the spell of a man named Vincent Lawrence. You probably associate him with the writing credits of a good many movies, and no doubt have seen his plays. But his influence in Hollywood goes considerably beyond the scripts he has written.... He has laid down principles that are pretty generally incorporated into pictures by now, and for that reason, as well as personal idiosyncrasies that are to say the least of it odd, has become something of a legend ... His banner wore a strange device indeed: *Technique*. Until then I had been somewhat suspicious of technique. Not that I didn't take pains with what I wrote, but I felt that good writing was gestative rather than fabricative, and that technique for its own sake probably anagrammed into formula, and perhaps into hoke. Also, I was for some time thoroughly suspicious of him. The charm, the strange viewpoint on life, were impossible to resist, but like most fanatics, he was incredibly ignorant, and I don't usually associate ignorance with profundity. For example, he talked quite a lot about the One, the Two, and the Three, not seeming to know that these were nothing but the Aristotelian Beginning, Middle, and End." He assumed he had invented them. "So when this wight got me by the lapel, and talked technique at me, I was a little hostile. Until then, my ideal of writing, as well as I can recall it, was that the story correspond with life, mirror it, give a picture whose main element was truth.... Lawrence ... insisted that ... if truth were the main object of writing, I would have a hard time competing with a $3 camera." If you want truth, write a case history.

"Writing, narrative writing, whether in the theatre, a book or a picture house, he said, must first make you care about the people whose fortunes you follow. Then he expounded to me the principle of the love-rack, as he calls it. I haven't the faintest idea whether this is a rack on which the lovers are tortured, or something with pegs to hold the shining cloak of romance," but it has had a great effect on Hollywood. Cain wanted to give the reader a sense of Lawrence talking, so he let him tell at great length a love-rack story in typical Hollywood story conference patois, the tough-guy-as-story-craftsman, theory in action, delivered theatrically, with the force of authority of a very lively human being. Cain respected this kind of literary talk.

"We both moved to Hollywood about that time, he to zoom to incredible wealth, I to hit the deck like a watermelon that has rolled off the stevedore's truck, and to become, briefly, almost as squashy. For I, who had found the newspaper business quite suited to my talents, and had usually been the white-headed boy of editors, now found there was one kind of writing I was no good at: I couldn't write pictures." Lawrence's gospel made sense to the movie business in the new talkies era, and he got rich. Lawrence provided a kind of moral and financial bridge for Cain from stage to screen.

Knowing that if he was going to stay out west, he would have to surmount financial obstacles, Cain began to think of technique in grim earnest. No longer content to listen to Lawrence, he began to interrogate him. "Why can't the whole thing be a love-rack? Why, if the main situation is pregnant, if it is such as to create an emotional area in which a man and a woman live, there has to be such special attention to an isolated scene in which they fall in love? Why can't every episode in the story be invented and moulded and written with a view to its effect on the love story?" Lawrence saw no particular objection, so Cain hesitantly revealed what he had in mind. "Murder has always been written from its least interesting angle, which is whether the police will catch the murderer. I'm considering a story in which murder is the love-rack, as it must be to any man and woman who conspire to commit it. But, they commit the perfect murder. It doesn't go, of course, quite as they plan it. But in the end they get away with it, and then what? They find that the earth is not big enough for two persons who share such a dreadful secret, and eventually turn on each other." Lawrence's enthusiasm gave impetus to Cain's urge. He wrote it as he had planned, with no love-rack in the Lawrence sense.

Lawrence always quarreled with him "about the first scene between lovers" in *Postman* ... insisting it is commonplace. A commonplace scene was just what I wanted. They were that kind of people, and I still proposed to be true to my ideal of truth, something theatrical people are inclined to be a little perfunctory about. But after this scene, as the dreadful venture became more and more inevitable, I strove for a rising coefficient of intensity, and even hoped that somewhere along the line I would graze passion. The whole thing corresponded to a definition of tragedy I found later in some of my father's writings: that it was the force of circumstances driving the protagonists to the commission of a dreadful act. I didn't, however, know of that definition at that time."

He had more he was eager to say. "Although only one of them is about murder, these three novels embody this theory of story-building, for they all concern some high adventure on which a man and woman embark. In the case of *Career in C Major* it is a comic adventure, but to them important. I discovered certain unexpected similarities between them. All three, for example, have as their leading male character a big, powerful man in his early thirties. This bothers me much less than you would think. I care almost nothing for what my characters look like, being almost exclusively concerned with their insides. Yet, when a number of people complained, after publication of my novel *Serenade*, that they had to read half the book before they found out what the singer looked like, I decided . . . to 'wrap that up in a little package for them so they've got it and will stop worrying about it.' My choice of what a character looks like is completely phony, and it may surprise you to learn that I haven't the faintest idea what he looks like. The movie writer's description of a character's externals, 'a Clark Gable type,' would do perfectly for me, and if you don't like the appearance of any of the gentlemen in these pages, you are quite free to switch off to Clark Gable, or Warner Baxter, who played Borland in *Career in C Major*, or whoever you like. All these stories involve women whose figures are more vivid than their faces, but this doesn't bother me either. In women's appearance I take some interest, but I pay much more attention to their figures than I do to their faces—in real life, I mean. Their faces are masks, more or less consciously controlled. But their bodies, the way they walk, sit, hold their heads, gesticulate, and eat, betray them. But here again, on paper, I am more concerned with what goes on inside them than with what they look like. So if you want to put Loretta Young, who played Doris Borland, in her place or Brenda Marshall, who played Sheila Brent, in her place, it will not affect things in the slightest.

"Reading these stories over, I get quite a surprise. I would have said, on the basis of how I felt after finishing them, that I liked *Double Indemnity* best, *Career in C Major* next, and *The Embezzler* least. Now my preference is quite the reverse. In *The Embezzler* I find writing that is much simpler, much freer from calculated effect, than I find in the other two. And for long stretches I find the story quite free of what Clifton Fadiman, writing about me, once called 'the conscious muscle-flexing.' The muscle-flexing is often there, all right, and it is real, but it is not, as so many assume, born of a desire to be tough. I had acquired, I suspect as a result of my first fiasco at novel writing, such a morbid fear of boring a reader that I certainly got the habit of needling a story at the least hint of a letdown. This bothered Edmund Wilson, too, in an article he wrote about me: he attributed these socko twists and surprises to a leaning toward Hollywood, which is not particularly the case. Recently, I have made steady progress at the art of letting a story secrete its own adrenalin, and I have probably written the last of my intense tales of the type that these represent. The trouble with that approach is that you have to have a 'natural,' as it is called, before you can start, and a natural is not to be had every day. If what you start with is less, if you shoot at passion and miss by ever so little, you hit lust, which isn't pretty, or even interesting. Again, the whole method, if the least touch of feebleness gets into it, lends itself to what is perilously close to an etude in eroticism. Again, love is not all of life, and I confess that lately, having got past the stymie of style that bothered me for so many years. I want to tell tales of a little wider implication than those which deal exclusively with one man's relation to one woman. In the future, what was valid in the technical organization of my first few novels will be synthesized, I hope, into a somewhat larger technique. What was bad will continue to drop off the cart until in the end most of it will be bounced out."

There were so many unsettling facets to his life at that time that he had plenty of excuses for being unable to put anything through the typewriter and call it finished, but the lawsuit over plagiarization of the church scene from *Serenade* was in itself a major distraction. Dwight Taylor had changed his story. He and Stahl persisted in their innocence. Cain finally lost belief in his own case. And he took a look at his earnings so far this year—$6,000—and his debts, over $4,000—and at the prospect posed by Cain vs. Cain, so what was he doing in this courtroom taking on a studio and two of its writers? He dropped the suit.

But how even to start to sue Mussolini, the son of a bitch who finally passed on an Italian movie version of *Postman* called *Ossessione* by Luchino Visconti, a flagrant violation of copyright laws? He heard it was hailed as a breakthrough masterpiece of realism. It sounded like one of those proletarian novels of the 1930s.

Then in October, the reviewers of *Love's Lovely Counterfeit* started bombarding him with everything but praise.

William du Bois, *New York Times*: doesn't compare with Cain's earlier work. "It is redeemed from sheer pulp melodrama only by his spine-tingling treatment of 'big' scenes, his wonderfully accurate ear for the rhythms of dialogue."

Milton Hindus, *Books*: "I don't have to talk, do I, of the felicities of pace, characterization and dialogue to be found in this book? The name of James Cain, by itself, has become a guaranteed trademark of swift entertainment."

Vincent McHugh, the *New Yorker*: "the dingdong daddy of that terrible-people school of novelists appears to be moderating somewhat. . . . According to the jacket blurb, you 'ought to worry about yourself if you don't find it exciting.' I'm a little worried."

Time: "an expert thriller . . . by the most literate U. S. pulp writer."

N. L. Rothman, the *Saturday Review*: "Mr. Cain has established, with a few books, a formidable reputation of furious pace, harsh and masterful realism, tough, raw speech right out of the mouths of the people. I do not think this story will add anything to that, and it may indeed raise certain questions which he will have to answer with a better book."

In November, with the sales at seventy-five hundred, Knopf pronounced the creature dead, but Mencken wrote to say it was one of the best things Cain had done.

He read with interest the entry on him in a new fat, black reference volume called *Twentieth Century Authors*. "Music . . . remains his favorite recreation." "He is a dark, burly man, with black hair worn in a pompadour and heavy black eyebrows, who looks more like a schoolmaster or an amiable priest than a sophisticated novelist." "His work is all of the 'hard-boiled' school fathered by Ernest Hemingway, but rather superficially tougher and faster-moving than his master's." Goddamn it, would they never stop that?

Then Darryl F. Zanuck came to the rescue with an offer of $1,000 a week to write a script set in North Africa glorifying the Signal Corps. He resented being investigated by the War Department, got jittery for our national security when they proved so inept at it, but once cleared, he went to work. Working at the studios, you'd have hardly noticed there was a war going on, had the air not been filled with war profit fever. Robert Bassler, his producer, read his script and called him in for what turned out to be lesson number one in how to write a film script. "You've written forty pages of script with no reaction shot." What he learned from him gave Cain a new confidence.

Another thing that set him up that December was seeing his "Montfaucon" story reprinted in the *Infantry Journal*.

And it gave a boost to his morale when Manchester Boddy, editor of the *L.A. Daily News*, rendered his judgment of the letters he'd written: "I have seldom encountered more stimulating, fine writing."

In February 1943, Swannie sent galleys of *Double Indemnity*, from *Three of a Kind*, around to the studios in another attempt to sell his most censorable novel. He liked to tell the story of how it came to legendary Billy Wilder's attention. One day when he had trouble finding his secretary, one of the other women said, "I think she's still in the ladies' room reading that story." "What story?" "Some story Mr. Swanson left here." Wilder took it home, read it, and told Paramount he wanted to make it. They all met, the offer was only $7,500 compared with the $25,000 it would have brought in 1935 had the Hays office not rejected it, and Swannie urged Cain to take it. He said okay.

So it would pass Hays, Cain made a few suggestions for changes himself, but Wilder wanted to stick with the original plot. Since his usual co-author, Charles Brackett, found the story disgusting, Wilder offered Cain the job. Said he wanted to make certain he got that famous Cain dialogue. But he was still under contract to do that Signal Corps script. Somebody recommended Raymond Chandler, Wilder read *The Big Sleep*, asked Knopf for his address, and was surprised to discover he was living in Hollywood. As a novice willing to work for too little, Chandler needed help, and Swannie took him on.

The reviews of *Three of a Kind* started reaching Cain in April.

New York Times, John K. Hutchens: Despite his faults—underdeveloped characters, for instance: "the pertinent fact remains: when he is at the top of his form it is all but impossible to put down the story he is telling."

A. C. Spectorsky, *Book Week*: "Cain's style—grit, gore and gusty lustiness—is as timely as war news, his plots are almost as exciting, and the nearest architectural analogy that comes to mind is a mile-high juke box."

The *Springfield Republican*, Middle West pulse-taker: No equal for "terrifically fast pace . . . command of dialogue and vernacular . . . skill and flexibility in the first person. . . . technical virtuosity" which save him from pulp or "Grand Guignol."

Dawn Powell, again, of the *Nation*, seemed to have read the preface as a challenge she was eager to take up. "This undergraduate dream, prevalent in Hollywood and correspondence schools, that the carefully laid technique catches the great story instead of the great story catching the technique has defeated other writers besides Mr. Cain. . . . Cain extracts nothing from characterization or place, he requires a constant drumroll of telling dialogue and action. . . . Here is Cain's musical obsession again." As for 'needling,' "I'd rather be bored but convinced. . . . This 'I' is the only character with which he is completely successful, though it is actually always the same man . . . the Mug ('I'), the Victim, and the Dame. These stock figures are set up methodically and then knocked methodically down by Fate, who happens to be Mr. Cain's bellboy. . . ." Good or bad, his women "push the button for the catastrophe." Even the best story, *Double Indemnity*, ends with "the tempo of fast farce."

"Validity in art is recognized by the after-effect, and the after-effect of a Cain book is a half-angry feeling of having been gypped. . . . This is not to say that Mr. Cain's art is not important in its own peculiar way, or that it is mere hammock reading. Rather it is something to read in the iron Virgin, for at its best the intensity of suspense successfully anesthetizes all other senses and might even induce a trance."

Time led off with: "It is popularly supposed that people go right on reading the thrillers of James M. Cain ... through five-alarm fires and the sudden inheritance of large blocks of stock. ... Cain's appeal is partly sheer narrative skill—and partly the fact that he is one of the world's most vivid tellers of dingy stories." In "his latest exhibition," all three novels have "the rancid air of authenticity." Cain screws "down his competent microscope on a drop of that social seepage which discharges daily into U. S. tabloids and criminal courts. And as in any drop of ditch water, the action ... is of infusorial violence." He skillfully uses "business routines to build suspense." He leaves his "readers hanging on Cain's hypnotic typewriter."

The reception of *Three of a Kind* made a big difference for Cain in Hollywood.

7

Past All Dishonor

THE DIVORCE SETTLEMENT HAD BEEN DRAGGING ON FOR ALMOST A year, because Elina's demands were clearly all out of reason, but in June 1943, when he had a little money, they reached a final lump settlement of $27,500, which in the divorce racket was quite a killing for her side, and put the freeze on any leftover friendliness.

In mid-summer after twenty-two weeks and $34,000, the Signal Corps project ended, with no picture in sight, Universal, the studio he had sued, hired him right away to do a script called *Gypsy Maid*, about a princess raised by gypsies, for Maria Montez. George Waggner gave him two weeks to turn this weird concoction into something passable, but he set his own sights a little higher than that.

"Cain," he said, "you're going to do the best script they ever read."

He thought movies had gotten better, and was actually studying them: *The Little Foxes, The Major and the Minor*, discussing them with film cutters, editors, and the more cultivated producers who had come on the scene. He turned in the script a little over the deadline, and stopped in to see Waggner.

"I see you're rewriting it," he said, with that sinking feeling.

No, Waggner said, he was only putting in the baby talk for Montez. "You've tightened and simplified it and tuned it and re-dialogued it and it's a beautiful thing."

That made him feel he was at a turning point in his script-writing career, so when United Artists sent for him, he took on *The Moon, Their Mistress*, based on Chekhov's *The Shooting Party*, at a higher salary—$1,250.

PAST
ALL
DISHONOR

A Novel by
JAMES M. CAIN
Author of SERENADE, DOUBLE INDEMNITY, and others

Then Benedict Bogeaus hired him to participate, just how, he wasn't finally sure, on the writing of Thornton Wilder's *The Bridge of San Luis Rey*, a writer and a novel he admired.

Billy Wilder, complaining that Chandler was throwing away Cain's nice, terse dialogue, got some student actors in from the Paramount school, and let Chandler hear what it would be like if Chandler would only put in the script what was in the book. It sounded like holy hell, to Wilder's utter astonishment.

Then Chandler explained to Wilder what the trouble was: "I could have told you," said Chandler, "that Cain's dialogue, in his fiction, is written to the eye. That ragged right-hand margin that you find so exciting, is wonderful to look at, and exciting, as you say, but it can't be recited by actors. Now that we've got that out of the way, let's dialogue it in the same spirit as he has in the book, but not the identically same words."

They had got Cain over there, purportedly to discuss something else, but he detected the real reason Wilder wanted to see him was in the hope he would contradict Chandler, and somehow explain what had evaporated when the kids tried to do his lines. But at once, he bore Chandler out, reminding Wilder he could write spoken stuff well enough, but on the printed page there just wasn't room for talky climaxes. Chandler, an older man a bit irked by Wilder's omniscience, had this odd little smile on his face as the talk went on.

In late August, William Targ, senior editor at *World*, which had just put out a cheap, "Tower" edition of *Serenade*, asked Cain to write an introduction to an anthology of short stories aimed at servicemen called *For Men Only*. He was glad to do it, but when he sent it in, he told Targ that if he had a chance to re-read those stories in the galleys, he might do a different and better piece. He sent Cain the galleys. He suggested that Targ add stories by Poe and Doyle, drop Michael Arlen's "Man with the Broken Nose" and add Dorothy Parker's "Big Blonde."

Fiction in American magazines and annual collections, O. Henry's and Edward J. O'Brien's, was in a precarious situation, "a suitable embellishment to the promulgations of those who said the short story was literature as well as entertainment, a bewildering piece of news to most of us at the time." "The critic in the last analysis is posterity's bookmaker, and the final critic is Time himself. . . . For the test of a grand vin is that it keep."

This was a good opportunity to reveal Doyle's influence and praise him. "In my youth, Arthur Conan Doyle was read by all and laughed at by all. If it had been suggested that he was important, like William Dean Howells, etc. . . . the suggester would have been thought painfully naive. Yet he lives on . . . I began reading him at the age of twelve, when I found a paperback edition of *The White Company* up in the attic; I have been reading him ever since, and expect to go on reading him until I die. . . . he is incredible, nonsensical, and pure, unadulterated magic."

"Bierce was the master of the eternal moment." "Jack London . . . occasionally turned out something neat, small, and terrifying." "Irvin Cobb, like many another, is fascinated by fate, by the struggle of some poor wretch to escape a doom which you know from the beginning he is destined to meet, not so much because he deserves it, but simply because his number is up," as in "Snake Doctor."

"One of the best authorities on fiction that I am acquainted with, the story expert for one of the big picture studios" (that ought to annoy the critics), said Cain was mistaken that Woollcott ever wrote fiction. "Woollcott, who applied himself assiduously to the task of becoming the most-hated man in the United States, died universally loved, and for a very simple reason. The cobra was phony. Inside he was a rank sentimentalist, and nothing he wrote so well exhibited that side of him as this little story, "Historie de France." "By Ring Lardner we have chosen 'Alibi Ike,' which takes its place beside 'Haircut,' 'The Golden Honeymoon,' 'Champion,' and his other celebrated yarns." "The Undefeated" is Hemingway's best, and "one of the best stories in the language." Important to point out that he didn't know Hemingway. James T. Farrell's "Twenty-five Bucks" will stand comparison with Hemingway's "Fifty Grand." Cain pointed out that he read O'Hara's first published piece, "The Christmas Speert," and republished it on the editorial page. "He so perfectly catches the inanity of the whole human race." John Collier "still hasn't jelled his amazing talent." "Parker's 'Big Blonde' is one of the great stories of all time, and I asked waivers to get it in."

Show research among works on the short story as a genre. Agree that it is "literature, or can be." "It is the one kind of fiction that need not, to please the American taste, deal with heroes. Our national curse, if so perfect a land can have such a thing, is the 'sympathetic character.' We love our Christmas Speert. . . . The world's great literature is peopled by thorough-going heels, and in this book you will find a beautiful bevy of them, with scarce a character among them you would let in the front door."

Then Wilder called Cain, Sistrom, the producer, and Chandler in for a conference to explain why they weren't using Cain's dialogue. That was not an issue with him, but he liked very much something Sistrom said, "All characters in B pictures are too smart." They only help the writer to facilitate his own story. That led to two different faults, both of which are bad: slickness and slackness. A helpful insight.

Chandler changed very little of the basic elements and came up with a story the Hays office could pass. Edward G. Robinson was the obvious choice for the insurance investigator. But George Raft refused to die in any of his pictures and Brian Donlevy turned playing Huff down for other reasons. Fred MacMurray was afraid the part would knock his type casting in romantic comedies for a loop, but for his own reasons said okay. Barbara Stanwyck was afraid of Phyllis, but Wilder bullied her into saying yes.

During the forty days of shooting that fall and the winter days that followed, Hollywood was in a state of thrilling anticipation of a shock.

In September, in this charged atmosphere, there was talk of *Serenade* and *Postman* as movies, and Jerry Wald at Warner Brothers asked him what he thought about his making a movie of *Mildred Pierce*. Wald wanted to open with the murder of Monty Beregon. Cain wrote him a letter pointing out how wrong that was and suggested alternative alterations. Wald wanted more from Cain, but he told him he couldn't rethink *Mildred* as a movie script. Wald got a treatment out of Thames Williamson and used that to develop the project.

The Knickerbocker was too loud for a settled work schedule. Paul Robeson, Sir Thomas Beecham, and other musicians lived there, and there were soldiers and cute but loud ladies all over the place. He wrote to his sister Virginia, "Time just seems to slide along without leaving a trace," and in September, he told Arthur Krock he still intended to write the one about the lovable little lady in the *World* morgue, but "I can't be persuaded a book by me at this time is of any consequence whatever." In a mood of self-appraisal, he concluded that he had "a mind of appalling usualness . . . full of special abilities and lack of abilities as it grapples with daily problems, but ideationally speaking, filled with trade goods right off the national stockpile."

In October, he promised Knopf a history of the Confederacy that would follow from the notion, what would have happened if Beauregard had not fired on Fort Sumter? But three days later he was informing Knopf of his intention to write the one about the lady in the newspaper morgue, "probably the best idea I ever had." Then he decided to go east and work on his old play *7-11*. He didn't do that either.

Early in December, Arthur Hornblow at MGM hired him at $1,250 a week to write a treatment for *Frankie from Frisco*, set in California, in the 1850s. So he had to write to his sister Rosalie to tell her he couldn't spend Christmas with the family in Baltimore, that this was a chance he couldn't pass up. He wrote Mama that this script would prove whether he was "a genius or a bum."

As his years with one woman who had meant a great deal to him ended, his fewer years with another special woman were about to end. By urging him to have surgery, Kate Cummings had saved his life, but then he became "God's masterpiece in the way of a drunk," and she couldn't take it, and in some ways he couldn't focus; maybe he was a little relieved himself. She had been a part of him in ways that no other woman had been. He owed her things he owed no other woman. She was shrewd and intelligent and he needed in marriage what she could offer him. But by the end of 1943, it was over.

Robert Nathan, who wrote novels and scripts, *Portrait of Jennie* in 1940 making him famous, invited Cain to a party in January 1944. This very good-looking older woman was holding court as if she were a famous picture star, but although he could see she liked to have fun, she was too witty to be a star. The more he listened to her, the more familiar she got, until he was looking at Aileen Pringle, the silent picture star of great magnitude who had done a series of sophisticated pictures with Lew Cody, and who had been somewhat romantically linked with Mencken before he married Sara. She had met Mencken at Joseph Hergesheimer's house in Pennsylvania, and was photographed with him when he visited Hollywood in 1926. She was legendary in Hollywood for her rare intelligence, independence, and biting wit. A friend of Gloria Swanson. A terror to producers and directors, who could not tame her. Because she thought DeMille was a tyrant who abused actresses publicly, she refused to work for him. She worked because she loved it, and so had fun. But she was always lamenting the passing of show business when it was fun. She was often seen walking, with three sheep dogs following her.

So he had to speak to her and was flattered that she knew who he was, some kind of Hollywood celebrity. But it turned out, she knew about writing, not just the names. They were immediately and powerfully attracted to each other. So he took her out to dinner, and they talked about mutual friends, Mencken, Arthur Krock, Jed Harris, and discovered they had just missed each other at parties most of their lives.

For Men Only came out in January 1944, and he liked imagining the boys overseas prowling through it. Targ was a little shy about paying him only $250, but Cain hastened to tell him that "I don't count money in connection with this kind of work, and I greatly enjoy it."

He was proud to be represented in *The American Mercury Reader* that Lawrence E. Spivak and Charles Angoff edited, with one of his old dialogues, "Trial by Jury," but not-so-proud that they stuck the label "hard-boiled" on him in the contributor's note.

Arthur Hornblow liked his treatment, but not his script for *Frankie from Frisco*. He had to agree with his criticism that it lacked a central idea, that Frankie's problems were not serious enough to carry the picture.

The Bridge of San Luis Rey opened in early February, written by Howard Estabrook and Herman Weissman, directed by Rowland V. Lee, with Lynn Bari, Alla Nazimova, Louis Calhern, Atkim Tamiroff, Francis Lederer, and Blanche Yurka as the people who meet doom on the swinging bridge in colonial Peru. The other United Artists movie he'd worked on in 1943, *The Moon, Their Mistress*, had been dropped.

He and Aileen were enjoying each other. They were in the same fix: recently divorced, passing through a dark period, and not sure where they were headed.

He got a note in March from Chandler about his dialogue: "Nothing could be more natural and easy and to the point on paper, and yet it doesn't quite play.... It had a remote effect.... It came to me then that the effect of your written dialogue is partly sound and sense. The rest of the effect is the appearance on the page ... the difference between photographable dialogue and written dialogue." Cain wrote back that he did calculate those effects, but that "I use a completely different system in picture work when I dictate for the ear and pay almost no attention to how it appears to the eye." He told him that in *Double Indemnity*, he was "trying to capture some of those bellowing unrealities you get in a fever dream."

And when he had a chance in April to see the movie, Chandler had caught the fever dream quality by a major change more fitting to a picture. MacMurray, wounded, speaks his story into a Dictaphone for Robinson's ears, and all through the movie we hear his cool voiceover. It was one of the finest movies Cain had ever seen. He sent inscribed copies of *Three of a Kind* to the three stars, all of whom were superb. MacMurray conveyed a tragic quality, Robinson had great authority, and he wrote to Barbara: "It is a very creepy sensation to see a character imagined by yourself step in front of your eyes exactly as you imagined her." He sent Billy Wilder a memo: "After several viewings, I woke up to a curious fact: I was *not* ahead of the camera.... I was, as the saying goes, *with it*. Through some magic, whatever illusion is made of, I was caught and stayed caught." This movie made him wake up to the possibilities of a medium he still thought little of, and he was determined to see as many pictures as he could.

Aileen went with him. They had hit it off in all ways and had become very close friends. They were a little leery of what they saw coming, so they broke up several times. But they had something for each other that they didn't want to pass up.

Jack Warner decided to risk *Mildred Pierce*, buying it for $15,000.

By spring, Cain and Aileen were talking marriage, with Aileen suggesting a trial marriage of about six months: "If I make you unhappy in any way, I'll give you a divorce and it won't cost you a cent."

He let her know that "I'm not entering a trial marriage and I don't think either of us should be in that frame of mind. So far as I am concerned, it is a life sentence and in your heart I think it is, too. But if it turns out differently, I have no doubt you will do as you say. . . ."

Meanwhile, he wasn't writing anything new. He got caught up for the first time in a damned political campaign for his state representative. And he was getting off a great barrage of letters to editors about the war and its implications, and doing everything he could to make contributions in time and effort and writing of every sort. But he was at least thinking about the Civil War novel set in Virginia City silver mines.

In May, Swannie reported interest in *Serenade*, but Cain wanted to wait until *Double Indemnity* came out and made a smash, then ask a higher price.

Mencken got his congratulations in before the wedding, in a letter dated July 25. "Of all the women now extant in this great Republic, Aileen is probably the most amusing. You may resent it when she tries to run you, as she undoubtedly will, for there is a Regular Army general hidden in her soft and disarming exterior, but you will never be bored. I am surely delighted that such old and good friends have come together."

They weren't married until August 12, in a courthouse in Santa Monica. They honeymooned in San Francisco where her mother lived and in Sacramento. He took the opportunity to research background details in the Sacramento library for his silver mine story.

They got back in time for the premiere of *Double Indemnity*. It got the great reviews he had expected, with Louella Parsons giving ticket sales a jolt by trumpeting "the finest picture of its kind ever made." And it was clear pretty soon that the careers of the stars, and of Wilder, Chandler, and Cain, had gotten jolts too. They were proud of themselves.

Jerry Wald at Warner Brothers was developing a script for *Mildred Pierce*, and one day on the Metro lot he ran into Carey Wilson. "You're going to say I'm crazy, but I'm going to do your *Postman*." Metro had owned it long enough, so now *Double Indemnity* had liberalized the code, why not risk it?

While Chandler had been writing the script that was getting so much praise, Cain had been over at Universal trying to turn his own dialogue into baby talk for Maria Montez to embarrass Jon Hall with. Chandler had made movie history, breaking the censorship code and starting a new kind of movie, while Cain had made exotic hokum, for all to see in early September, with his name flashing on the screen, his third fractional credit, along with three others and the director, Roy William Neill. Having told his followers, "Set your brain at zero when you go see this one," Bosley Crowther in the *Times* ribbed him a little for having his name on a picture with no Cain elements in it.

To add insult from a stranger to their self-inflicted injury, they all got sued by some obscure writer for plagiarism. In the courtroom, he kept looking at this fellow who obviously had no case, sitting alone there as he had done when he sued Universal himself. Cain thought, "Why should you have to sit there all alone, except for your attorneys, and sue me, assisted as I am by moving-picture money, lawyers, and witnesses. Other writers ought to see your business as their business and come to your aid."

When the judge threw the case out, Cain tried to get a committee started to create a procedure that would advise writers when they had unwinnable suits and go all out for them when they stood to win. But it didn't go over.

In September, Max Lerner wrote a piece called "Cain in the Movies," in his "Public Journal" column. Police in the city were confiscating detective magazines and other contributions to the fact that "We . . . make violence part of our daily imaginative fare." That led Lerner to Cain and the movie *Double Indemnity*, which was better than a "worthier" movie, *Wilson*. "Cain is known as a novelist of the 'hard-boiled' school, but the designation strikes me as covering too many other diverse writers and not saying anything about Cain's essential quality." Cain was glad to read that his preface to *Three of a Kind* was revealing. The theme of Cain's novels is "of love and death coiled up with each other like fatal serpents. It is love-in-death and death-and-rebirth-in-love. Cain's idea as a writing technician is that you mix a potion of love with the powerful ingredient of murder, then you get the strongest light possible shed on the love story . . . more than any other contemporary writer, Cain has become the novelist-laureate of the crime of passion in America. He takes his task seriously, and aims at getting his characters caught in the same grip of fatality that the Greek tragedians did. If he fails it is partly because of the phony tensions in a Cain story. . . . Cain thunders ahead like a movie of an express train rounding a series of curves at full speed." Critics all seemed to reach for a vivid metaphor that expressed the impact of Cain's pace on the reader. "I am left not enriched, but with a sense of emptiness." He ends by saying he is "waiting for the tales of a little wider implication" Cain promised in his preface to *Three of a Kind*.

Since January, *Mildred* had been giving a regiment of writers fits: Thames Williamson, Catherine Turney, Albert Maltz, Margaret Gruen, Ranald MacDougall, Louise Pierson, and William Faulkner. And from the beginning, Cain had tangled with Wald over the murder gimmick as the story-frame, over the concept of Mildred and Veda and of their relationship, until he could believe the rumors that Wald was the model for Budd Schulberg's *What Makes Sammy Run?* Wald knew most moviegoers were women, and during the war, he had done so well with men's action movies, he was out to save his career with the right women's picture, starring the perfect actress, without being true, as Wilder had been, to Cain's novel.

Cain reminded him that the keystone of the novel was the implications of having a big coloratura soprano in the family, that Mildred's problems came from the fact that a dream come true may be the worst possible thing that can happen, that she could never understand a creature like Veda. And that Veda would never accept her. The book was selling so well in popular paperback reprint because this fable had great appeal, especially for mothers, for all of them have aspirations for their favorite child, though not perhaps so obsessively. But the movie script made Veda a cheap little tart who lacked the guts to shoot Monty, as Wald intended her to do, and Mildred's effort to get Veda back was simply a moral question, without passion or obsessiveness. The murder clouded the whole issue, which was one with a wider implication than Cain's other works. He told Wald he was exploiting his literary reputation as a writer of thrillers and spoiling a serious story. He was trading on *Double Indemnity*.

Joan Crawford had been looking for a comeback vehicle, and she loved Mildred, so that got the casting off to a good start. And over at Metro, Lana Turner and John Garfield were set to star in *Postman*.

In September, Cain wrote a treatment of *Serenade*, making Sharp's problem alcohol instead of homosexuality, so it would pass the Hays office and encourage MGM to buy it, but Warner's bought it for Wald for $35,000, the highest so far for a Cain movie.

Cain had spent a year at Metro on *Frankie from Frisco*, a filthy job, as he told his sister Rosalie, that "drags on past all reason or sense ... a protracted, painful, and laborious job," and in December, he told her, "we approach the end of this dreadful tale," an end that racked up another failure for him, and he asked Hornblow to take his name off the credits. But his income had been $80,000 for 1944, his greatest ever.

He went to Baltimore to spend Christmas with Mama and his sisters. He'd just gotten used to being a celebrity in Hollywood, glamorous, if a man said to look "like an ex-sheriff of San Bernardino," a huge, "shaggy figure of a man with beetling eyebrows," indicates glamour, but he was surprised to be greeted in Baltimore as a returning celebrity, with his old *Sun* putting out interviews. As a reporter on the *Sun*, he had been "a lean, dour chap, who seemed steeped in bitterness and was known to intimates ... as old sourpuss," and he had come back twenty-five years later a 230-pound glutton. He talked with Hamilton Owens about writing on post-war politics for the *Sun*, but nothing came of it.

Look asked him to be guest author for a "Photo-crime" feature.

He was glad to hear that Chandler and Wilder were nominated for the Academy Award for their *Double Indemnity* script.

Carey Wilson told him to report to MGM in February to work on *The Common Sin*, which turned out to be a young man's inclination always to fall for the very type of woman who is out to take him.

Wilson asked Cain's advice about several aspects of the *Postman* script, especially the intricate trial sequence, and encouraged him to work on his Civil War novel while under contract to MGM, but finally, unable to do that, he took a leave so he could write.

He also made a few suggestions to Wald about *Serenade*, which he knew would have script problems. He had turned down several requests to stage it, even Sigmund Romberg's and Oscar Hammerstein's offers to do it as a musical.

To economize, he gave up his office at the Knickerbocker Hotel and tried to write in Aileen's house, but it was a small house, and Aileen had her routine, and he was always underfoot, so she claimed anyway, and it turned out the maid's work was more important than his own. She loved the house, but he didn't, because he didn't like the house being provided by the wife, and he had tried to get her to sell it for a larger one. It figured in every quarrel they ever had.

That summer, when the boys started coming home from the war, he knew he had made some contribution, though not nearly what he wished he could have, but what gave him special satisfaction was knowing, partly through their own letters of appreciation, that in armed services editions his books had given thousands "two hours of forgetfulness, of excitement and entertainment that had nothing to do with war, or ideologies, or indoctrination, or anything of that kind. It is the way I would like to have it."

The *Postman* script by Harry Ruskin and Niven Busch, a friend of Cain's whose western *Duel in the Sun* showed traces of *Postman*, passed the Hays office. As Tay Garnett, the director, stated in a piece called "James M. Cain Amazes Hollywood by Becoming Top Screenwriter," in the *New York Herald Tribune*, "We've lifted it from the gutter up to, well, the sidewalk."

He got to work on *Past All Dishonor*. He'd been a history major, he'd always read history passionately, he was interested in the past for its own sake, so it was natural for him to do, finally, a historical novel. But while he had been writing his present-day novels, Edna Ferber, Walter D. Edmonds, Ernest Boyd, Margaret Mitchell, Hervey Allen, and Kenneth Roberts were establishing the historical genre that became very popular during the war, along with newer works by Thomas B. Costain, Van Wyck Mason, and now Frank Yerby, with *The Foxes of Harrow*. Novelists may seduce audiences, but audience demands also seduce novelists, so maybe that was an added inducement to put this one through the typewriter, more than once, as it always turned out. He would evoke the Civil War era in Virginia City, not in a typical massive volume, but in the same economical way his modern novels evoked contemporary times, and the first person seemed one way to keep him on a straight and narrow line. His hero would write his own story.

Getting that straight line was difficult at first because he tried, in four versions of the early chapters, to make Morina a nice girl whose aunt runs a whorehouse. As soon as he made her a whore, like one he'd met the year before, whose black eyes would bring some man a load of grief, it took off. This is how the equation finally looked: Roger Duval, a Confederate soldier, falls in love with Morina Crockett, a mining-camp whore, in Sacramento and follows her to Virginia City. They go on the love-rack. Before they can fully enjoy each other, Roger must kill his wealthy rival, Brewer, and rob and kill other men for Morina, who gets sexually aroused by it. But in the end, their wishes having come true, Roger accidentally shoots Morina. The best dramatization of that theme he had done.

"I first met her, this girl you'll find soon enough, when she fished me out of the Sacramento River on an occasion when I was showing more originality than sense. I was taking the day off from my job, which was secesh spy, though I may as well say right away there was no bravery attached to it, or anything like what they put in the novels. Last year, when Lee got kicked out of Maryland, I figured it was time to quit griping at how the feds ruined Annapolis, and do something about it."

Roger learns that "if you give people everything they want, and nothing they ought to have, that'll wind them up in hell." "I'm at the end of the plank. Other dogs will be along soon, and they won't be chasing deer. They'll be after me. But when they get here, I'll be out there with her, where she's covered up from the birds and wolves, in the snow, with the gold piled up at my feet, and this story at my head."

"Here they come."

He left the implication that Roger will die shooting it out with the posse. All his writing those days sounded terrible to his ear, but he could say he was proud of that last chapter.

And he was proud of the accurate, exhaustive research he'd done in many libraries and on the scene before starting to write. "I set out to do a book that would cause people to rub their eyes and ask: Can these things be? Was this world so modern, so rich, so industrialized at the very moment Grant was taking Vicksburg?" He felt he had combined elements of the historical and the western, and given them more serious implications. And he expected reviewers to agree with him that it was his best novel.

His MGM secretary typed it at a snail's pace, because she was on a love-rack of her own at the time.

Knopf did a slow burn over time wasted when he could be capital-izing on the notoriety the movies of Cain's novels had generated. He was having an interlude where all he could do was gnaw his fingernails.

He happened to tell *The Butterfly* to Aileen who listened, reflected for a time, then looked at him peculiarly and said: "Now I understand the reason incest never gets written about, or almost never."

"Which is?"

"Because it's there, not in fact very often, but in spirit. Fathers are in love with their daughters. It's like what you said in *Serenade*, about there being 5 percent of a homo in every man, no matter how masculine he imagines himself to be. But if a father happens to be also a writer and cooks up a story about incest, he's in mortal terror he'll be so convincing about it all his friends will tumble to the truth. You, though, you haven't any children, and I personally think you're a fool to give this book up."

"After the Joad family trip in *Grapes of Wrath*, if I had a Tyler family trip I'd never live it down."

"Well, if you don't mind my saying so, I think that Tyler family trip is just dull, and that California stuff so phony you'd throw it out yourself after you'd worked on it awhile—a wonderful, hot conflict between your description of the look in their eyes and your description of the scenery. That story is the story of a man's love for his own daughter, and the more it stays right up that mountain creek where it belongs and where you can believe it, the more it's going to be good. And look what you're throw-ing away for the damned California sunlight. That abandoned mine you told me about just makes my hair stand on end, and it's absolutely in harmony with that fellow's disintegration. What does California give you that compares with it? California's wholesome, and maybe it's O.K., but not for this. You go to it and pretty soon you'll have a book."

So he set it along the creeks of the West Virginia Mountains on the Eastern Kentucky border, finally realizing his minefield material. Jess Tyler, a farmer, and his "daughter" Kady desire to make love. They go on the love-rack, and their wish comes true. Sex in a mine—or other confined place, isolated by a storm in a church or an unfinished house—had become one of Cain's favorite sex situations. Later, Jess kills Moke Blue, a loafing banjo-picker, who stole Jess's wife and seduced Kady earlier. As an old Greek discovery device, he used the butterfly birthmark that ran in Elina's family. By that sign, Jess discovers he is not after all Kady's father, whom he has killed. A fable of the consequences of supposed incest. Betrayed by Kady, Jess is about to be killed by Moke's kinfolk as the novel ends.

He started to work and it began to come, slowly at first.

"She was sitting on the stoop when I came in from the fields, her suitcase beside her and one foot on the other knee, where she was shaking a shoe out that seemed to have sand in it. When she saw me she laughed, and I felt my face get hot, that she had caught me looking at her, and I hightailed it to the barn as fast as I could go. . . ."

It began to move along at a faster clip.

"It's been raining for a week, they've been out there for a week, and I've been writing for a week." First time the reader will learn that he has been writing.

"I'm cut off. Ed Blue is out there and"

The endings of the two novels were perhaps a little too similar, but in other novels, too, it had been forced on him by his first-person method of narration. And bit-by-bit, traces of this long suspended novel had appeared in other books: *Mildred, Love's Lovely Counterfeit.*

He surprised himself by getting a first draft in two weeks, and surprised himself even more when he reread it. "This is it."

When the typist delivered the manuscript for *Past All Dishonor*, he made Knopf wait until he had had the experts review every possible question of historical accuracy, involving not only events but minute details. Aileen looked it over too. He dedicated it to her, and sent it to New York in August. Bernard Smith at Knopf said it was "really terrific—rough, tough, fast, and dirty—the Cain of *The Postman Always Rings Twice* and *Serenade*." The Knopfs agreed, in the shape of a $5,000 advance.

He had to suspend work on *The Butterfly* to make changes in *Past All Dishonor*, but soon he was back on it, and after the usual interminable rewrite, it was done.

He was glad to see another old *Mercury* dialogue, "Will of the People," called "Legislature" in *Our Government*, reprinted in *Best American Humorous Short Stories*, edited by Robert N. Linscott for Modern Library.

Cain thought Knopf was getting too big a cut of picture and reprint rights, so he wanted to talk contract changes, and he wanted to meet his new New York agent Harold Ober. By train, he went east for the first time since the war started. Knopf gave him an acceptable rationale for the old terms, and Ober, though not very sociable, inspired confidence.

His sister Virginia read both novels, liked *Past All Dishonor*, didn't even slightly believe *The Butterfly*, "I want you to throw that book away." Her passionate reaction temporarily undermined his confidence.

New automobiles were scarce, but he found one in October and drove down through West Virginia, which he had not seen since 1939, but found nothing to contradict the facts and the speech used in *The Butterfly*. He wanted to see the South because he was planning that nonfiction project *If Bori Had Blundered* or *If Lincoln Had Been Late*. The South he saw was poor land producing poor people. Driving along, he got to thinking about doing a Civil War trilogy.

But back at the keys, he felt an urge to take on his picaresque tale of the kid who wanders America during the Great Depression.

Rafe wrote to Cain that when Sinclair Lewis was visiting him he had re-read *Postman*. "It was treated with the casualness one gives a classic."

On October 20, 1945, Warner Brothers released *Mildred Pierce*, screenplay by Ranald MacDougall, produced by Jerry Wald, directed by Michael Curtiz. The reviews of *Mildred Pierce* were terrific, except one in *PM* that charged the three principles were "the slimy teratology of a literary monster-monger." James Agee called "the tawdry, bitter *Mildred Pierce*" one of the finest of the year, and Crawford's performance her best. Reviewers of the novels had seen quite clearly their congruence with movies. It "took a while for the little men who make movies," said Jay Adams "to recognize the wonderful possibilities of *Mildred Pierce*."

Maybe *Past All Dishonor* could be made safe for pictures, too, even with the red light over Morina's door. He was dreaming of a six-figure Christmas.

They came up with this ad line, "Please don't tell what Mildred Pierce did!" What's to tell, was Cain's reaction, but it more than did the job.

Cain was one of the movie's severest critics, but then he realized that maybe the book wasn't so hot—"two novels in one scrambled in a confusing way . . . something for a woman serial writer," but not for the kind of writer he was when he was hot.

Then Paramount sent for him. If he didn't like the claptrap of most movies, *The Great Gatsby* was literary claptrap. He had liked some of Fitzgerald's stories, but always felt he was overrated, that "his thinking was dull, his writing all diction, cadence, and accent." So when they handed him Owen Davis's play script and someone's botched, unedited film script, he started with zero enthusiasm. One major suggestion he made was for a new ending in which Gatsby is mistakenly thought to have died in the famous car crash, but he shows up at his own funeral, and nobody comes except a girlfriend he left behind in the Midwest years ago. Tricky, but Paramount didn't want to try it.

Then Columbia asked him to adapt *Carmen* for Rita Hayworth. His love of opera didn't blind him to the dated absurdities in the story itself, compounded by their star vehicle rationale. Not for him.

Mildred made him hot in Hollywood. Joan had won the Academy Award. And a third smash hit was on the horizon, *The Postman Always Rings Twice*, they all hoped, and to help that come true, Cain wrote a promo article for *Modern Screen* on Lana Turner, after a very friendly meeting in which she expressed her admiration of Cora's honesty, a new one on him, so that was the angle for "Lana," that she understood Cora better than the author did, and so could be expected to turn *Postman* into a hit with her performance.

When he got an early look at *Postman* over in Glendale, he crawled up the aisle on his hands and knees to avoid his good friend, Carey Wilson, the producer.

In April, Swannie got him on at RKO at his highest salary, $2,500 a week, to work on *The Glass Heart*, about a pious girl who starts "a little lighthouse cult, so common in California," for homecoming soldiers.

That was when *Postman* hit the screens, and *Past All Dishonor* hit the bookstores.

In late April, Metro released the movie Edmund Wilson and Max Lerner and many others believed could never be filmed, *The Postman Always Rings Twice*.

He saw it again after the opening and saw good things in it, but not enough.

The *New York Times*, for which in '36 he had written an article about the novel, "The Postman Is Below," now asked him to write a piece explaining how his three censorable novels had broken through the Hays barricade. In "The Postman Rang Thrice," he pointed out, against popular assumptions to the contrary, that "all three stuck closer than the average picture does to the material from which it is adapted." The lack of sex in the movies was no change, either. His readers have only the illusion, one he worked hard to create, of reading about sex, violence, and profanity.

He liked what Bosley Crowther said in the *Times* a few weeks later in May, that the movie gave reason one could expect more realistic movies in the future. He called both novel and movie "a Greek tragedy in modern dress."

Reviews of the movie were mixed, with this Agee fellow, who had good insights into the other two, chiming in with the nays.

People who had seen *Double Indemnity*, *Mildred Pierce*, and *Postman* on the screen were, Cain expected, likely to pay attention to the publication of *Past All Dishonor*. Thirty thousand advance sales was a major advance for his books, and six-figure picture money was whispered as a possibility.

Knopf held off on *The Butterfly* to give it a clear field for next year. He wanted changes in the ending.

The reviews of *Past All Dishonor* were coming in.

Kirkus: "does not rank with his best." Fatiguingly familiar.

C. V. Terry, *New York Times*: Has a "dime-store moral." "Camera angles suggested neatly.... But why should any literate lover of novels waste his time reading the notes on a director's cuff?"

Charles Poore, the *Times*: "One of the most preposterous and enter-taining books of the year."

The *Boston Herald* and *Louisville Courier-Journal* called it "Cain at his best."

Herbert Kupferberg, *Weekly Book Review*: Cain is a master at this. He "generally has the reader breathless from trying merely to keep up with the conniving that goes on. . . . Roger Duval's machinations become so involved that at times they confuse as well as astonish the reader."

Time: "deadpan savagery suggests that it was written with the tip of an icicle. . . . features enough lust and mayhem per page to shame a pulp novel."

Newsweek: "timeless as a classic," "the equal of Conrad's *Lord Jim*."

H. W. Hart, *Library Journal*: "perfunctory moralizing. Shows careful research. . . ."

Jay Adams, *Saturday Review*: reviewed *Postman* all over again, cited Hemingway and Dos Passos as influences, claimed Cain spawned a school. The new novel shows "his wonderful ability to convey excitement plus a rare knack for spinning a yarn plus excellent writing, a combination that makes it essential to read the book in one sitting . . . revised version of *The Postman*, with an historical twist . . . it certainly does not fit into the tradition of historical novels. . . . To be sure, Cain has not written an important book. If we are lucky, he never will." Like Maugham, he's a superb storyteller.

Malcolm Cowley, who was getting famous making Faulkner famous, *New Republic*: "Soft music and soft tears . . . for James M. Cain, who used to be a writer before he got so tethered in celluloid." From the same issue, a double-barreled blast.

John Farrally: "simply his old story. . . pretentious claims. He says, 'I have tried to explain as plausibly as I can how a gunman got that way'. . . . The characters are puppets pulled out of the old box of melodrama to go through their wooden routine to the tune of Mr. Cain's particular brand of Fate. . . . All the research necessary for this work could have been gath-ered in an afternoon at a third-rate movie house."

Edmund Wilson, the *New Yorker*: "The characters talk post-Hemingway. . . . I laughed more times in the wrong places than I usually do with Cain." Blurb on the jacket: "'Here is Cain at his peak.' Poor fellow, he is at his nadir. The worst is that he seems utterly unconscious of it. . . . he has been eaten alive by the movies."

Reviewers noted that it was very unlike *Forever Amber* and other historical novels of those years. That encouraged him to keep mining that vein. He hadn't read *Gone with the Wind*, but in his Civil War books, he would "explain where Rhett Butler got his money." That would be his focus, not the costume-plantation approach.

Two charges he found infuriatingly ironic: that his research was bad and the book was deliberately composed of elements that would ensure a movie sale. His jacket statement, "I have tried to present the life of the time as it really was, and as few people nowadays seem to realize it was," had been an assumption of success, not a screen for weak research, and the red light over the door, as Stanwyck said when it was offered to her, had killed it, he assumed, for pictures. The three current hits had been made his way, hadn't they? Joseph Henry Jackson of the *San Francisco Chronicle* was the reviewer most expert in this field and he praised the novel's authenticity. As far as he was concerned Edmund Wilson was an "intellectual snob, a humorless son of a bitch."

To have to wear the eaten-alive-by-the-movies brand on his forehead and then not sell the damned novel to the studios, beginning with MGM which, according to their agreement when they gave him leave to write it, saw an outline, was galling, to put it mildly. If you put in a room all the producers who asked to see, then said no to *Past All Dishonor*, you would not likely ask, who's missing?

the
Butterfly

a novel by
JAMES M. CAIN

author of PAST ALL DISHONOR, MILDRED PIERCE,
DOUBLE INDEMNITY and others

8

The Butterfly and *The Moth*

At RKO, nothing had come of *The Glass Heart*, but he did do a little polishing on *Out of the Past* for this French guy Jacques Tourneur, about a fellow with a dark past, who owns a gas station, and a desperate girl who get caught up in a murder.

Mary Morris came over to RKO and did a long interview with Cain for *PM*. She knew how to conduct an interview and got out of him stuff nobody else could have. "I get hired on, as they say, to enrich the story. Style, manner," ability to dialogue in ways that make the crucial difference. "Also they hire me for excitement. . . . I can fiddle around with it, raise the intellectual interest a bit, give it some attractiveness to cultivated people, but on the principle of high suspense." "We take the story elements, lay 'em out on the desk, beat 'em with a maul until they break up." About his characters: "This country is filled with worried souls—people who may not have education or culture, but they *ain't tepid*. My stories mirror life much more than they're given credit for."

Bayard Swope saw the interview and praised it: "Thus are Gods made."

In March, as a member of the Screen Guild's Committee on the Sale of Original Material, Cain got involved in a typical case of a producer's abuse of a screenwriter. David Selznick, seeing a resemblance between Henry James's *The Wings of the Dove*, a property to which he owned picture rights, and Ketti Frings's adaptation of her novel *I Know You*, which she had submitted to Selznick, loused Frings's sale by suggesting to other studios that if they bought her script he would take legal action. It was Miss Frings who sued, and Cain agreed to testify on her behalf.

Meanwhile, he wrote an article, "The Opening Gun," for *The Screen Writer*, the Guild's official organ, parsing the implications her plight had for other writers. His premise was that "any case involving property rights and their enforcement.... involves all writers.... And some of you, who read this, I expect to see down there in court, when Miss Frings' case comes to trial, going on the witness stand with me."

After a year and a half, Cain realized that friendship, no matter how close, how gay, how pleasant, isn't the stuff of which marriage is made. He and Aileen woke up the next morning total strangers, and though both had tried, conscientiously, honestly, and high-mindedly to make a marriage out of their wedding, it wouldn't come alive. Aileen refused to consult him about their joint finances, or anything to do with activities in the house. About half their married weeks were spent apart. She claimed he was a drunk, and she had never experienced a drunk before, and that he abused her, and generally acted like a monster, grim, moody, melancholy. But he knew he *had* become a drunk, and that made all other problems insolvable. "My main cruelty consisted of stuffing $1,000 bills down her throat."

He checked into the Shoreham Hotel and they formally separated.

"Of course, I am perfect," he wrote Mama, "and the other two failures were surely the fault of the ladies involved, but three divorces is getting into the funny coincidence department." Was he capable of a close relationship with a woman?

He separated from RKO at about the time Aileen and he parted. Maybe now was the time to take that Civil War research trip to New Orleans, several times postponed, or maybe he'd go to England and write a picture, as he had an offer. Maybe he would go to this tea party at the home of a famous Hollywood singing coach. No, he didn't think he would, so he dropped by his close friend Bert Parks's house to tell him to give her his regrets, but when Parks happened to say Florence MacBeth was going to be there, Cain was hooked, because he was seeing this idol of his youth in the Wagnerian costumes she had worn in the music magazines he read in 1914 when he was studying singing in Washington. The Chicago opera star he had never seen but whose image he had consecrated privately.

At the party, he saw no divinity among the guests, and was too disdainful of this chic bunch to ask. Somehow a lady pouring drinks, the caterer, he supposed, pale, with a haunting beauty, a slightly stocky figure, caught his eye. The hostess flowed by and introduced the lady as Florence MacBeth.

At first, back in 1914, her name intrigued him. In her photographs, she looked too much like a musical intellectual. But he had followed her career through the years quite closely. Praised for her accuracy and adherence to score, she had sung many famous solos. She had a light, sweet, golden voice. For twenty years, she was first coloratura soprano of the Chicago opera, a somewhat legendary success. She was listed in *Who's Who in America* and in various encyclopedias on music. She came from Mankato, Minnesota, a descendant of the MacBeth of Shakespeare, and resembled queen mother Elizabeth who also came from the MacBeth family—the slight retroussé nose, the somewhat stocky, yet soft figure. She also resembled Jenny Lind, and had toured, doing a Lind repertoire. She debuted in Germany under Richard Strauss's sponsorship, in England under Beecham's, in Chicago under Campanini's. He learned that that intellectual photo had been a case of mismatched captions.

The face at the party haunted him for several days. He called her up and they had dinner and sat in Cain's car by the sea watching the moon come up, and told their stories, discovering they were both going through dark times. She was recovering from a nervous breakdown, living in a cottage on the singing teacher's property, taking lessons, preparing for a comeback, possibly on radio.

He was happy to learn that Ward Morehouse, writing in the *Baltimore Sun*, had quoted Mencken as saying that he was "the most competent writer the country ever produced." Fine, if true, but if not true, fine anyway that he thought so.

Edward G. Robinson's portrayal of Keyes, the insurance investigator, had gotten him so much praise, he asked Cain if he might not have another insurance story that could focus on Keyes. Cain had thought through a variation, *The Galloping Domino* story, which wasn't selling, set in Reno, involving the murder of the husband of an actress, but with the emphasis on the insurance investigator, and Keyes came into it as a third character. So aiming at a magazine serial and a picture sale, he wrote *Nevada Moon*, telling it in the first person, as Huff had told *Double Indemnity*. The great adventure for Ed Horner and Jane Delavan, movie actress, is their effort to solve the murder of her husband, whom she is in Reno to divorce. Ed's secondary wish is to win the award cup for the best salesman.

"At the desk, when they said she was in 819, I knew hubby or pappy or somebody was doing all right by their Jane, because 19 is the *de luxe* tier at the Washoe-Truckee, one of our best hotels here in Reno, and you don't get space there for buttons. . . . I didn't state my business, or mention insurance, in any way when I rang her. No smart agent would. I just said I was Ed Horner of Edgar Gordon Horner, Inc., and that her husband had asked me to talk to her in connection with a certain matter, so she said come up. And waiting for me, at the door of her suite, a cigarette in one hand and the knob in the other, so she could step inside if she didn't like my looks, was the Jane Delavan you read about in the papers.

"Maybe you saw her pictures. . . ."

When he finished, he realized that he had given the label boys an excuse to keep calling him a mystery writer. He had written several crime novels that employed similar concepts, but this was the only one in which the reader doesn't witness the crime, and this one, like *The Galloping Dom- ino*, ends happily. A mystery romance.

In July, three months after "The Opening Gun" had appeared, Cain, disappointed by what his call to arms had turned up, decided nobody else was going to do anything. He drew up a complete plan himself. His own experiences, his observations of the experiences of others, and, he wouldn't disallow a stimulation of his social consciousness by the war, had put him in the driver's seat. Florence was back of him, having proposed and helped organize a Los Angeles Opera Guild herself in 1940.

The members of the executive board of the Screen Writers Guild asked him to present the plan in the July issue of *The Screen Writer* for the membership's consideration, and with their recommendation that it be the collective program of writers in America.

Trying to make the thing as readable as possible, Cain used strong language and wit to put it across. In every situation, the writer was forced by contract, by a united front of publishers that amounted almost to a conspiracy, to give up a number of rights that should always belong to him. Often the holder of the rights just "sits on them," to keep others from using them. The motion picture situation was the worst, for the writer gave up his rights forever, for a small sum compared with the profits, with no added earnings from remakes.

A worst persecutor is the government, which favors almost everybody but the writer. His writing is adjudged "stock in trade," his earnings as "ordinary income," in spite of the fact that the writer "has just so many of these ova in his belly." He is really a capitalist who produces a property.

But a writer's most formidable enemy is himself. "No tricks, except determination on one side and supineness on the other, have been played. It is right there on the table, six pages in a neat blue cover. And if we sign it as it is, it is strictly and only our fault."

"A gang of plumbers can sew up a city with extortionist regulations and hang together like wolves. But anybody who has tried to get three writers to act as a unit on the simplest matter knows what the difficulties are." Writers have illusions of invulnerability and infallibility. Since the answer to the question of remedy is copyright, the AAA, for the writer, will always own the copyright, and lease the rights separately. "Now here, it is manifest, if the Guilds only stick together and act tough, is a potential source of incalculable strength." Using funds collected from 1 percent of each work copyrighted in its name, the AAA will lobby for a new copyright law and fairer tax policies. It will bring lawsuits against corporations.

The four guilds should create this central body and "take the power that awaits them, a massively powerful organization is possible in a very short time, with a $1,000,000 kitty and a full-time tough mug at the head of it."

Cain's proposal had the backing, in discussion, of George S. Kaufman, Russel Crouse, Howard Lindsay, Clarence Day, Dalton Trumbo, Herman Mankiewicz, Lawrence Lipton, Craig Rice, Ring Lardner Jr., and Emmett Lavery, among others.

Unable to get the love story focused in the Civil War novel, he put it aside and dealt with questions three people had raised about the ending, which was too similar to *Past All Dishonor*'s. And over Knopf's objections, he wrote a preface for it, taking up the charges of hatchet men, such as Wilson and Cowley, and trying to get rid of the Hemingway thing.

Cain set to work on his preface to *The Butterfly*. "This story goes back to 1922, when I was much under the spell of the Big Sandy country and anxious to make it the locale of a novel that would deal with its mine wars and utilize the beautiful bleak ugliness . . . as setting. I went down there, worked in its mines, studied, trudged, and crammed, but when I came back was unequal to the novel." Not until ten years later did he try a novel again, "for I had at least learned it is no easy trick, despite a large body of opinion to the contrary."

After publishing *Postman*, the earlier idea "began recurring to me—not the part about labor, for reflection had long since convinced me that this theme, though it constantly attracts a certain type of intellectual, is really dead seed for a novelist," as the proletarian novels proved. The "countryside itself" was appealing. "And then one day, in California, I encountered a family from Kentucky, running a roadside sandwich place. Certain reticences about a charming little boy they had led me to suspect was the reason for the hegira from Harlan County, and the idea for a story began to take shape in my mind . . . and presently I had something fairly definite: a girl's disgrace, in a mountain village, which causes a family to make the grand trek to California, this trek being the main theme of the tale. The bitter, brooding unhappiness of all of them over California, with its bright, chirpy optimism, its sunshine, its up-to-date hustle. Finally, a blazing afternoon, when the boy who started it all blows in, orders an egg malt, and finds himself staring into the murderous eyes of the girl's father.

"Quite pleased with this fable, I drove to Huntington early in 1939, and cruised up and down both forks of the old familiar river, stopping at the old familiar places, picking up miners, visiting friends, noting changes, bringing myself down to date. Back in the West, I started to write, and the thing began to grow. And then Mr. Steinbeck published his *Grapes of Wrath*." He had been scooped. "Giving the project up was a wrench, but I had to, or thought I did."

"Re-reading it, now the final proofs are in, I like it better than I usually like my work, and yet I have an impulse to account for it. For most people associate me with the West, and forget, or possibly don't know, that I had a newspaper career of some length in the East before I came to California." "The many fictions published about me recently bring me to the realization I must relax the positivist attitude I carried over from newspaper work ... for as a polemist I had acquired a fairly thick hide." "But when these assumptions are repeated and I still don't deny them, I have only myself to blame if they become accepted as fact. Elaborate major deductions may be made from them. This may be an appropriate place, then, to discuss some of them, and perhaps get them discarded in favor of the truth."

"I belong to no school, hard-boiled or otherwise, and I believe these so-called schools exist mainly in the imagination of critics, and have little correspondence in reality anywhere else." Young writers often imitate, as when my brother and I as soldiers exchanged letters in the style of Lardner's *You Know Me Al*, and Lardner's influence shows in *Our Government*. "Yet if he can write a book at all, a writer cannot do it by peeping over his shoulder at somebody else, any more than a woman can have a baby by watching some other woman have one. It is a genital process, and all of its stages are intra-abdominal. It is sealed off in such fashion that outside 'influences' are almost impossible. Schools don't help the novelist, but they do help the critics. Using as mucilage the simplifications that the school hypothesis affords him, he can paste labels, wherever convenience is served." "Although I have read less than twenty pages of Mr. Dashiell Hammett in my whole life, Mr. Clifton Fadiman can refer to my hammett-and-tongs style and make things easy for himself. If then, I may make a plea on behalf of all writers of fiction, I say to these strange surrogates for God, with their illusion of 'critical judgment' and their conviction of the definitive verity of their wackiest brainstorm: You're really being a little naïve, you know. We don't do it that way. We don't say to ourselves that some lucky fellow did it a certain way, so we'll do it that way too, and cut in on the sugar. . . .

"I owe no debt, beyond the pleasure his books have given me, to Mr. Ernest Hemingway, though if I did, I think I should admit it, as I have admitted various other debts, mainly in the realm of theory. . . . Just what it is I am supposed to have got from him I have never quite made out, though I am sure it can hardly be in the realm of content." Show how we are very dissimilar. "He writes of God's eternal mayhem against Man, a theme he works into great, classic cathedrals, but one I should be helpless to make use of. I, so far as I can sense the pattern of my mind, write of the wish that comes true, for some reason a terrifying concept, at least to my imagination. Of course, the wish must really have terror in it. I think my stories have some quality of the opening of a forbidden box, and that it is this, rather than violence, sex, or any of the things usually cited by way of explanation, that gives them the drive so often noted. Their appeal is first to the mind, and the reader is carried along as much by his own realization that the characters cannot have this particular wish and survive, and his curiosity to see what happens to them, as by the effect on him of incident, dialogue, or character. Thus, if I do any glancing, it is toward Pandora ... and often helps my thinking.

"Nor do I see any similarity in manner, beyond the circumstance that each of us has an excellent ear, and each of us shudders at the least hint of the highfalutin, the pompous, or the literary. We have people talk as they do talk, and as some of them are of a low station in life, no doubt they often say things in a similar way.... He uses four letter words.... I have never written one.... We are quite exact about the conventions we offer the reader, and accept Mark Twain's dictum that it must be made clear, in first-person narrative, whether the character is writing or talking, all small points being adjusted to conform. We each cut down to a minimum the he-saids and she-replied-laughinglys," which make dialogue so monotonous. Ask writers to drop this convention overboard. "Slip a little, not too much of course, but just the right subtle amount, of ominous glint in the speech," not in stage directions.

Resemblances "do make for a certain leanness in each of us, as a result of all this skinning out of literary blubber." Prove by chronology of my career that Hemingway did not influence me. "The style" of "Pastorale" "is pretty much my style today." "Although for convenience of expression I have thrown what appears to be a very chummy 'we' around his neck, I intend no familiarity and claim no equality. This, as I well know, is a Matterhorn of literature, while my small morality tale is at best a foothill. But small though it be, it is as good as I know how to make it, and I take some satisfaction in the fact that it is made well enough to reap some of the rewards mainly reserved for the small fable: It translates, so that it is known all over the world. Its point is easily remembered, so that it passes easily from mouth to mouth and so lives on from year to year. I don't lack for at least as much recognition as I deserve, which is a fortunate situation to be in. But it does strike me as a very odd notion that in setting out to make it good I would do the one thing certain to make it bad."

"I am not particularly close to the picture business," not successful in it. Though my "stories have made legendary successes when adapted for films. . . . I have learned a great deal from pictures, mainly technical things. . . . Picture people . . . usually feel I earned my pay. But they don't do my scripts . . . we discuss the riddle freely. Moving pictures simply do not excite me intellectually, or aesthetically, or in whatever way one has to get excited to put exciting stuff on paper. I know their technique as exhaustively as anybody knows it, I study it, but I don't feel it." "I wrote only *Love's Lovely Counterfeit* with pictures in mind. It didn't sell. Others had censor trouble, as I knew they would. In *Past All Dishonor*, Morina was not a whore in four versions." "Putting the red light over the door, I knew, would cost me a picture sale, and so far it has. It is in there just the same, and it made all the difference in the world with the book."

It was a "startling experience" to read eastern critics who said he has been "eaten alive by pictures, as one of them put it." "That I had done my research in projection rooms and that this story was simply the preliminary design for a movie." "I do my research as all writers do, in the field and in the library," . . . whatever I need for the story. For *Past All Dishonor*, I used my own copy of *The Official Records of the War of the Rebellion*. I checked "to make sure the terse, short-cadence style I had in mind for Roger Duval had justification in the writings of the time." Grant's writings and court testimonies support my usages. I wanted to delight the modern reader by turning the lights up "on a world he possibly had no idea had ever existed. That my integrity would be doubted, that it would be assumed that I got all this from picture sets, I confess astonished me." I can't let the pat statements of the New York critics "pass uncorrected, which is the reason I ask your indulgence for this visit to the words-of-one-syllable department."

"Yes, I have actually mined coal, and distilled liquor, as well as seen a girl in a pink dress, and seen her take it off. I am 54 years old, weigh 220 pounds, and look like the chief dispatcher of a long-distance hauling concern. I am a registered Democrat. I drink."

He dated the finished manuscript August 6, 1946.

In September, Harrison Smith responded to Cain's AAA in an editorial in the *Saturday Review*. "Throughout the literary centers of the country a controversy is raging over a proposal by James M. Cain." Smith noted that Cain's "startling proposal" was front-page news. He announced that fifty prominent writers had formed The American Writer's Association to combat such a monopoly. "This glamorous proposal is written with all the enthusiasm and confidence of a wildcat oil company's prospectus," and it is a "'blue sky' proposal with a vengeance." Cain was naïve in his claims, said Smith, who anticipated that all the independent writers in the country would resist such an organization, for it seemed obvious that any agency with such power would strangle free speech and free literary enterprise. Smith aligned himself with those who questioned the political ideology of "the backers of this fabulous scheme.... Whether there are Communists in Hollywood and in radio studios or not, it is our opinion that the American Authors' Authority is dangerous and unworkable."

Too soon to answer Smith specifically, Cain wrote a clarifying article, "Just What is A. A. A.?" He reviewed the opposition and impressed upon his readers the fact that the meeting of the Guild membership to consider the plan in July was "the biggest meeting of writers ever seen in Hollywood, and I imagine the biggest in the history of writing." One man finally joined Cain because he decided that the project is "simply one gang of capitalists trying to get more dough out of another gang of capitalists." For the same reason, Cain expected that the New York opposition would blow up. He modified his own stand. Before, he had said that the authority would handle only material by its members, thus compelling others to join. Now, he said that it would accept anything from anybody, but to have a voice in the management of the Authority one must be a member of one of the four guilds. Cain's slogan is taken from Philip Goodman's response to an inaccurate cashier in Paris: "And remember, it's not the principle of the thing, it's the money!" The article came out in

October's the *Screen Writer*. Philip Dunne and other screenwriters commented on the plan in the same issue, and the editors stressed the lack of political control.

Immersed out of personal interest in direct action, writing, speaking, working, Cain arrived in New York in October for a meeting of the Authors' League, sympathetic to Cain. But it was cancelled. Dorothy Thompson, Red Lewis's wife, captured the small audience that showed up anyway and took them to a theater, secured overnight, where she attacked Cain.

When the League finally held a meeting, Cain looked out on six hundred writers, the largest number of them ever assembled in one spot in the history of literature, so far as he knew. James T. Farrell's objections to AAA were greeted with "scornful laughs" and "boos."

In November, the *Saturday Review* set up a debate between Cain and James T. Farrell, featured on the cover. Farrell saw AAA as a struggle between rich and poor writers and charged that the materialistic, inartistic commercial Hollywood writers would control the market to keep out independents. A major reason for artistic decline in America in the first place was this overemphasis on money. "This idea is stamped in the crude conceptions of the artist which Mr. Cain holds, the notion that the artist is a kind of idiot who thinks that he is a God, but who has only the defects and none of the virtues of a God."

In his rejoinder, Cain observed that his opponents conceived the issue in terms of freedom versus control. Ironically, this freedom was illusory for reasons that prompted the proposal in the first place. He saw arrayed against the AAA established, wealthy writers: Louis Bromfield, Clarence Budington Kelland, John Erskine, Clare Boothe Luce, Philip Wylie, Katherine Brush, Ayn Rand, Dorothy Thompson. Fear of reprisals from publishers was the real cause of opposition from well-to-do writers. Farrell's argument was "twittering nonsense." He did not believe, as Farrell did, that "art can be consciously 'created'... these ideas, to me, are simply weird, and downright silly.... I believe the conscious creating of art is a form of literary smugness."

In the winter of 1946, Vincent Lawrence died. Cain wrote a tribute to his mentor, using a tough tone, writing as he would if Vincent were listening. "Various writers have become legends in Hollywood . . . but no writer that I know of has become so fantastic an epic, the subject of anecdotes that take such long hours in the telling, as this Vincent Lawrence who has just died. Incredibly enough, most of the anecdotes are true . . . he was one of the most valued writers in the business, and the reason . . . was one of the clearest, coldest, hardest minds that ever faced a confused, divided, and desperate story conference and got order where only chaos had been. He was a screwball, but the screwball wins ball games."

"If you heard he was ignorant. . . ." Use that device to ring off his characteristics. Profligate with money . . . that he drank . . . of his panto-mimed act—the Ball Game—he was more so than you heard. As I wrote *Postman*, he gave not only encouragement and technical advice, but put his money on it, too, handsomely.

"He worked steadily." *Test Pilot* was his best picture. He had made an exhaustive study of the theater. George Jean Nathan called him "the first high comedy writer of the American stage." "Lawrence took nothing on faith . . . at the center of this knowledge lay a conviction, partly instinctive but buttressed by study, that the love story was the foundation of every-thing." With his love-rack theory, "he was the first out here, I think, to articulate the philosophy of the love story into the intellectual whole. . . ." "The core of his thinking is also the core of my novels. If ever a man had an intellectual parent, at least so far as this narrative part of my work is concerned, I must acknowledge such a relationship with Lawrence. And in closing this little tribute, I might say I have the most indescribably lost feeling doing it. I have hardly written the symbol—o—which closes all my stories, in the last twenty years, without wondering what Lawrence was going to think of it. That such a speculation can no longer enter my mind is, believe me, something I shall be a long time getting used to."

"Vincent Lawrence" appeared in the January 1947 *Screen Writer*.

With a thirty thousand first printing, a second printing before January 23 publication, and a third printing coming up, *The Butterfly* had an exhilarating start.

Now what about the reviews?

Kirkus: sordid, not for conservatives.

Library Journal, H. G. Kelley: "The author's preface was comic."

New York Times, Richard Gorham Davis. "Stories like 'The Butterfly' are not dubious social goods because they consider incest and murder. The major tragedies have done that. But what hard-boiled fiction, in and out of the movies, increasingly does is to train its audience not only to accept violence and perversion, but to take a callous pleasure in them. Thanks to this technique, violence and perversion are made to seem so isolated from normal consequence and meaning, from the audience's own social and spiritual concerns, that it feels no tragic fear or pity, but only the excitement of shock. Hard-boiled literature makes entertainment out of suffering by dehumanizing it." It may "end by dehumanizing the audience."

Stephen Stepanchev, *New York Herald Tribune*: "contrived," but "you are likely to enjoy the neatly packaged violence."

Joseph Henry Jackson, who had praised *Past All Dishonor*'s authenticity, *San Francisco Chronicle*: "remarkably able writer ... electricity ... not an imitation."

Lloyd Lewis, *Chicago Sun*: "*Butterfly* had me at its end turning out my study light and crawling on hands and knees to my bedroom, butting my head into chairs and hall walls, all for fear someone would wing me with hillbilly rifle bullet through a window."

Time: "about as incestuous as *Tarzan and the Apes*."

Walter Havighurst, a novelist, *Saturday Review*: "good writing hard, lean, nicely weighted. The pitch is just right and the pace is the Cain pace, sustained and pressing.... The little book is all one ... suspense ... used like a weapon ... control and timing. You won't forget this story ... good writing ... on practically no material at all ... a triumph of technique over substance, and you wonder why a man who can write this edged, tonal, actual dialogue should choose people who have so little to say ... completely identify narration with character," even though limited persons are his material. In a "half-trucelent introduction," Cain says he appeals to the intellect. "I first read Mr. Cain on shipboard nine years ago, along with some other books that I cannot now remember. I remember 'The Postman' very well, but not because it made an appeal to my mind. And what I will remember from 'The Butterfly' is the kind of thing you can't any more forget than you can forget the wreckage of a car in the roadside with the glass shattered and the steel top crushed like a kicked-in derby and the upturned wheels still spinning."

Hamilton Basso, another novelist, the *New Yorker*: Cain is the "best comic-strip artist in the country," except that Tracy and Canyon have more credibility, make more skillful use of language. Cain's preface gets "a hammerlock on the whole process of literary creation." "I dislike making sweeping statements, but nowhere in the whole field of aesthetic inquiry can this paragraph be matched . . . his central argument, of course, is irrefutable. Can a woman have a baby by watching another woman have one? Think it over." Cain takes up several pages to deny emphatically that he and Hemingway have anything in common except an "equal measure of talent." "The sum of Mr. Cain's argument is that he is a pure, unadulterated original, of the sort that turns up once in a century. I certainly hope he is right."

Meanwhile, *Past All Dishonor* had sold forty-five thousand copies.

Cain's reputation, his essay "Camera Obscura" in the *Mercury*, and the knowledge that he was negotiating to write a script in London prompted a request from The New Theatre there that he write a piece on the Hollywood writer. They expect me to get off my chest my lament for the suffering, intelligent, sensitive artist vs. the producer. I am going to have to disappoint you. The new breed of producer is not boorish, but as intelligent and sensitive as the writer. On another subject, why does the British public reject British films so admired by critics? They have failed to solve the love problem. "Any open emotion became distinctly bad form, and matter-of-factness a sort of cult. Now this certainly has charm . . . if we know that under the calm, great volcanoes are smoldering. . . . But if under the calm there is nothing but more calm, then we have only a set of very hollow people betraying their complete futility." There is no such futility in the English people themselves. Hollywood gives people what they like, and what they like is "what has life in it, i.e., what is good." Analyze the relation between art and public taste. Movies are commercial products that should satisfy public tastes not ignore them.

By February 1947, Cain, no longer at the center of the storm, felt a swansong was indicated. He went over the story of the effort, and pointed out that nobody else had offered a solution to the desperate plight of the American writer, who works on an archaic copyright law framed in 1909. What was needed was a full-time tough mug, for "pugnacity would help more than a calm, reasonable disposition." "Respectfully Submitted" appeared as a supplement to the March 1947 issue of the *Screen Writer*.

He had strong doubts now about the possibility of writers ever being able to band together. Even back in the fall, at that meeting in New York, the expression on one reporter's face had made him feel in his guts that something was going wrong with the proposal and his own advocacy of it. He now began to see more and more clearly that communists really were heavily involved in pictures and radio. He was apolitical, with some liberal and some conservative positions that shifted with the men and the developing facts involved in any issue. He knew he had a reputation as a loner with guts. He had long belonged to but had not gotten active in the Screen Writers Guild until recently.

Cain, like a burned child, hesitated at fifty-five to make a fourth attempt at marriage. His "little opera singer" had been widowed four years, after a happy marriage, and was reluctant to risk that memory in a new venture. But they discussed the possibility and she seemed receptive. When they talked of his future as a writer, she encouraged him to concentrate on writing novels. They dreamed of a high, exciting adventure together, writing her autobiography and his novels.

The image that had long ago inspired the tale of the Great Depression continued to haunt Cain. The road from Warner Brothers studio to the main street of Burbank (the town where he lived from 1932 to 1934) leads past a railroad station at the edge of town, and here, night after night, Cain would be held up by a freight, shunting off cars, or taking on water, or something. As he waited, the motor running, he would see, silhouetted against the Verdugo Hills, heads on the tops of the cars—not just two or three, but hundreds of them. He used to think with horror of the human beings up there, with no place to lay their heads, nothing to eat, no gleam of anything in their lives—all through no fault of their own. And gradually he had felt he might write a book about them.

To get the dope, he went to great lengths, going to the missions on Los Angeles Street, and finally connecting with a mentor, a tutor, a guide to Hobohemia who was willing, for a consideration, to take him in hand

and teach him. The most erudite man Cain ever met, the tramp got his knowledge of literature from the public library in which he took refuge from the cold.

In April, at fifty-five, he started his twelfth book in fourteen years. Like *Mildred Pierce*, *The Moth* would be a character study. In *Mildred*, he had presented a detailed picture of the Depression's middle class, a portrait of one of its most convincing female archetypes: the divorced self-sacrificing mother. In *The Moth*, he would present a detailed depiction of the life of a hobo, a migrant worker who makes good. Neither novel fit the tough-guy mold. Maybe they were closer to the proletarian novel, but what mattered was that he was putting into *The Moth* his own elements. In the 1920s, war-weary America's wish for prosperity and freedom had come true. The Depression was a massive expression of the futility of the wish-come-true. He would let the Great Depression happen to one man, Jack Dillon. He expected this simple but ambitious intention to produce one of his finest novels.

Jack Dillon is a man of many wishes, one of which is to embrace his mysterious mother, another is to avoid making love to a twelve-year-old girl, a Poe-like problem Cain remembered having himself several times when he was a young man. The love-rack concept takes many other forms as Jack wanders for a decade. Then he comes home to discover that Helen has grown up. His wish comes true, and his many trials end happily. With the algebraic equation set, though a little wobbly, how was he to begin?

He had decided to start Jack from Baltimore, first to tell something of Jack's childhood. That brought into play some memories of Cain's own Annapolis and Chestertown years. Cain's earliest memory is an enchanting vision of a large green luna moth on an overcast summer day. He called his mother to come look. But when he returned to it, a thick-legged boy was beating it to pieces with a club—a moment of horror that had remained with him ever since.

That night, his mother, perhaps to cheer him, recalled his frequent boast that he could beat his father running. She announced a race from the house on the college grounds down to the foot of the campus. With a flourish, the race began. But, instead of running, his father walked, with long strides, looking back with a giggly grin, not even bothering to throw away his cigarette. From the bench in front of the house came waves of laughter, for his mother and Aunt Mary were overcome with the spectacle of a three-year-old boy trying to outrun a tower of muscle. Jamie collapsed in tears upon a world that for him had suddenly caved in.

This double-horned day had left deep and lasting wounds. The race had a great effect upon his writing. His six-foot father might have foregone the funny feat of beating a small child, and thus allowed him the illusion of victory that night. Cain always remembered this incident in his relations with children, small animals, and his readers. For instance, his left hand was constantly cut and scratched from the attention he gave his cat. For he never forgot that being enticed with a string or a finger isn't much fun for the cat unless he *wins*. In his fiction, Cain put his reader in place of the cat.

For the reader hopes to win, too, and *must* win. Whether he is enticed by the prospect of sex, riches, violence, or whatever, the reader must be indulged, must get a good full bite of what has been promised. This payoff, rather than any penchant for "violence" as such, dictated much that was in his novels. Where other writers might use indirection, Cain plunged the action along, without flinching, to give the reader what he came for.

The luna moth had figured frequently and significantly in his work. Such rare moments of beauty and peace momentarily dispel the aura of evil Cain created.

Jack began his story. "The first thing I remembered was a big luna moth. I saw it in Druid Hill Park, which is up the street from our house, in Baltimore, on Mt. Royal Terrace. On cloudy days it's a little dark out there, and things like fireflies and bats and swallows get their signals crossed up and come out. Well, one day when the sky was about the color of a wet slate shingle, I was over there with Jane, my colored nurse, and this thing began flying around. I followed it quite a while, to a wall and a hedge and a bush, and then I ran off to find Jane so she could see it too. When I got back, there was a boy, I guess ten or twelve years old, but to me bigger than any Yale guard was, later. He had a stick, and he was whacking at the moth to kill it. Never in my whole life, in a dream or on a battlefield or anywhere have I felt such horror as I did then. I screamed my head off. When Jane got there she told the boy to stop, but he kept right on whacking. She jerked the stick out of his hands. He kicked at her, and she let him have it on the shins. Then he spit, but I didn't pay any attention. All I saw was that beautiful green thing, all filled with light, fluttering off through the trees, alive and free. It was a feeling I imagine other people have when they think about God in church. It makes no sense, does it, to say that a few times in my life, when something was happening inside of me, I could tell what it meant by the pale, blue-green, all-filled-with-light color the feeling had?"

Jack always feels guilt as the pink, hot-faced sensation associated with the pear he didn't give his teacher. Another episode in Cain's childhood inspired that distilled image of guilt. Bushrod Howard, a languid, aristocratic, handsome boy, three years older than Cain, was dragged one day into assembly at the Annapolis School by the principal and commanded to "apologize." The third-grader not only refused, but in a hysterical, weeping blaze of ferocity let fly with his heels against the shins of the principal, who was holding him up bodily, in front of the whole school. And when the principal was utterly defeated, clobbered 100 percent, Bush went charging off through the door at the side, and disappeared. Cain never discovered what Bush's offense was. He thrilled to his triumph over his stupid, cruel schoolmaster, and when he went home, he looked up the word *apologize* in the dictionary. Finding out what it meant frightened him even more than the scene itself. For he had a terrible, horrible suspicion that he *would have* apologized—though he didn't even know for what! Cain's sense of guilt over what he *might* have done had stayed with him all his life. But the incident made a double impression: It was his first encounter with gallantry. When things got tough, he always remembered Bushrod, and the courage it took to smash up that principal, and he acted in loyalty to that courage.

He was written up in *Current Biography* for the first time, the 1947 edition, the occasion being all the racket he had raised with his American Authors Authority. But it led off declaring that by early 1947, his novels had sold over one and a half million copies. They cited his estimate that the *Postman*, *Mildred*, and *Double Indemnity* pictures had sold for a total of $45,000 and had made $12 million, and that he felt there was something wrong with such an equation. And they wanted the world to know that he had beetle brows, a bush of gray hair, and weighed 220 pounds. And that he admired Ring Lardner, John O'Hara, Ernest Hemingway, and Sir Arthur Conan Doyle, who held him "bug-eyed."

One day, he got a letter from Wheeler Sammons, the publisher of *Who's Who in America*, asking him to write a preface for the 50th Anniversary Edition. He had first heard from him in response to a feature in the *Chicago Daily News* in 1945. They had asked various authors to recommend a Christmas book, and he had chosen *Who's Who in America*, his favorite reading since he first plunged into one in his father's study back in 1903. Writing the preface was an honor he was delighted to accept, but *The Moth* had to wait.

"Institutions, if they be actual and not merely nominal, will be found, I think, to possess some element, some simple, pregnant aspect, easily comprehensible to the popular imagination, which sets them off from other members of their class and gives them special status. 'Who's Who in America,' though a gospel, a heresy, and a raging polemic in one, and thus potentially suspect, is at the same time a Dun, Bradstreet, a Social Register, and a Hall of Fame, all merged into a grand consolidated National Glory Highway, and thus unique in the eyes of the American people." The policy had changed over the years "until even what a man had done began to take precedence over what he had been born to." Give a history of the book. "It began to seep into popular consciousness that the Marquis statement was true: You couldn't in the case of this book buy in." If you get in, it's because "You are a success." Page 1 stories in small towns tell who got in each year.

"In the course of an ordinary writing day, one consults the 'World Almanac' at least once, the 'Britannica' three times, the 'Webster Unabridged Dictionary' six. But 'Who's Who in America,' in my case anyway, is thumbed every hour on the hour."

He finished the introduction in June. In that edition, as in all previous ones he listed his occupation as newspaperman.

In July, Mencken wrote, "I am delighted with protests from various literati against your Authors' Authority scheme. The charge is made that you have been taken for a ride by the Communists, and some of the brethren even hint that you have gone into the Communist tank yourself.

What is the present status of the proposal? I seem to hear nothing about it save from its enemies."

Cain gave Mencken a report, but by then the first full-scale drive in US history to organize all writers had wandered down a country lane somewhere.

Then Farrell's book *Literature and Morality* came out with the first full-scale essay devoted to Cain's fiction alone. In "Cain's Movie-tone Realism," he blew the same note Wilson had blown on his horn. "James M. Cain's novel, *Mildred Pierce*, wantonly squanders what could have been a very good and representative American story. It could even have been a great one. Because there are so many indications that Cain has empirically grasped some important details of the modern American scene, and because this book has been distorted into movie-tone realism, it may be rewarding to discuss and analyze it."

And then that was just what he did, in agonizing detail. "One of the striking and promising features in the early portions of the novel is that the two main characters are presented with reference to objects." Things, "commodities," become the basis for "the spiritual content of Mildred's life. . . . Much has been written about standardization of human beings in modern American society. But here was the promise of a vivid . . . well-presented fictional account of the structure of American standardization. . . ." But Mildred's problems are falsified by "plot involvements," distorted by "cheap glamour and cynical melodrama."

Farrell stressed the fact that Cain's background was intimately associated with "the twenties of Mencken," and observed that in the early 1940s his writing still suggested the sophistication of the *Mercury*. But, while Mencken encouraged a more serious exploration of American experience in fiction and created an audience for it, Cain failed to grow with the positive side of Mencken's approach. "I think it is not unfair to say that writing like Cain's exploits rather than explores the material of life in America." It was not enough that Cain depicted American life, he must render, as Farrell did, some judgment on what he depicted. Cain possesses "the taste for reality" which he acquired in the 1920s. But "to it he has added lessons learned from Hollywood. Cain now shocks with his calculated thrills the yokels he attacked in *Our Government*." If Cain once suggested that the yokels got what they deserved, "These same yokels deserve the realist they now have and that realist deserves his audience." An audience of which Cain hoped to be worthy.

The divorce became final. Even though Aileen had hindered his writing in every way she could, she would get one third of the income from the two novels he had written while they were married. Cain didn't feel she had blackjacked him in this settlement.

After the divorce had been granted, Aileen rang Cain up about some small thing, and suddenly over the telephone, now that the lawyers had done their stuff and it was all settled and done with, they were the same warm friends as they had been. If they had let it go at that two years ago, instead of trying to force it, they would have both been spared a heartbreak.

One night, driving home after dinner, Cain cued Flo for one of those scenes that change your life. He asked her point blank to marry him, and she, sitting apart from him in his big Packard, said abruptly: "You go home now and hold your head under the pump. I don't want to see you for a week. You think things over, and if you still want to marry me, come back, and we'll talk. You don't have to marry me. Do you hear what I say? You don't have to. If you don't want to, just don't call any more and that'll be that. I'll live. I admit, giving you up will be a wrench, but I'll survive. Much better I get over it now than later, when it will be much more of a wrench. Now, drive home directly, without any circling around."

She had given him a full, fair chance to say no. He wished he could tell the whole female gender what a difference that makes, because the man rarely has this chance to say no. When he got home, late though it was, he called her. "I don't want any week. I know already how I feel, so do we have a date for tomorrow night?" A little breathlessly, she said all right, she guessed she was glad, a little bit.

They were married September 19, 1947, with many factors in favor of its lasting. Flo herself, most of all. She had made one happy marriage, and was capable of making another. Another factor was their chemistry. Physically, she delighted him, and did not get on his nerves. It was something more elusive than sex, some harmony of touch, sound, even of smell, that makes for peace, for tranquility, and at a tremendous change in one's life, in one's outlook. Three failures had made him begin to think of himself as a nut, a queer, an unstable zany, incapable of what normal men are capable of. One success would wipe that away.

The autobiographical elements entering into his conception delayed *The Moth*'s thrust into the Depression episodes. With its numerous sub-plots, it had become a picaresque novel, his longest.

Another interruption in writing *The Moth* was a $3,000 commission by Argosy Films to write an article about John Ford to promote *Fort Apache*. He was to sell it himself through his agent. He sent "Minstrel Boy" to Harold Ober, but he was not able, as Cain had warned Argosy Films, to sell it.

And he was also researching Florence's career, gathering material on file cards for her autobiography, *La Picina*. Her notices had been such raves, he couldn't understand why she was not one of the big legends of our time.

The Moth survived all those interruptions. Cain finished the first draft in December—nine months' fitful labor. The Knopfs accepted it, with the understanding that much work had to be done.

Rosalie objected to Jack's falling for a twelve-year-old girl, so Cain revised to remove all suggestion that Jack and Helen had done anything physical about their avowed love for each other.

He had decided that he was through with pictures forever, but late in 1947, Lou Brock, an independent writer-producer, hired him to write a treatment for *Forbidden Game*, an original story about an American couple who get involved in a mysterious game called Pato in South America.

It was a shock to see JAMES M. CAIN above the title SINFUL WOMAN, "A BRAND NEW NOVEL," "The Avon Monthly Novel #1," the artwork crude, two-toned, rust and hot pink, an oversized pulp, stapled along the spine. But he had asked for it. Knopf had objected to his having original paperbacks floating around out there. Avon was one of the tackiest of them all, seeming to specialize perversely in mixing indiscriminately the world's best, past and present, with the world's worst, their only common denominator being definitely the trashiest covers.

The Embezzler and *Love's Lovely Counterfeit* were already appearing as Avon Murder Mystery Monthlies. And *Double Indemnity* and *Career in C*

Major were on the stands in another Avon series, slotted in among Avon's de Maupassant, John O'Hara, D. H. Lawrence, John Steinbeck, Erskine Caldwell, A. Merritt, Raymond Chandler, Damon Runyon, Donald Henderson Clarke, and Jack Woodford titles. Knopf had turned down his first novelization of his play *7-11*, so he hadn't offered the second version, *The Galloping Domino*, in which Sheriff Lucas Parker tries to solve the "murder" of Sylvia Shoreham's husband, whom Sylvia is in Reno to divorce. His wish to meet his favorite movie actress, Sylvia, comes true. But he is miserable for a while, as he suspects her of hoodwinking him concerning her own involvement in the "murder." Comes out in the end that she was only shielding her slightly demented copycat sister, and that her husband was shot accidentally, making a happy ending possible. The title *Sinful Woman* went on over his objection, and he had gotten a $500 advance.

In its second issue of 1948, *Publishers Weekly* included a piece called "Cain's Books Popular in All Editions" that read like a market report. Knopf had paid him $22,500 in 1947, $3,500 advance on *The Moth*, but most of it for reprints. He noticed that *PW* quoted all the info given on the copyright page of the July 1947 second printing of Pocket Books' edition: "The Publishing History of *The Postman Always Rings Twice*." Knopf "rang the bell of popular favor to the tune of ten printings by May 1946." Then: Knopf, paper edition, October 1935. *American Mercury*, January 1937. Blue Ribbon, February 1938. Grosset and Dunlap, July 1943, nine printings in four years, to 1947. Garden City, February 1944. Editions for Armed Services, October 1945, reprinted, 1946. World, January 1946, with *Serenade* and *Mildred* in a single volume. Tower, August 1946. Fiction Book Club, October 1946, with *Past All Dishonor*. United Kingdom editions. Translations in French, Swedish, Norwegian, Hungarian, Danish, Italian, Spanish, Portuguese. "Cain's other books have not established quite such an impressive record, but are still in active demand."

Mildred: Knopf out of print since January 1944. Tower: 1945, about 150,000, no appreciable drop thereafter. Penguin (Signet): April 1946.

Serenade: Knopf, out of print since 1944. Tower: August 1943, reprints in first half of 1947, slight decline, '46. Penguin: February 1947.

Avon Editions of *Embezzler*, *Double Indemnity*, *Career*, Knopf edition of *Three of a Kind* still sold well, despite Avon's success.

Sundial, Triangle, Garden City Publishing Company, and Dollar Book Club published other editions. *Mildred Pierce* in all editions, paper, and cheap hardcover had sold 733,000.

Cain himself took stock of "The Baby in the Icebox," which had been reprinted in Ellery Queen's and Rex Stout's mystery magazines, Alfred Hitchcock's *Fireside Book of Suspense*, and Charles Grayson's *Half-A-Hundred, Tales by Great American Writers*. "Dead Man" had been reprinted in Charles Grayson's *Stories for Men*, Frank Owen's *Murder for the Millions*, Peter Arno's *Bedside Tales*, and *The Avon Story-Teller*.

In London, Robert Hale was bringing out an omnibus, *Love's Lovely Counterfeit, Past All Dishonor*, and *The Butterfly* called *Three of Hearts*. To express his special interest in the Southwest, in Sacramento, in ghost towns such as Virginia City and Port Tobacco, Maryland, and to clear up popular misconceptions about ghost towns, Cain wrote a preface, mindful that many reviewers and critics seemed to quote from his prefaces out of sheer delight, though sometimes with intent to ridicule. For his English readers, he also wanted to describe the Middle West and the culture and dialect of West Virginia. And he wanted to make further comments on his own approach to writing.

"These novels will come as a surprise to readers of my previous work, for there is a never-never-land quality in all of them. A flight, not so much from reality as from actuality, not to be found in any of my previous work. . . . Each story, in its own way, recoils from the present as it existed at the time it was written. . . . The reason was the war, which swept away the intellectual co-ordinates of American writers. . . . we were equally depressed in the realm of the spirit and wanted to know what had become of those principles, those truths, those beacon lights which had seemed so eternal to our fathers, and to us in easier times, but which now seemed gone, condemned as naïve saws to be believed only by gulls. . . . As of, say 1941, it seemed impossible for those of us who wrote novels to work at our trade at all. . . . *Love's Lovely Counterfeit* was begun in the dark days of 1941. What, a year or two before, had seemed a gay idea, seasoned no doubt with a pinch of malice, to write of some colorful goings-on in the city where I lived, suddenly seemed somehow a dirty trick, one not likely to be appreciated by my neighbors. . . .

"By 1942 anything current had become a complete impossibility, and like many of my colleagues I turned the calendar back many years to find a time when at least the values that men cherished were fixed and comprehensible. *Past All Dishonor*. . . . an idea of many years' cogitations seemed unassociated with the perplexities then plaguing us, *The Butterfly* was the result. . . . The worst offense of narrative, in my belief, is tepidity, and in my work, God willing, you will never find it, whether I write of past, present, or future. . . ."

"The locale of *The Butterfly* is the Appalachian Highland. . . . The people are the mountaineers of whom so much is written in the United States. You will find them more accurately depicted in *The Butterfly*, I imagine, than in much of what you read about them. . . . there is one thing not commonly known about them. . . . To the philologist, the region is rich in material for study, constantly examined by American scholars, for here and there in secluded hamlets are our last surviving remnants of Elizabethan speech. . . . I do very little about this in the novel, for in my observation too much concern with local speech usually results in distraction from the tale, to which all dialogue and action, in my belief, should be subservient. But the mountain drawl, the quaint syntax, the melancholy humor of these people is suggested, and the reader may accept it as authentic."

By 1948, his AAA proposal had been reduced to the status of an excuse for communist baiting. Cain wanted to see communists run out of the Screen Writers Guild, too, not because they were communists, but because he abhorred secrecy in political affiliation. He was a registered Democrat and that was public knowledge, even if he did campaign for Dewey in 1944 and was ready to stand behind California's Governor Earl Warren in the 1948 presidential campaign for his courageous stand on racism, which made them both more than a little leftist. When the ten writers who defied the Thomas Committee returned to Hollywood, he objected to the use of Guild funds to defend them in court. He asked Albert Maltz, who had worked on *Mildred Pierce*, in an open meeting: "Are you or are you not a Communist?" to stress the importance of open declaration in such matters if his supporter money was being sought to back that position. Maltz refused to answer, Cain was ruled out of order, and his letter of protest went unanswered. But he didn't approve of the House Committee on Un-American Activities, either. Call him leftist, if you want to be absurd, call him conservative, if you insist, but a loner is what he had always been, and a few at least knew that.

On March 1, he delivered a 110-page synopsis of *Forbidden Game* to Lou Brock, having earned $5,000, and prepared to travel with his new wife by automobile to Washington, DC, where he intended to research his Civil War novel in the Library of Congress.

9

Galatea and *Mignon*

CAIN AND FLO GOT SITUATED IN A MOTEL JUST OUTSIDE WASHINGTON, then visited friends in Baltimore and New York. Over dinner at Sardi's, he and Leonard Bernstein discussed Bernstein's proposal that Cain write the libretto for a grand opera rendition of *Serenade*. Cain told him to go ahead with the music, but to count him out as the librettist.

It pleased him that in mid-February, while he was still in Hollywood, he had already made a footnote to history in the nation's capital. The Honorable Emanuel Celler of New York had entered Cain's preface to the 50th Anniversary Edition of *Who's Who in America* in the *Congressional Record*, from which Cain had taken verbatim one of the most devastating chapters of *Our Government*, the one on Congress.

After some research time in the Library of Congress, Cain and Flo set out in June on another research trip for the Civil War novel. Among other things, he wanted to find out how his hero would travel. *The Moth* had just come out and in many of the towns where he did research in libraries and on the scene, newspapers wanted to interview him. He started out in Parkersburg, West Virginia, as "a dynamic individual," and by the time he hit Houston he looked like "a refined, middle-aged Irish bricklayer." In between, they stuck around Alexandria, Virginia, one of the novel's major settings, a long time.

He told a Houston reporter that he was "still writing to entertain people, and I'm not searching for any of this social awareness in my stories," but that he had "made an effort" in *The Moth* and in the Civil War novel "to examine the chief characters' surroundings and environments and their effects on the characters more than I have ever done before."

GALATEA

a novel by

JAMES M. CAIN

The *Houston Post*'s review of *The Moth* said it was "dull to the point of irritation." Few of the other reviews buoyed them along in their travels.

Kirkus: "Sentimental, rather than elemental."

H. G. Kelly, again, *Library Journal*: great improvement over *The Butterfly*, "should regain many readers for the author."

New York Times, James MacBride, a Cain fan since the days of his *World* column dubbed it Cain's most ambitious novel, but "Dillon remains a vaguely glimpsed stranger who has talked you to death, and beyond." Famous pace "lost in verbiage."

Lewis Gannett, "Books and Things," *New York Herald Tribune*: another reviewer-as-reader testimonial as to Cain's power to grip a reader. "Mr. Cain uses the American language as skillfully as any living writer . . . he never forgets that the business of the novelist is to keep his story moving."

Sterling North, syndicated review: "There is a streak of authentic poetry in James M. Cain . . . a real love for humanity hidden under his cynical, self-protective shell . . . he is headed for the first rank of American novelists."

Stephen Longstreet, *Los Angeles News*: "*The Moth* is American. . . . A great book by a great artist."

Jack Conroy, who wrote the proletarian classic, *The Disinherited*, in the *Chicago Sun*: "his determination to write a more ambitious type of novel has caused him to deviate from his usually tight and efficient narrative structure." The effect is not breadth and depth, but choppiness and disorder.

New Yorker, brief notice: "Excellent in its reportorial chapters . . . but disappointing as a psychological study."

Novelist Merle Miller, the *Saturday Review*: "Occasionally James M. Cain writes like an angel—a slightly malicious, dyspeptic, and ribald angel with a lust for gore."

Time: "In *The Moth*, Hollywood's hoary old sensation-monger James M. Cain tells the story of a nice boy. . . . The best things in the book are like the best things in all Cain's books: clear, fast-moving narrative passages in which Jack Dillon tells you step by step how he bluffed, fought and figured his way out of jams. . . . Cain's writing is too proficient and disciplined to be classed as pulp, too intelligent to be classed as trash, and some of it certainly ranks with the classics of shock fiction. It is nevertheless essentially near-adolescent."

Charles J. Rolo, *Atlantic Monthly*: "The maestro of the slim, sex-propelled shocker has taken himself too seriously. Cain's story is essentially the Superman comic strip on a different literary level." Cain gives the reader "courses on the know-how of oil drilling," etc. "Pretty silly without often being dull."

While they were still on the road, the *Saturday Review* published the American Library Association's list of books by American writers most popular with their readers over the past twenty-five years, and *Three of a Kind* was Cain's only book on it. He liked knowing that his comments on his own work in the preface had been part of his ongoing readership.

But it appeared that *The Moth* would not hit twenty-five thousand copies.

When he got back to Washington, in early September, he was ready to start writing the Civil War novel. The Library of Congress was right there when he needed to do further research. It had proven far more helpful than research trips had. An interim stay of about a year was indicated, so they had their belongings in California put in storage and rented a little white house in College Park, a suburb in Hyattsville, Maryland, convenient to the Library of Congress, to the University of Maryland's library, and to Mama in Baltimore. They were also quite close to the most maddening summer climate in America, so although he was through with pictures, he wasn't beyond persuasion. A trip west might make them feel human again.

He set about writing this novel with higher hopes for its bestseller possibilities than anything he had ever written. He'd chosen a great story of the Civil War, the Union's ill-fated Red River expedition of 1864. He wrote Joseph Lisser at Knopf that it would be "quite a romantic tale, full of skullduggeries involving large sums of money."

He went almost daily to the Library of Congress. After he'd read *Ordeal of the Union*, he wrote his old *World* colleague Allan Nevins, now a major historian, to tell him his idea for a book on the question, what if the Civil War had never been fought? He corresponded with Joseph Pennell, whose novel *The History of Rome Hanks* was very well researched, and to many other people involved in the field.

Eating, drinking, and weighing too much made work sluggish, but an irritant out of the Hollywood setting also distracted him. A woman wrote in late September accusing him of stealing her script *Nothing to Live For*, using it as the basis of the movie *Mildred Pierce*. She claimed she had submitted it to him in 1937 for his comment and advice. He told her his longstanding policy had been never to read or advise on manuscripts submitted by amateurs, but he did advise her that plagiarism suits were expensive and frustrating. She decided to risk it, and filed suit against Warner Brothers and Cain in January 1949.

In February, the State of Massachusetts took Cain to court on obscenity charges for *Serenade*, which also dated back to 1937. The massive logjam at the heart of the Red River Campaign held fast while he tried to blast this logjam in his life.

It was the lead item in *Publishers Weekly*'s "News of the Week" department, March 29 issue. "Experts Testify in Boston for Cain, Caldwell Books." "Testimony for and against 'Serenade' by James M. Cain and 'God's Little Acre' by Erskine Caldwell began in Massachusetts' Superior Court, Boston, on March 15, in separate trials before Judge Charles S. Fairhurst, under the Massachusetts Obscenity Statute." New American Llibrary (NAL) were defendants.

"Three school teachers ... said they had caught children reading it behind books they were supposed to be studying." "Harold Strauss, editor in chief at Knopf, gave the publishing history of the book since 1937, and mentioned its reprinting in editions by World, Sun Dial, and Penguin Books (now New American Library) and its many foreign editions." Two covers were shown, Robert Jonas's abstract, replaced for sales-appeal reasons by the head of a woman, both conservative, with limited low-key advertising.

Theodore Morrison, English A director at Harvard, former Atlantic Monthly Press editor, testified that *Serenade* was "a psychological novel in which the sexual episodes were indispensable to character portrayal." A good example of the serious "hard-boiled novel." Ralph Thompson, *New York Times Book Review*, gave similar testimony. Robert Gorham Davis, associate professor of English at Smith College, also defended *Serenade* as a work in the realistic tradition. Thompson and Gorham had attacked other novels by Cain in reviews. Murphy, the prosecutor, cited profane words, grammatical errors, sexual episodes, and sacrilegious elements.

The *Mildred* suit took time, and labor. And a toll on his health. After a minor but painful operation, he was well enough to waste more and more time and energy, and nervous tension, imagining how even a $5,000 judgment against him could annihilate him. His income in 1948 has been almost $30,000, but 1949 was shaping up as a painful contrast.

He was all along repeatedly writing himself into problems on what he was now calling *Ghost Riders on the Red River*, and getting himself out of them, requiring supporting research at the Capitol.

They had dug in, as he told a friend, and were thinking of staying, because they couldn't face another move. "Making this trek," has been a God-awful wrench, to both of us, and leaves us somehow suspended in mid-air because we really don't accept this dreadful little state, take no pride in it, and want no piece of it.

But he drank too much and he ate too much. He weighed 250 and thought of himself as a hog-fat, pink caricature of a man, and knew he had come to a point in his life. He drank because he liked it, because he wanted it, because he had to. When he discovered one day in the fall of 1949 that he couldn't climax an anecdote about his friend Mostyn Thomas, the baritone, with the second verse of *La Traviata*, he knew his brain was soaked in alcohol.

One night, he told Flo, who took no interest in liquor, that he thought he'd skip the evening cocktail, for it had come to him that if a drunk is always only one drink from disaster, he's equally only one drink away from salvation. So he didn't quit drinking, he just kept on skipping the next drink.

Health problems had always influenced his life and affected his literary output. Alcohol had helped to undermine his health over the years.

When he heard that Mencken had had a stroke, he wished he'd gone up there to see him, but Mencken's not knowing him had made Cain fainthearted. Mencken was in and out of the hospital. Finally, in October he went to see Mencken and he looked so good, Cain's spirits were lifted, even though Mencken just had to say that he was almost seventy and so would be dead within a year.

He was glad to see a book on one of his other mentors, *Walter Lippmann, A Study in Personal Journalism* by David Weingast, with an introduction by Harold L. Ickes, from a university press. Weingast quoted Cain's "End of the *World*" article and a long passage from his response to his query back in 1947.

Career in C Major was still alive on the page in the library favorite *Three of a Kind*, and in November the movie version, *Wife, Husband, and Friend*, was resurrected by Twentieth Century Fox as *Everybody Does It*, the new script by Nunnally Johnson, directed by Edmund Goulding, with a new man, Paul Douglas, in the lead, supported by Linda Darnell and Celeste Holm. The rave reviews told moviegoers it was a hilarious comedy romance. NAL put out *Career* and *The Embezzler* together under the movie title *Everybody Does It*. Book and movie sold each other, Cain imagined.

The Butterfly, for which NAL had paid a $2,000 advance, had come out in July and was in its third printing by December. *Past All Dishonor* also came from NAL, in 1948, and *Serenade*, in its seventh printing, still earned rack space. Avon advanced $1,000 for *Nevada Moon*, which he'd revised so that all Edward G. Robinson and *Double Indemnity* tie-ins were out. Avon changed the title to *Jealous Woman*, which did not strike him much more inventive than *Sinful Woman*. It was to come out as the Avon Monthly Novel No. 17, with titles for its four parts: "The Playboy's Second Wife," "Dishonorable Intentions," "The Willing Widow," and "Hush Money." Avon wanted to put out a collection of Cain's stories, but except for "Dead Man," "Pastorale," "Coal Black," "Brush Fire," and a few others, they were little stinkers, written quickly when he was hot, to cash in on the magazine trade, which was, compared with hardcover books, no more important to him than pictures, or original paperbacks. But even with all this reprint activity, he had earned in 1949 only half the 1948 figure. And the *Mildred* suit, postponed until May 1950, still hung over his head.

The feel of paperbacks in his hand made him aware of millions of readers in a way that hardcover books did not. Signet's motto, Good Reading for the Millions, had a trumpet sound to it.

Cain and Flo were so down, they thought of going on back to Hollywood. But when a producer asked Cain in January 1950 to meet him in New York to discuss an idea he had for a movie for Rita Hayworth, even though he liked the idea, he told Swannie to hold out for $10,000 even at the risk of not getting it. It worked. Cain didn't get it. They took a longer lease on the house, until August 1950.

As his own health mended, with the loss of weight, now that he was skipping the next drink and eating less, Flo's energy was diminishing, her problem diagnosed as high blood pressure.

When Francis Brown, editor of the *New York Times Book Review*, asked Cain to review Edgar Kemler's *The Irreverent Mr. Mencken*, he "got a case of the shakes," as he wrote Brown, "for fear of Henry's reaction," for fear of losing him as a friend, because he still had "an intellectual reverence" and "a wrenching personal affection for him," while also feeling that he owed the reader a fair report. But his review, he was glad to learn, pleased everyone concerned, and so pleased him.

In late June 1950, he went to New York to receive a Silver Kangaroo from Pocket Books. *Postman* had passed the one million mark.

Helen Markey called him one morning in July. Morris had died; his funeral was the next day. Cain was totally unprepared for the death of a man he had felt was like a brother, with whom he had worked on the *World*, who had gotten him the *New Yorker* job, who had been out in Hollywood with him for a while, whose commentary on the Texaco Saturday afternoon opera concerts he'd often enjoyed, who had left Hollywood and then New York in disappointment, to retire in Halifax, Virginia, close to his hometown in North Carolina, whose drinking was excessive, whose health was bad, who had never finished his novel, *Doctor Jeremiah*.

But when he got down there, he discovered that Morris had been shot, "death from causes not determined," which left three choices up to the townspeople: suicide, homicide, or accident. Morris had often told his wife that when he went, it would be an accident, hinting at insurance benefits for her. But the bullet had struck from behind, leaving the event in a mysterious limbo. As Cain headed home, he knew it would haunt him the rest of his days.

Feeling the need for another research trip, Cain and Flo set out again in September for a tour of the South. Did he need another research trip? He didn't know. He did know he needed to get out of Maryland. He wrote to Swannie, "In this neck of the woods, except as a base for research, I don't fit in at all." And war was about to erupt in Korea, and Washington was too close. Cain asked Swannie to be on the lookout for a scriptwriting job. In September, the Supreme Court, which had reversed the decision against *God's Little Acre*, upheld the earlier decision that *Serenade* was not obscene.

That was the month NAL came out with the abridged version, cut from 373 down to 189 pages, of *The Moth*, trumpeting "By the Author of *Serenade*." Length had been one of the novel's problems. A sexy, but nice cover, a class above Avon's. "What was the matter with Jack Dillon?" the inside cover asked, suggesting a bounce off *Serenade*, for it asked about the twelve-year-old girl, about too many nights in hobo jungles, about the mother who deserted Jack. The jacket quoted Lewis Gannett, whose angle was always how much he hated but couldn't resist reading Cain's tales.

In 1950, Cain continued to crash: $12,000, $5,000 less than the previous disaster year. And still, the woman with the claim on *Mildred* continued to drain his time and energy, all for a settlement in January 1951 of $7,501. But not from Cain, from Warner Brothers. Cain still had legal expenses.

Driving through the rain one day on the Eastern Shore, Cain skidded into an army truck, the second collision of his life, both his own fault, but this one made him and Flo wonder about the effect of his age on his driving ability.

Cain got back to work on the Civil War novel. But after several months, Ober tempted him with work in a different medium, radio, on a subject treated in his first book—a series called "Congressional Investigator." He met in New York with the people who were packaging the series, went home, and spent two weeks preparing a twenty-page treatment, featuring an intellectual investigator, a dumb blonde as his half-hostile foil and confidant, set in an average-sized town, somewhat like the one in *Love's Lovely Counterfeit*. It was a unique, worthwhile approach, he thought, free of claptrap. The big money lure collapsed to a $200 level for the outline, $1,000 for a sample script. Cain and Ober decided this was a fly-by-night outfit, and Cain did not work on speculation anyway. Other radio prospects came along and proved unfeasible.

He needed another book for Knopf after four years without, but he also needed fast money, and to go after that, he had conceived a magazine series with a neighborhood focus, "about an eight-year-old boy, his squirrel, his mother who wins diving contests, his father who teaches Greek, his uncle who tells the stories." He told Ober he had a gift for this kind of thing, "and used to make the *Ladies' Home Journal*, believe it or not." Ober seemed to like the idea, but pointed out that magazine series were out these days, and that discouraged Cain.

He saw another dead-end detour up ahead when *The Theater of Famous Authors* TV series asked him for an original story. He needed the $2,000 but foresaw endless attempts before he could come up with what they wanted. He had done so much detailed and intricate research, he knew that only in a trilogy would he use everything that interested him. That plan probably contributed to his inability, after three drafts of the *Galatea* novel—*The Lady Is a Pirate*, *The Slim Girl*, and *The Silver Mountain*—to make even one novel work.

He was exhausted, and his doctor forecast a nervous breakdown. Flo was depressed again, for they both saw that their dreams of glory in the East writing novels and her autobiography were still only dreams that mocked the daily reality. He even had to tell Mama he couldn't send her any more money for a while. Cain and Flo took a brief trip to Lake Champlain to rejuvenate themselves, and then he returned to the novel. He had asked Rafe to read it, and that request in itself told him he had trouble. Vincent's advice would have been to focus on the love story. That's what he did.

A Union officer conceives a cotton-trading scheme that will finance a conspiratorial movement to sweep General Banks into the White House in 1864. To advance the career of her husband, a Secessionist, the heroine helps the Union officer with his plan. Her husband is killed. The Union navy seizes the cotton as a prize of war. The lovers' plan is smashed. But they devise another plan for money and glory, and that fails too. The hero helps to build the dam on the Red River at Alexandria, and in that exploit he is regenerated, and the lovers finally get each other. A tale of an adventure in treason.

He was glad to find himself written up in *American Novelists of Today*, though it was a rather routine recital of the facts of his life and the plots of his novels. The author, Harry R. Werfel, was a Noah Webster, Charles Brockden Brown, and local color scholar.

The Washington scene was beginning to stimulate a few ideas. What if a twenty-five-year-old code clerk met a payoff girl for bookies and tried to free her from her boss? He let the man tell it. "I met her a month ago, at a little cafe called Ike's Joint, in Cottage City, Maryland, a town just over the District line from Washington, D. C. As to what she was doing in this lovely honky-tonk, I'll get to it, all in due time. As to what I was doing there, I'm not at all sure that I know, as it wasn't my kind of place. But even a code clerk gets restless. . . ."

He wrote two other stories in 1951 but only "Pay-Off Girl" sold. *Esquire* paid $400 for it. That didn't keep his income from declining once more, this time by $1,000.

The Root of His Evil. A lurid cover, a blonde with a black slip sliding off her shoulder: "They call me a tramp because I made a sucker of a millionaire." There it was, after fifteen years, his 1937 serial, *A Modern Cinderella*, called *When Tomorrow Comes* in the movie version. His own title, to head off another *Sinful* or *Jealous Woman*. Had Avon considered *Greedy Woman*? On the back: "In spite of everything she was called, Carrie felt she had to set the record straight . . . pass judgment on her only after you've read *her* story," as opposed to the newspapers. "It is hard to write on the deck of a sloop that is anchored here, off the Bay Islands, for if a swell . . . the interruptions are many, but I want to tell my story, partly because it is my story, and partly to correct false impressions. Yes, I am Carrie Selden, the Modern Cinderella, but if a girl emerges who is different from the girl the newspapers pictured, then all I can say is that the newspapers printed a great many surprising things. . . . My story really begins, of course, with the appearance of Grant. . . ."

Carrie Selden gave some idea how Mildred Pierce might have sounded if she had told her own story. Carrie was a waitress who devoted her energies and employed her feminine wiles to make a great deal of money to win back the man she married and divorced. Too much money was not the only "root of evil" for her husband, Grant Harris, who would rather study Indians than make much money. The main obstacle to matrimonial contentment was his possessive mother, a society priestess. But Carrie triumphs over her, wins Grant back, and the fable ends, as those other two studies in character, *Mildred* and *The Moth*, happily. In all three, the audacious endeavors of the chief characters were rather solitary. And he had employed the love-rack and wish-come-true concepts rather diffusely. He had started Carrie's story before Mildred's, so *Mildred* was really a variation on Carrie's story, in a way.

He'd kept the serial structure, so the four parts had titles: "The Girl in the Beanery," "Knife Under the Tongue," "The Snake," and "A Mink Coat." His third for Avon. And they still advertised, on a full page in the back with the other two titles, *Love's Lovely Counterfeit*. On the opposite page, they hawked four titles by Jerome Weidman, and on their backlist were Tiffany Thayer, Philip Wylie, Howard Hunt, John O'Hara, D. H. Lawrence, Nelson Algren, and Stephen Longstreet whom they also quoted up front: "James M. Cain is the master novelist of the American scene." Yes, and those millions of readers were holding their breath, waiting for him to tell them all about Prince George's County, Maryland.

One day, he told Flo his research needs at the Library of Congress were over; they could go back home to Hollywood. She said it wasn't there anymore. TV was there, but not the Hollywood where he had earned big money, and she had sometimes earned big money. Better to be poor here, than poor among rich Beverly Hills friends. On her logic, they stayed put.

John Garfield re-awakened Cain's passion for writing plays when in 1952, he asked him to prepare a new version of the *Postman* play for a summer stock tryout in which he would star. Cain cleared a space in his warehouse of Civil War notecards and books to breathe new life into a long dead project; then Garfield died suddenly.

But his desire to write a hit play was alive, and he returned to another postponed project, *The Guest in Room 701*. Harold and Helen Reed have not been in New York City for ten years. He is to give a speech. He is such a famous lawyer the newspapers prominently report he is staying at the Dijon Hotel (similar to Cain's favorite, the Gotham). Now what if their old friends and lovers were to come to their room one by one, dredging up compromising relationships and events of ten years ago? Each entrance would, in the nature of theater, especially of the one-room set, raise audience expectations and each exit would enhance the effectiveness of each confrontation, and the rhythm of entrances and exits would facilitate a pace that would sweep the audience along, enhancing their interest in developing relationships.

Helen's old boyfriend is rich enough to tempt Harold with an offer: Sell me your wife. Harold's old girlfriend comes into his life again. Harold's old pal blackmails him. Harold agrees to sell his wife, partly to pay the blackmail money. Then a woman, who has been waiting outside to see him, shoots him. The police shoot her. Helen's old boyfriend does not buy her after all. He has fallen for Harold's old girlfriend.

Remembering that novelists go broke writing plays, especially novelists on the brink already, he took up another idea for a novel that had come to him rather fuzzily while he was still in California but that came into sharper focus after he quit drinking in '49 and had lost sixty pounds by '52. His editorial experience had taught him years ago how surefire food and diets are as items of interest to American readers.

Duke Webster, ex-boxer and trainer, does not wish to make love to his boss's wife, Holly Valenti. But after he succeeds in transforming her from "a tub of lard" into a trim and lovely woman by having her use a special fighter's diet, he falls in love with her. Their audacious adventure is the diet itself, conducted in secrecy because Holly's restaurant-keeper husband had deliberately fed her abnormal appetite to imprison her in blubber and thus keep a hold on her. Duke impulsively kills his creation, Holly. Another love fable, with grotesque and comic elements. "I chopped, grubbed, and shoveled, and the deeper I dug the keener I felt it: I was being watched. At first I tried not to mind, as a holdup case, his first day out, on a cockeyed probation deal, could expect watching, especially if left alone on the farm he's been put to work on. . . . And then, as I reached for the ax, there she was not ten feet away.

"Not counting her eyes, which were big, black, and pretty, or her expression, which was sweet, she was the most sickening sight in the way of a woman I think I'd ever seen . . . so fat she was deformed."

This was a concoction that, remembering he'd written *The Butterfly* in five weeks after the long haul on the other Civil War novel, *Past All Dishonor*, he hoped he could turn quickly into an advance from Knopf.

By the end of 1952 he sent it to Knopf. Knopf didn't think it one of his best, but would publish it, and Blanche liked it but wanted a happy ending. While thinking it over, he realized how deeply he cared for this book, and that a happy ending for Holly would satisfy him too, so he would knock off a few pages in which the husband's attempt to murder Holly and Duke fails, and he is accidentally killed instead, a switch from the pattern readers of his novels knew perhaps too well by now.

In a way, most of his characters were like Pygmalion, who sculpted a woman so real he went on the love-rack, and when his wish that she come alive was granted by Aphrodite, the results were startling. In *Career in C Major*, a woman opera star had transformed a contractor into an opera singer.

He finally negotiated a $4,000 advance from Knopf, but $5,700 for the year was his lowest income since 1933, the year he was writing *Postman*.

The *Galatea* rewrite was more difficult than he had anticipated. He had become cold in Hollywood, maybe lukewarm around the nation, but at obscure Washington College, where the library had refused to shelve his early books, he was hot. The president there wanted to cite him for this and that achievement, but he found it all very embarrassing, and so declined.

Having put the Red River logjam behind him for the time being, and written *Galatea*, he was vulnerable to other new ideas—a novel set on the great Susquehanna River in the Pennsylvania coal mines.

He and Flo went up there as part of his research, and visited with his old army buddy Gilbert Malcolm, provost of Dickinson College. Then he gave a lecture to the graduating class of a branch of William and Mary in Norfolk, Virginia. It was on world affairs, not, as requested by William Seward, creative writing, and what he walked away from was, he felt, a disaster.

Back to Hyattsville for some short story writing, quick bucks from *Manhunt*, which accepted "Two O'Clock Blonde" and "Cigarette Girl," the fruits of his attempt to use a Dictaphone. Ober, like Knopf, thought it undignified of him to traffic in the realm of the second-rate, but he told Ober, "The fact is, it's the first magazine in a long time that has shown much interest in my writings, and I think it is worth cultivating." What he told Knopf about Avon applied to *Manhunt*: "The only novel that hurts you is no novel at all." That was proven by the editor of *Manhunt* himself, who rejected three other stories, and expressed fear that he was seriously slipping.

Fast writing, fast money, equal instant praise? *Galatea*'s reviews came in that summer.

David Demsey, *New York Times*: style like the heroine, lean and spare as ever.

E. L. Acken, *New York Herald*: "skill at creating tension, as he proves once more."

Washington Post: "James M. Cain at his best."

Stephen Longstreet again, *Daily News*: "best novel he has written ... he has no peer ... rated just under Faulkner and Hemingway. ... That Cain is one of our best writers has been hidden from us by our critics, who are often snobs and logrollers ... best tough yarn of the year, maybe of the decade." Fine, if true.

Saul Pett, syndicated review: "242 pages. I read all of them, I reread some 2 or 3 times, I still don't know quite what Cain is talking about."

W. K. Harrison, *Library Journal*: sordid but placid Cain.

The *New Yorker*: "not human enough to be affecting and not grotesque to be interesting."

Nation: "Cain is running down." Banal.

Harper's: The water tower scenes again. "I read and reread these scenes and could never understand what happened."

Charles Lee, *Saturday Review*: "Cain's fans may like it, but the writing is dull enough to make the authors of *The Congressional Record* seem the very models of clarity and charm ... usual hard-boiled hocus-pocus." Boomerang.

B. F. K. Springfield, *Republican*: no less well written than Cain's best.

Galatea closed out at around twelve thousand copies.

While writing *Galatea*, he had continued work on the play *The Guest in 701* and, when the producer's interest was still keen after Garfield's death, further minor revisions on the *Postman* play. Tom Neal and Barbara Payton, third-rate actors, were cast in the leads in the hope that the first-rate publicity over their notorious Hollywood love affair would draw crowds, and make them all some money. The actors were rotten, but *Variety* threw him in the same bin, calling him a first-rate novelist who was a "pedestrian playwright," and the *Chicago Tribune* said it was such a crude dramatization somebody ought to perform a mercy killing on the theater in general. He had witnessed the whole process, having gone up to New York and Connecticut to work with them, and he was there on opening night in Pittsburgh, and toured with them to Chicago and St. Louis. The play shut down in October.

And he had made less than $500, but as he told Mama, he had also come out of it with a firm resolution that if he ever again made the slightest movement toward reviving that double disaster, he hoped somebody would shoot him.

In 1954, he was back on the banks of the Red River, contemplating those bales of illegal cotton and that logjam to see what he could, at last, make of it all. But his memory was sluggish, he made far more typos, the dank summers stupefied him, the winters scraped his bones, his thinking about plot was confused, and he just didn't always give a damn whether the guy got the doll or not.

But he now had a title, *Mignon*, and, in the spring, an urge to soak up more atmosphere on the scene. When he got back to Hyattsville's climate, he dug in for the last long siege. He had his love story in focus, and the young man was telling it in the first person.

Bill Cresap, recently discharged from the Union army with a leg wound, dreams of cutting a canal to the Gulf of Mexico but civilians draw him back into the war. In New Orleans, he falls in love with Mignon, a beautiful, fiery widow. If his wish to have her is to come true, he must reject his other dream and devote his time as a lawyer to freeing her father from the jail where he is held on a false charge as a traitor. Frank Burke, a wily Irish trader, a masterful liar and murderer, stands between Mignon and Bill. He repeatedly tempts his partner, Mignon's father, a merchant of dangerously wavering patriotism, and Mignon herself into scheming for a rich shipment of "hoodooed" cotton.

The conflict ends with everyone dead except Bill. Though he loses Mignon, another wish—to serve his country well—comes true. "It was Mardi Gras in New Orleans, February 9 of this year, 1864, but the extent to which I partook of the merry fun was not visible to the naked eye. I was there, I was lodged at a good hotel, I had cash in my jeans, but had reason for taking it easy. For one thing there was my leg with a sword-stab in it, my souvenir of Chancellorsville, which had got me a discharge from the Army but compelled me to walk with a stick and discouraged any jinks—high, low, or medium. . . ."

In August 1954, the paperback of *Galatea* came out, with a cover a cut above all the others, except for the old *Serenade* by Robert Jonas. "The New Novel" "by the famous author of *Serenade* and *The Postman Always Rings Twice.*" "Fatal Transformation" was a good teaser for the description inside. Seven other books of his were still in print with NAL, listed and described inside. He had passed through several transformations himself since the professorial photo they had used on all their editions of his books was taken.

And in October, NAL put a new cover on *Serenade*, its third, on the occasion of the tenth printing.

Otto Preminger took an option on *Galatea* for $1,000.

In 1954, Robert Hale in London brought out a hardcover reprint of *The Root of His Evil.* The cover was an imitation of the cheap Avon style, but better artwork. *Galatea* and *Postman* were advertised on the back. *Truth*, on *Galatea*: "Mr. Cain is one of my favorite authors . . . toughness and sentimentality." And praise for *Postman* from *News Chronicle, Spectator, Manchester Guardian*, which said, "We associate this story with the masterpieces of its genre . . . the directness of the narrative is masterly."

He had worked on *The Guest in Room 701* off and on until 1955, when he made his final revisions. Rafe was living up in Bucks County, not far at all, obsessed, to the sore neglect of his writing, by photography, so Cain finally accepted one of his invitations, his intention being to ask him to read the play, Rafe's to do a portrait of Cain and Flo. Flo was getting weaker and weaker from her blood-pressure problem, so Cain went alone. Rafe got his picture, and Cain, in the nicest language that could be devised, got a critique of his play that should have discouraged him, but that didn't, not entirely.

He stirred up some interest among producers, and kept at it.

He had done *something* right in 1955, because his income quadrupled to $21,000, including what the sale of *Love's Lovely Counterfeit* to the movies brought in. Preminger had dropped his *Galatea* option.

Robert Hale in London brought out a double-decker in 1955, *Jealous Woman* and *Sinful Woman*, taking Avon's sleazy cover, showing Grant's mother intruding upon Carrie, half-undressed, and Grant, fully suited, in their bedroom, as the model for their more sedate sleaziness. They continued to promote their editions of *Galatea* and *Postman* on the back.

Paperbacks coming in the mail like that gave Cain a lift in these years of relative bleakness in his creative output, of his finances, of the status of his health, and Flo's.

Kunitz's *Twentieth Century Authors, Supplement, 1955* had more to say about Cain. "Although none of James M. Cain's later novels has had the tremendous popular success of *The Postman Always Rings Twice*, he has gained a new and even wider audience in recent years through motion picture versions of his works." "*Double Indemnity* is a landmark in the history of the cinema." Much on AAA, copped from *Current Biography*, 1947. His later novels showed the same pattern: They were hard-hitting, fast-paced, sordid, violent. It distorted statements from the preface of *Three of a Kind*, quoted Edmund Wilson and W. M. Frohock, cited Cain's influence on the French novelist Albert Camus.

In late January 1956, Cain marked the end of an era with the funeral for Henry L. Mencken. By his own decree, only a few attended, Hamilton Owens of the *Sun*, Frank Kent, Alfred Knopf, among them, and no ceremony, as when Mencken quit the *Mercury*. Afterward they went to the appropriate place to reminisce, where Cain said very little, but later he wrote to Krock: "Somehow, we were made to subserve a gag, and the effect wasn't so much bleak as blank. The minute of silence didn't quite say it."

The novel Mencken thought was Cain's best, *Love's Lovely Counterfeit*, became *Slightly Scarlet*, though not in title alone, on the screen in

February. Written by Robert Blees, directed by Allen Dwan, starring John Payne, Rhonda Fleming, and Arlene Dahl (Stanwyck had pulled out), it got this from Bosley Crowther in the *New York Times*: "an exhausting lot of twaddle." He had seen what Cain hoped everyone else would see—no resemblance to his only novel written for a movie sale.

In 1956, *60 Years of Best Sellers, 1895–1955*, by Alice Payne Hackett presented some exciting figures on *Postman*, *Serenade*, and *Mildred Pierce*.

Hardcover: *Mildred Pierce*, 1,436,252

The Postman Always Rings Twice, 1,435,000

Serenade, 1,428,765

Paperback: *The Postman Always Rings Twice*, 1,410,000

Serenade, 1,402,765

Mildred Pierce, 1,112,161

So his works were only in the first million, selling an average of about one and a half million, with his paperback readers showing different preferences.

Only two months later came the *Serenade* movie, retaining its own name, but little else. Not even Cain's suggested changes to gain Hays office approval were left unscathed. Joan Fontaine got into the act somehow, and became the hero's and the picture's main problem, in addition to the alcoholism. After considering Ann Sheridan, Maria Montez, and Katy Jurado, the decision was for Sara Montiel as Juana. Mario Lanza, like John Sharp, was making a comeback, having wrecked his career with problems like Cain's own, drinking, eating, and being overweight. Ivan Goff, Ben Roberts, and John Twist wrote the script, Anthony Mann directed it, an incredible mutilation of the novel. But Warner's had made money. Cain had spent his own share ten years ago. That year, 1955, he earned only $6,000.

So while Cain was taking a dive, he watched the movies usurp his reputation as a novelist, although they did keep his name in lights.

When people asked him what he thought of what *they*, the movie people, did to one of his books, he was ready for them. "They haven't done anything to my book. It's right up there on the shelf."

If the old Cain black magic wasn't working so well for Cain, other writers, on the name alone, were cashing in. Publishers in blurbs coupled his name with that label so detestable to him, "hard-boiled" or "tough guy," to pedal the books of writers whom reviewers then said were either much better or far less effective than Cain himself. He was glad to say that Jay Dratler's *Ducks in Thunder*, admittedly modeled on his style, was good. That was a decade earlier.

In September 1957, *When Tomorrow Comes* appeared on the screen again, resurrected as *Interlude*. Daniel Fuchs wrote the script. Douglas Sirk directed it, and June Allyson and Rossano Brazzi starred.

As they neared their tenth wedding anniversary, all those titles, including *A Modern Cinderella*, but not *The Root of His Evil*, seemed to apply to Cain and Flo and to their move from Hollywood to Hyattsville, in some ways with heavy irony. In *Who's Who* and other record books, he may be listed as having married four times, but to mean it and have it take, he had married twice, the first time to Elina, the second to Florence MacBeth. The other two were doomed from the start. After a decade, he and Flo were as close as ever. He was especially grateful to her for being able to call him Jamie, his childhood nickname, which he loathed, without embarrassing him. She had unkinked him in all sorts of strange ways.

They were both in a physical decline, though. In his life, he had survived several physical wrecks to begin again. Always his health had direct and indirect effect on his fiction. The "new life" theme was one of his favorites. But this was a serious decline. Flo's blood pressure problem and a dislocated shoulder necessitated a regimen of absolute quiet, and no chores whatsoever. He had to keep her away from people because she liked to join in, and got excited, then had to stay in bed for days afterward.

He kept trying to bring in some fast magazine money. He did sell one story, "Death on the Beach," to *Jack London's Adventure Magazine*, for $200. But he couldn't make it even with the pulps.

In 1957, Avon reprinted *Sinful Woman*, with a new cover. It had continued to outsell his other two Avon originals two to one.

Cain was still trying to find a producer for his play *The Guest in Room 701*. The Theater Guild and several producers had come close, and he had earned $1,000 option money. Swannie advised him to focus on the rich man who tries to buy another man's wife, a Gatsby-like figure who had great appeal.

A television series based on *Mildred Pierce* was dangled in front of him for a while, and then one day was not there anymore.

Interior, Hollywood, Fade Out ... Fade In, Interior, Hyattsville, a decade later, early 1957, Cain, now a recluse, finishes *Mignon*. And sends it to his publisher of a quarter of a century, who rejects it. His first major rejection came when he was sixty-six. "The story is altogether too complicated, and yet perhaps not involved enough ... you hit on a little backwater episode in the Civil War which is completely unfamiliar to almost everybody likely to read your book.... I think your lady character is weak.... Cain enthusiasts will expect a little more sex ... the motivations of the hero and heroine are by no means always clear." If true, disastrous. With his income not likely to exceed $3,000 for the year, he was glad Ober liked it and wanted to show it to magazines. But what if Knopf were right? Looking it over again, he couldn't convince himself Knopf was wrong. He promised a revision soon.

In 1958, at the age of ninety-five, Cain's mother died. Now, the only person who could call him Jamie without embarrassing him was Flo.

He had no children. The Cain line ended in him. His three sisters were elderly. He had no friends, except in correspondence. He had Flo.

Then Genevieve, his youngest sister, who like Cain had always been withdrawn and literary, ill at ease with people, and who had worked with Rosalie at a radio station, died a few months after their mother.

When Virginia died, a few months after Genevieve, only Cain and Rosalie remained.

Nickie, the cat, who meant more to Cain and Flo than animals should, died that year, too, and they buried him in Bonheur Memorial Park in Elkridge, Maryland.

In the spring, Cain came across a piece in *Newsweek* about cholesterol, consulted his doctor, who diagnosed a high cholesterol condition, and put him on a special diet. And in forty-eight hours, he was feeling great, saved again by a recent, new technique. And he had a good explanation of his poor health—his depression over the past several years. From having been a "nitwit," who couldn't remember anything, or think to any purpose, he was himself again.

But his agent, Harold Ober, died.

Walter Lippmann had moved to Washington, and he had gone out to visit him at his house, but because he had to tend to Flo, they couldn't make much of their friendship. In April, he had lunch with Marquis Childs who with James Reston was preparing a book to commemorate Lippman's seventieth birthday. When the book came out, he listed Cain with a "constellation" of "witty, brilliant, sometimes even searching and profound" men, whose names "evoke a time that today seems more distant than the Stone Age." Uplifting on the one hand, depressing on the other. If "Stone Age" applied, maybe that was the reason he'd turned down Carey McWilliams' invitation to write for the *Nation*, where his second article had appeared in 1922.

In June, a Hollywood radio station wrote to ask for an interview to be broadcast in a series called "Living Legends." Also from California, from UCLA, came a request for help from E. R. Hagemann and Philip C. Durham, who were compiling a bibliography of Cain's writings, 1922–1958. It had a monumental ring to it. Just when he had come back from the dead, he was tripping over tombstones all over the place.

But also in June came interest in his work from Hollywood in harmony with his rejuvenation in body, and so at the typewriter. Jerry Wald, who had his own company now, wanted to see whatever he had cooking. He bragged he'd helped Grace Metalious get rich with *The Return to Peyton Place*. "James M. Cain means far more than Metalious and is far more worthwhile merchandising to the world audience." If he made $2,000 this year, a record low, he would be lucky. So with stars in his eyes, he took a cue from Wald's movie lingo and ended his description of the Civil War novel by promising "plenty of color, music, dancing, and, of course, sex," and a complete "script," in novel form, by end of August.

By June of the next year, he was still working on *Mignon*, and the work on it was all his life amounted to, except for taking care of Flo, with whom he now shared a new kitten, Mittens.

One morning in June 1960, the postman delivered a letter from David Madden, from Boone, North Carolina, which showed up on the map as a little town, the highest in the Appalachian Mountains. For a graduate course with Norman Holmes Pearson in Yale's American Studies Department, he was doing a study of the novels of James M. Cain. He had just finished a year at Yale Drama School and he was acting in an outdoor drama called *Horn in the West*, living in an old farm house without running water, finishing his first novel, set in Eastern Kentucky, and another, based on his youthful experiences in the Merchant Marine, that Random House was going to publish next year, also a detective novel called *Hair of the Dog*, and also a literary book on Wright Morris to inaugurate a new series called Bison books from the University of Nebraska Press.

How do you talk to an academic who is also a novelist, or vice versa? Cain replied on June 26, starting off by noting the similarity in their typing styles, drifting immediately into a sidelight on Raymond Chandler's work on the script of *Double Indemnity*.

Enough of that. Tell him what's in the works now. "What I am doing now is trying, in the frame of the Red River Expedition of 1864, to do a period novel about the cotton racket back of the whole thing, and the terrible awakening that came to those who had got themselves mixed up in it. It has been a long, dreary pull. I had read of writers who took years, and did draft after draft, on some period novel, and thought of course that couldn't be me." But is. "The other day, off on one of my lunges at harmony, I tried what's called 'numbered base,' and ancient exercise for those who dabble in music. Numbered bass looks like this:

—8	3	—8	5
I	I	LV	I

"The lower numerals are the chords in the problem, the upper ones their position, which if followed will yield a treble, or melody. Working the above algebra out, it becomes Old Black Joe, which is not much of an achievement, for so much calculation, having nothing to do with music, in any lyrical sense. Well, a period story is like that. The given events, which can't be changed of course, as to wind, weather, tide, or number of soldiers killed, correspond to the numbered chords, and the characters to the treble. It becomes indeed a sort of etude in algebra to fit the characters to the events, with no possible relation to proper narrative, so you come out with something that looks like fiction, and with luck may be mistaken for it. I shall never, as long as I live, try a period novel again. It is like a sentence in the penitentiary. Even if Earle Stanley Gardner puts Perry Mason on it, and gets you out on a writ of improper conviction, you refuse to leave your cell until your time is up, by then having got to the point you must finish Old Black Joe, even if it's not so much by the time you get done.

"*The Moth*, I thought, had some vitality as an etude in the love life of a twelve-year-old girl, but in many ways it was faulty. I may be taking another try at a similar theme, perhaps really carrying on with that story in a different setting, with a project I have in mind, of a civil engineer in California, under a TB lung sentence, dabbling around with an underground river (they have them out there, they flow in gravel, like the Los Angeles River, a source of the city water) and winding up with a swimming pool his divinity is attracted to. No, I'm not rewriting *Lolita*, though it was a pretty fair book. But why in the hell, when Nabokov finally got the girl in bed with the guy, after establishing her love for him, did he turn around and have her announce he was just a filthy old letch? It was like an expedition for the Koh-I-Noor diamond that threw it away after finding it. I'll ring down now. Does this help?"

He showed *Mignon* to Knopf again in the late fall of 1960, and when he again rejected it, Cain was hurt, and somehow also felt that he had let Knopf down. But Knopf had a history of faintheartedness about his novels, so Cain rejected his criticism of this new version, and told Ivan von Auw, who was running the Ober agency now, that he needed a publisher who had faith in his work. Von Auw's suggestions for revisions made more sense than those of any agent Cain had known. He looked again at the ending. Maybe Willy Cresap shouldn't return to Annapolis, Cain's own hometown. He changed the ending.

What if a suburbanite woke in the night to find a runaway tiger staring into his eyes? A humorous, though rather absurd notion that called for an ending in the same key: He would subdue the tiger with a plastic bag. Yes.

So he began "The Visitor" in the third person: "Looking back at it, sorting his recollections into something resembling order, Greg Hayes is sure now that the first warning he had, of a presence there in the room, was a smell—a pungent, exotic reek that was strange, yet oddly familiar."

And it sold to *Esquire*, his second story to be accepted there.

By March 1961, he was ready to show *Mignon* again, and who he showed it to was Knopf. And Knopf rejected it for the third time. Cain told von Auw, "I would hate to confess how much time, labor and money it represents, and something to show for it would help, psychologically: I have a horror of abandoning something after getting so deep into it."

Then in May, Dial said yes, they wanted *Mignon*, if Cain would make changes. Jim Silverman's suggestions were "shrewd, sensible and helpful in every way," Cain told him in December. "On an intellectual level that commands respect." And they were close to his own feelings.

The buyer for a large department store in Maryland attempts through her daughter to gain the place in the sun she herself never attained. A little too close to *Mildred* some might say, but he got to work on it.

In April 1961, a year after his first letter, Madden sent him a flimsy carbon of the essay he finished in a shed in the mountain and had sent to Professor Pearson at Yale.

"Among writers, critics, and other serious readers, James M. Cain enjoys a reputation which is unusual for an essentially popular writer who has never, according to several critics, written anything entirely out of the trash category. Cain's major interest for the student of modern American literature, and the reason for the respect accorded him, is the compatibility between his rather unique style and technique and his timeless themes and timely raw material. Because of the style, one, reading all the works of Cain, is struck by the author's sensibility, at times as vividly, but never as deeply, as one feels Faulkner's. It is his art, more than anything else, that moves the serious reader to almost complete emotional commitment to the traumatic experiences Cain renders.

"He has influenced those writers who have created the shallower parts in the stream of American, and perhaps French, fiction, but he has also influenced such writers as Albert Camus, who has stated that it was Cain's style, not Hemingway's, that he imitated in *The Stranger*. . . .

"While there seems to be no serious intention nor artistic conception at the heart of any of his eleven novels (1934-1953), his works exhibit a strange mingling of serious and of popular elements, which he has made his own. Cain's themes are often inherently serious, his character relationships are at least potentially complex, and the milieus of his novels often promise the kind of richness of association one finds in Faulkner. But Cain never quite steps over the threshold of art. Still, without his finest novels, *The Postman*, *Serenade* (1937), *Mildred Pierce* (1941), his first three, and *The Butterfly* (1947), the cream of our twentieth century fiction would be thinner. Frank Chambers, John Howard Sharp, Mildred Pierce, Jess Tyler, as well as Walter Huff and Jack Dillon of *Double Indemnity* (1943) and *The Moth* (1948), are fascinating characters representative of certain aspects of our time, but embroiled in universal predicaments. . . .

"Critics first write him off as a popular novelist and then proceed to reproach him for failing to rise to the level of artistic achievement toward which they have felt him striving. . . .

"Cain's own comments about his work reveal a serious concern for the craft of fiction and a clear understanding of his intentions as I have been able to discern them. His comments also convey a sense of the kind of man who would write the novels that have caused such an ambiguous impression. . . . Cain is a dramatist who writes in the novel form. He has a story to tell, always about a man and a woman, and all his energy is directed toward getting the story told as briefly and with as much impact as possible. . . .

Frohock "feels that Cain's technique is fraudulent. 'In a Cain novel, it is clear that Cain's opponent is his reader. He feints us into position and hits us before we can get our feet untangled.' Frohock: "Frank Chambers is not tragic because Cain's violence is not endowed with any moral significance. Writers like Cain 'exploit the sensibility which informs the serious novel of violence.' Although Frank Chambers is like Meursault of *The Stranger*, Cain's work lacks 'the large philosophical view that Camus has.' *The Postman*, Frohock declares, is an immoral book because of the behavior it incurs from the reader. 'We have been tricked into taking the position of potential accomplices,' because we want Frank and Cora (ourselves, that is) to escape.

"It seems to me that Cain's style is less like Hemingway's than the general aura of his books is like Faulkner's in their elements of horror, despair, terror, and grotesquerie. . . .

"Frohock claims that Cain's characters are uncomplicated, a judgment which recalls my suspicion that neither he nor most other critics have read many of the novels. . . .

"*Love's Lovely Counterfeit* is among his two or three least convincing novels. . . ." *Mildred*: "If Cain had told it in the first person, probably, the book would have been much better, for it is Cain's language that generates much of the excitement in the explosive character relationships, presented in incendiary situations. . . .

"Pace, always brisk, terrific, is almost a comment in itself on the aspect of life, of truth, that Cain has focused upon in his field of vision. . . .

"Cain thinks *The Butterfly* comes closest in theme and treatment to art, and I agree. . . .

"Ironically, Cain's novelistic dialogue has had a tremendous effect on successful movie writers.

"My study of the novels and other writings by Cain has convinced me that he has always been serious about his craft. While he seldom rises above certain commercial elements, I feel that his themes, too, are serious and of interest, especially as they are compatible with the concept of the 'pure novel,' to the discerning reader." Elements: love-rack, Lawrence, sex, abnormal sex, bizarre scenes for sex, pace and sex, appeals to our prurience to express something about it, animal aspect of sex, money, aura of evil, pagan, superstition, shark symbols of evil and violent death.

"I think Cain is a rare instance of a writer who can use effectively the method of extremes to render a truthful aspect of human nature and experience." Moments of beauty and peace, strange attitudes toward religion, love mystique, characterize his fiction. "Religion, food, sex, are one." "Sex, the desire for purity, the desire for money, and the necessity to kill or to use violence are related. Love, food, and God are intricately related." Signs of evil, birthmark, etc. The narrator usually writes his story, but sounds as if he is telling it. A touch of confession, but never officially one.

"But Cain seems, on the whole, interested less in the murderer's relation to society than in his relation to himself or himself and his lover. . . . Even in Cain's short stories, one finds the confessional or social-purpose motive for first-person narrative."

That Cain puts himself in, in various ways, makes his work less commercial: opera singers, much music, often not incidental. "Cain, it would seem, is making up for the career he has never had—the wish that didn't come true."

Glendale is one among other recurrent locations. He focuses on California, but his interest in the general American scene enables him to capture the feel of America. His characters have a streak of physical or moral cowardice, as part of his concept of a real man—"the inner conflict that gives off enough heat to propel him through various adventures. The wish comes true, but the weakness in us finishes us off."

The tough hero's "romantic view of life" is exploited by women, who are stronger. The hero audaciously steps into situations requiring real know-how. "Most of the men are romantics, who see life as one fierce adventure, who plunge into every situation with no regard for realities." "Cain had the journalist's curiosity about a number of various things." Like Hemingway. One character explains to another.

"He deserves more serious study than a first glance at his novels or his reputation may deem necessary."

"Cain seems to me an interesting example of a man who has let his American, journalist temperament blur his creative field of vision. . . . Like Tennessee Williams, another Southerner, and perhaps like Faulkner, Cain has a certain vision of life that never gets sharply focused, controlled, or conceptualized, but that is heightened and exaggerated for a purpose and creates an effect that is almost poetic. Straddling realism and expressionism, he gives us a true account of life on the American scene as he has observed it and, in his finest moments, he gives us the finer vibrations afforded by the aesthetic experience. As an entertainer, he may fail to say anything important about human life, but he takes us through experiences whose quality is to be found in no other writer's works."

On May 12 Cain wrote to Madden about his article, to Danville, Kentucky, to which he had moved and where he was teaching English at Centre College.

"Your article makes me feel as though I had paraded myself in the police line-up in a Bikini suit or less, but it touches me, nevertheless, indeed shakes me up. If I am worth all this close analysis I don't know, but it is very penetrating, and nails the truth in more places than I would like to admit." "As you say you intend to rewrite it, I enclose a set of notes." He cited three Avon titles Madden had not mentioned: *Sinful Woman, Jealous*

Woman, and *The Root of His Evil*. "For some reason not known to me I don't list them in *Who's Who in America*." First off, he wanted to know, "What is a 'popular' novelist, and who writes these unpopular novels? The aim of art is to cast a spell on the beholder, it has no other aim—or in other words, the whole object of a novel is to get itself read. . . . I know of no point at which the novelist is supposed to abjure popularity as though it were something discreditable."

Influences. Add Philip Goodman "for a vast backlog of ideas on what works, and what doesn't work, in the field of narrative. A man of vast erudition, he was the one who impressed me with the idea that though the author should be, ought to be, as erudite as he can get, it ought not to show through his tales. H. L. Mencken, for the importance of journalistic vitality, the illusion of being real, that ought to mark any story. Conan Doyle, a writer never mentioned in connection with me, but probably a greater 'influence' than any, though I never knew him personally. I very often, wondering whether some small thing is too tiny to include, or perhaps has its claim to effectiveness, refer to Dr. Watson, and in him find justification for those decimal-point distinctions that often mark my style." Madden had indicated echoes of Ring Lardner in "Pastorale," "The Baby in the Icebox," and others. "This influence, however, if it was vivid, I purged myself of, or tried to, when I moved to California and took up the 'educated roughneck' as my prose model. . . ."

Re Max Lerner's comment: "Which of my tensions are 'phoney?' I hate unparticularized indictments. I try to test all tensions for their soundness, and if they're phony, to my knowledge, I throw them out or work them over."

Re Frohock: "Making the reader an 'accomplice' of Chambers and Cora somehow seems to say it is up to me to act as an indignant commentator on what they are up to . . . if the idea of the story is to sit with the criminal, hear his account of what he did and why, and suffer and sweat and fear as he suffers and sweats and fears, how can we do that and at the same time stand apart, taking no interest in what he does? If we feel his danger, we care how he feels, we can't help it. Criticism, in this country, is incorrigibly moralistic. Who says we must have admirable characters?" He directed Madden to his preface to *For Men Only*, of 1944.

Faulkner and Hemingway again. "I can't read Faulkner, and know almost nothing about him. Actually, I don't know too much about Hemingway." He cited the best Hemingway—"The Undefeated," "Fifty Grand," "The Killers," *A Farewell to Arms*, and the worst, "The Short Happy Life of Francis Macomber," the rest of the 49 stories, *To Have and Have Not*, *The Old Man and the Sea*, *Across the River and Into the Trees* ("God what ghastly titles"). "Writers, I think, must be measured by their best work."

"My clichés are more or less deliberate. I hate narrative that is 100% distinguished, like Cabell's. To me it evokes utter unreality. Many of life's most moving things are banal—what more banal than a steak? What more beautiful, when you're hungry? I try, in using a cliché, to set it up so perhaps it gains its own awkward, pathetic eloquence."

"How Mildred would have told her story in the first person can be gleaned from *The Root of His Evil*, where little Carrie tells her story in the first person—my only excursion of this kind. It always seems to me that a man trying to be a woman, or a woman vice versa, gets a certain falsity into it. For some reason we can't really cross this chasm."

Symbolism. Madden had brought up subjects Cain had never had the opportunity to read and respond to in his work before. This was a fresh and interesting experience. "My symbolism, if I have any, is never conscious, and in fact symbolism is one of the things Phil Goodman warned me off of, like poison. He felt it intolerably literary, as I do—and easy. Who can't think of symbols? . . . Once, discussing with my wife the end of *Past All Dishonor*, I said: 'Why the snow I can't tell you. But for some reason it wanted in—the thing wasn't complete without the picture of that girl, all dressed up in her finery, wearing priceless jewels, smiling there in the snow, dead.' She seemed utterly startled. 'But don't you know?' she exclaimed. 'I got it at once—in death, at last, she was purified, and the snow makes you feel it.' So perhaps you are right, and lurking in me unconsciously is the compulsion to some sort of symbolism."

"Money is an element all can react to. Sex is another universal theme in my books, but not as much as is thought. As you note I seem to imply it even where it's not directly brought in, and this is somewhat deliberate. About sex, I think, in stories, if you earn it you don't have to claim it. If the situation is hot, pregnant, and passionate, you needn't get too explicit. It's a sort of inevitable corollary to some things in life, such as triumphs shared by two lovers. . . . "Food figures in my stories, again as a universal element—we all eat, don't we? My lovers share food in hunger. Food, I found out writing newspaper editorials, is a topic of compelling interest to the whole human race." His characters sometimes eat "with almost religious fervor."

Music: "Real dramatization is focused on their minds, their skill at reading music, at improvising to cover an emergency, at comprehension. This, I suspect, is all a bouquet on the grave of my mother."

Masculinity: "Anyone shooting for masculinity had better think hard before depicting a tough guy. . . . People, actually, all have weaknesses, and no man is exempt from fear. My men get scared and admit it. If this makes them 'effeminate,' I hope also it makes them real. . . . You're right that my heroes have to have some know-how, to solve certain situations. It is built into them, and their being equal to a situation, their rising to their challenges, is a conscious element, on my part, in developing them. There must be something positive that characters do, else there's no emotion."

He couldn't stop mulling over some of the insights Madden had put into his essay. Three days later, he expanded on two points: "What Morina did with the beer bottle, in *Past All Dishonor*. It was not what you say, but something entirely different. I have to know what it was, of course, and do know, but I prefer not to say, and it was so different from your conjecture that I cannot back you, in case your conjecture gets you into trouble, as it might. So I suggest you take it out." Cain felt compelled to lecture this young man. "In which connection, let me give you a tip you may find valuable: Do not, ever, let such conjectures run away with you, in a thing of this kind. They can only make trouble for you, specially with your sources." He described a case in point, a man whose book on Mencken was marred by indiscretions and inventions, based on sources who were now sore with him. Use judgment, so you can go back a second time to your sources.

"This question of why my characters tell their own story. With me, I found early on, I am like those actors on TV who have no capacity to be themselves, but like Ronald Reagan, have to work from a script. But,

I also found, if I pretended to be somebody else, i.e., the character, I was a wholly different writer, and could be natural, simple, and easy. That is why I use the first person, so much. But, at the end, the reader may ask himself: How could this man be so frank? Why would he involve other people, such as women? ... often the why of that gives me more trouble than anything else in the plot, and I have to invent some reason."

Several days later, he received from Random House galleys of Madden's first novel, *The Beautiful Greed*, a sea yarn. It held him from start to finish, he read it in one sitting, and sent off a comment, glad to help a young writer. "Madden goes beyond the sea of Maxfield Parrish, of Winslow Homer, of Joseph Conrad, who appealed chiefly to the eye, and offers a sea of his own, with much for the eye, to be sure, but more for the ear, nose, and taste—some of it beautiful, some chillingly gross, but all of it authentic. It is an engrossing tale, whose main characteristic is vividness." He sent a copy to Madden. "For your info."

He learned later from the dust jacket that Madden had been born in 1933, the year in August, that *Mildred* came out in a new, classier cover, the sixth printing.

In September, "The Visitor" appeared in *Esquire* with a head note that undercut the suspense raised by the question inherent in the situation: Does the main character get eaten by the tiger? "The problem facing Greg Hayes, suburbanite, was not to choose between the lady or the tiger. When he awoke he had the tiger in his room and she was no lady. The lady who almost ruined everything was his wife. A simple escape story." But *Esquire* was a prominent showcase, good exposure, on a level much higher than *Manhunt* and *Jack London*.

Since *Galatea* in 1953, not much had been heard from James M. Cain, except on the Avon original paperback level, and in other paperback reprints internationally. What had he accomplished since 1953? A lot of goddamn research. "Whatever happened to James M. Cain?" Well they might ask.

When he had finished the *Mignon* revisions, he had a new and much better work, a major novel that would justify earlier literary estimates and that would put him on "sugar hill." 1961 had put him in a hole: only $1,000 advance from Dial, $700 from *Esquire* for "The Visitor."

But one deflating sign was Wald's decision that *Mignon* was not for him.

When he met the postman on the walk one day in late February, he delivered a letter from Madden, who requested that Cain teach with him that summer in a writer's workshop at Morehead, Kentucky. That request caught him by surprise. He'd thought that he'd put all that behind him. He knew how it was done, but he ought to warn Madden that he had definite ideas on the subject, not all of them corresponding to the ideal prevalently held in the colleges themselves, "and it would be best all around if they knew what they were getting and I knew what they were wanting." He asked for more particulars.

March 2, he wrote to say no. "I hinted at some reservation, and 'creative writing' is the nub of it. I don't believe it can be taught, and helpful though I might be, to some writer facing a problem, and helpful as I have been, as a matter of fact, to various writers facing problems, I couldn't face a class of young hopefuls, full of ideals and nothing else, and not betray what I felt—that they'd be a great deal better off to get back to the hardware store."

Madden's assigned review of *Mignon* for *Saturday Review* had been rejected. "I can only say, I'm hot and I'm not hot—as every writer is." In homage to Cain's gesture at MGM, in 1934, Madden had returned *SR*'s kill fee.

In early April, a fellow came down from *Newsweek* to interview Cain. They met in a Washington restaurant to avoid disturbing Flo. Cain declined a drink proposed as a send-off for *Mignon*. "It leads to no good." He ordered shad-roe for lunch, and explained his years of silence. "There was a period of four or five years, 1957 to 1962, when I didn't feel worth a damn. I wasn't worth a damn. I was sick. It wasn't booze. I dropped that about twelve years ago, when I decided the only way to get rid of the stuff was to skip the next drink. I've been skipping it ever since." "I was frightened. My father died a blithering idiot, and for a time I thought the same thing was happening to me." His weight skidded, from 245 to the 186 pounds that now hung on his six-foot frame. Two years earlier, his doctor had prescribed a low-cholesterol diet. "Just forty-eight hours later, I knew I was going to be fine." Almost immediately he went back to work on *Mignon*. To get the background right, he had gone through four hundred books, traveled thousands of miles, to the actual scenes, starting in the spring of 1948. "A man who slights off his background can make a fool of himself. Take *The Old Man and the Sea*—it could never have happened the way Hemingway describes it. It's obvious the man never sailed a boat."

Just as reviews were starting to come in, favorable so far, Cain got an almost indecipherable working copy of Madden's *Saturday Review* review. "James M. Cain's admirers have waited fifteen years for a book which would show the further development of his special talent promised by *The Butterfly*, his best book. But *Mignon*, Cain's first novel in ten years, develops the historical interest that resulted in *Past All Dishonor*, not one of the best of his fourteen novels. Neither is *Mignon*."

April 19, Cain responded: "If you didn't like it you didn't like it, and that's all that can be said . . . if it caused you such night sweats, I don't see that you had to review it. So far as keeping it from some gibber goes, it is being sent to several hundred gibbers."

The *Newsweek* interview, "Cain Scrutiny," appeared April 23. "In the 1940's, the tough, tight-lipped novels of James M. Cain made the author rich and the movies richer." "For the past fourteen years, however, Cain has published nothing except a slow seller called 'Galatea' in 1953." The rest was a description of the interview and the conversation they had had.

In May, Lewis Nichols did a telephone interview with Cain for his "In and Out of Books" department. "Postman's Assistant" appeared in the *Sunday Times Book Review*. "All that reading and labor, and a kind of mouse is born . . . and if we could just get rid of rewriting." Nichols noted that Cain continued to set himself down as a newspaperman in *Who's Who*. He had written no other books for nine years, Nichols wanted everybody to know. "My characters always have gotten scared. My guys always get the girl in their arms and then are too scared to do anything about it."

The reviews of *Mignon* came in.

Martin Levin, *New York Times Book Review*: prefers Mr. Cain in modern dress.

Baltimore Sun: "hard to imagine what Cain had in mind with this mish mash . . . too confusing for mindless entertainment and anachronistic and sketchy as to background for enlightenment."

Harnett T. Kane, *Chicago Sunday Tribune*: "Cain gives us a highly colored, sharply focused, sometimes complex narrative."

J. C. Pine, *Library Journal*: "This is an unusually inept performance even for this day and age. (One is almost tempted to say marvelously inept, so ludicrous is it.). . . . Not even for libraries that buy everything."

Cain had poured into this novel, and then for the most part extracted from it in revision, over twelve years of research on the Red River expedition and the cotton racket of the Civil War, but the elements wouldn't cohere. Originally, he had been attracted to the idea, which he discovered by accident, that the war between the Union and the Confederacy was nothing, during the Red River expedition, compared to the war between the Union's army and navy. It had seemed a promising thing, just up his alley, with sardonic overtones and everything he liked to deal with. But though he had finally gotten the book out, he had failed to pull it off. It had sold fifteen thousand copies. *Mignon* was the most ill-starred venture he had ever embarked upon.

JAMES M. CAIN

Author of *DOUBLE INDEMNITY*
and *MILDRED PIERCE*

THE MAGICIAN'S WIFE

10

The Magician's Wife

THE ATTENTION GIVEN *MIGNON* LURED CAIN AND FLO OUT OF THEIR self-imposed seclusion a little, and because their health was a little better, especially his, he felt they were up to it. Cain had radio, TV, and newspaper interviews to do, becoming a kind of local celebrity.

He was about a hundred pages into the story about the buyer for a large department store with family conflicts, when he got a letter from Jerry Wald, saying he and Joan Crawford were talking one night about *Mildred Pierce* and how they wished Cain would do another woman's story for her, and Wald even outlined a plot in great detail. It was incredibly close to the novel Cain was working on, except that Wald had the woman running the department store. Excited by this coincidence, Cain tried to come up with an approach that would keep Wald's interest hot.

The paper the next day reported the death of Jerry Wald. Cain wrote quickly to Joan Crawford, told her about the coincidence, and described his novel. Trying to tempt her, he said of his heroine, she's "an ominous creature."

In September Cain had another automobile accident, his second in only a year. Flo and he decided it was not only too risky to continue driving, but that his use of the car had not proved worth the expense anyway, so he sold it, and that made their life even more reclusive.

Madden wrote from his summer mountain cabin on Hot Holler Road in Deep Gap near Boone, inviting Cain to stop by if he ever got up that way. He told Madden about the accident. "Not my fault of course, except that it was, 800%. . . . I don't take road trips anymore."

Cain's 1962 income of $12,000 was his best in seven years.

Ramon Gordon wanted to dramatize and produce *The Butterfly*. Cain had dinner with him in New York. But when he sent Cain his script, it was utterly naïve. Cain was terrified of getting involved in another theatrical disaster, so he let this one fade away. He still hoped though to develop a TV series of his own.

Even though Joan had encouraged him to finish and show her the novel about the woman department store buyer, Cain put it aside. Despite all the misery *The Magician's Wife* had put him through, and the fact that it did not differ enough from *Mignon*, and without his one-thousand-book Civil War library that he'd sold, he started another saga about the cotton trade: A man and a woman share the adventure of fighting nature to survive on the Desierto Muerto between Texas and Matamoras, Mexico. But after 250 pages and a rewrite, the same problem stopped him near the end, and he had failed to make *The Pink Buttercup* work. The Civil War had defeated him again, but he knew that someday he would return to it.

He stood a better chance in the department store. But not really, because that one got bogged down, too. And he had a next-book commitment to Dial that he was eager to satisfy. In June, he lost a very understanding editor when Jim Silberman left Dial to go to Random House. Henry Robbins came in, and Cain explained to him why he was having trouble keeping his promise to deliver a new novel.

He wanted simply to write a story about a masculine, average guy in the meat business, which he knew a little about through a brief venture into it, before he became a newspaperman in 1917. He'd always had a sense of affection for Swift & Co., especially after they gave him the red carpet when he sought their help on *Galatea*. They gladly helped on this one, too.

From the start, he consciously modeled the story on the pattern of *Postman* and *Double Indemnity*, lured on by intriguing variations on the formula. He meshed the story of the woman who was a buyer for a department store with this new conception. Clay Lockwood, a meatpacking executive, lusts for Sally Alexis, a waitress. More than sex, she craves money. And she uses Clay to get it. Together, they murder her husband, a magician, to collect insurance. Clay is on a double love-rack, for, midway in the novel, he falls genuinely in love with Sally's mother, Grace, a buyer for a department store. His wish comes true, but he kills Sally and commits suicide.

A letter came from Max Gissen, the editor of Time-Life Books. Would he write a two-thousand-word introduction to *The Treasure of Sierra Madre* by B. Traven? Set in Mexico, as *Serenade* was. "Also thought you might know Traven." Cain read the book. It was sort of interesting. He looked up Traven, a literary mystery man, who struck him as a fourth-rate nitwit. But he wrote the piece, thinking a little promotion at Time-Life might help along future projects. Gissen suggested he rewrite it. Cain told him he didn't write blurbs, nor did he write for nothing. "You owe me $500." Gissen sent the check, maintaining that a blurb was not what they had in mind, but that what he had written was "simply an astonishingly poor piece of copy." Cain returned the check with a directive: "Let's have an end of it."

In June, Swannie lifted Cain's hopes with news that the sale of *Past All Dishonor* to a studio for $30,000 was a distinct possibility. Then Kraft Theater showed interest in making a pilot for a series built around the Keyes character from *Double Indemnity* for Broderick Crawford.

But neither project panned out.

For thirteen years, ever since Morris Markey's death in 1950, Cain had been haunted by the mysterious circumstances. Feeling the need to share his thoughts with someone who was also close to Markey, he wrote a very long letter to Laurence Stallings, and told him to burn it, but kept a copy himself in his files.

In November Cain finished *The Magician's Wife*. While Von Auw was reading it, Cain wanted to try an idea for a period story on Dorothy Olding at the Ober agency. With the sesquicentennial of the War of 1812 Battle of New Orleans coming up in January of 1965, this one might have special appeal for magazine publication. Reading about Andrew Jackson, he had come across this "little nugget": The compassionate wife of a New Orleans lawyer took a wounded British officer into her home. The ladies of New Orleans having heard of the toast the British officers were drinking, "Beauty and Booty," the idea arose among them that a wounded officer was quite a prize, for out of gratitude he would protect them, so the ladies set out to capture one for each household. "And that's what my story's about." He would produce an awesome battle scene, with the loss of fifteen hundred British lives in twenty minutes. Miss Olding responded that there was no market anymore for serials.

Cain was determined to write "Beauty, Booty, and Blood" anyway. But first, he re-read *The Magician's Wife*, approaching it with the assumption he'd done a fine job. But the ending and a few other elements left a bad taste in his mouth. Von Auw reported that he thought the book had serious problems, character credibility and thus reader identification. Cain replied immediately, asking him to wait until he had written a new ending.

It was pleasant to have an account of his work in Geoffrey Grigson's *Modern World Literature*. Cain "wrote one remarkable book, *The Postman Always Rings Twice*, which . . . deserved its immediate fame . . . in a terse vernacular completely suited to the characters and the setting. . . . Cain's novel obliquely condemns the lonely amoral civilization which produces it." It "had its relatives in a thousand dime novels and movies, and in the more complex and sophisticated books of Raymond Chandler. But Cain simplified matters to a single classic situation; and the book is distinguished by brevity, inevitability, and savagely poetic writing." According to Grigson his other best were *Serenade* and *Double Indemnity*.

A tumor developing under his arm worried him so badly he finally had it removed, and it proved benign. That improved his general physical state and his spirits. But he had little inclination to venture outside the house.

The president of Washington College tried again to cite Cain for something, but, always mindful of how the college mistreated his father, he continued "not interested." But when the University of Maryland asked him to accept a "Distinguished Service Award," he was happy to. The self-enforced seclusion with Flo made him choose outside events very carefully but only more radically stimulated Cain's life-long inclination to carry on a vast correspondence with old friends, newspaper editors, his agents, his publishers, and his readers.

It was too much that their own lives as deteriorating recluses mutually depressed them, but too many of their friends were dying. Galli-Curci's death stunned Flo. Cain's old army buddy Gilbert Malcolm, his St. John's buddy, Edward Sirich, and his *World* buddy, Malcolm Ross, left him with memories only. He and Flo grieved for President Kennedy together.

It had not been a good year for writing income either—$3,000.

Cain wrote to Silberman at Random House, darkly hinting that they might work together again before too long, and telling him a nonfiction idea he had, a personal account of his effort to give up smoking. He would develop the implications of the fact that "Nobody was ever born with a taste for tobacco."

From Albuquerque, he was surprised to get a card from Madden whose play version of his novel-in-progress, *Cassandra Singing*, was being world-premiered by the Little Theater there. Here was another parallel between Madden's interests and his own, for he still wanted primarily to write plays.

Then from Louisville, where Madden was now teaching creative writing part time at the University there, came Part I of his initial essay, revised and expanded, in *The University Review* out of Kansas City, Missouri.

On January 20, 1964, Cain gave Madden further reactions: "Many thanks for the article, which is well-organized, well-written, and full of a sharp penetration that I find in some places astonishing. For example, you detect that my hospitality to banal matter is due to a desire to keep things in the frame, rather than have them slop over it, through a misplaced lunge at originality, and that is correct. Originality, in the literary sense, is usually exhibitionistic, the author showing off his virtuosity, rather than bringing the reader to the story without jarring dissonances." Your observations on "the pure novel," and the word "experience," as corrective of "story," "come as a supplement to some of my own, made very recently."

He had discovered what had gone wrong in *The Magician's Wife*: "What I try to do is satisfy a theme, the fault of this novel being it didn't do that, but satisfied a character. That is, provided a man with a happy ending ... trying to do nice by the character, it did dirt by the reader by denying him his expectations." Lewis, in *Babbitt*, makes the character himself the theme. "But I, using characters off the top of the pile, plain average people scarcely worth describing in detail, people everyone knows, nevertheless have a theme to think about, that acquires rights as the thing goes on.

"My tastes in music are thematic, not melodic or programmatic. Beethoven, Mendelsohn, Puccini, Mascagni, Bizet, and such men are my favorites, all different emotionally, but similar in the logic of their musical approach. Wagner, Richard Strauss, Debussy, and such men, who depend on an overpowering gush of tone, harmony, and color, tend to bore me. It even carries over to the popular side, for Vincent Youmans interests me more than any American composer, as he is the only one that I know of who makes tunes out of themes, as such. 'Tea for Two' is a thematic building of a tune out of three notes treated as theme. It therefore, to my imagination, is exciting, all the more so because of its leanness, and the avoidance of any surplus even to one grace note. . . . The novels which were thematically worked up, along the lines you assumed, were hits: *The Postman Always Rings Twice*, *Past All Dishonor*, *The Butterfly*, and *Double Indemnity*, where those which proceeded more from character and character's destiny, *Mildred Pierce*, *The Moth*, *Serenade*, and *Mignon*, didn't do so well." Although they made the best-seller list.

Madden was wrong to attribute the power of "the pure novel" to the first person. He told Madden about *Sinful Woman*, written in the third person, which outsold, two to one, every year, *Jealous Woman* and *The Root of His Evil*, written in first person. All were Avon originals. He had written it in compliance with Lippmann's cure for literary paralysis: "When I get in a state like that, I make myself write something."

On the element of confession: My characters don't confess "for large, emotional, mystical reasons. Constantly, repeatedly, I ran into the question: Why should this man, telling things so utterly discreditable, things which if known could destroy him, take the cover off at all? . . . Trying to answer this had tied me in more bowknots than any other single phase of my writing. . . . *Mignon*, which you didn't even like . . . presented that difficulty very much, and I can't say I ever solved it. Having *Mignon* come back as an apparition, giving Cresap some kind of compulsion to write things down, was a pretty thin stratagem. The result being that in this new effort, *The Magician's Wife*, and probably most future efforts, I shall go into the third person, which has no such pitfall awaiting. If it be objected that novels are supposed to be tough, and that a difficulty is a thing to be overcome, not circumvented, I can only say that this difficulty is mainly technical. So I am probably off to a more conventional way of writing, accepting the likelihood that 50,000 novelists can't be wrong—not all of them."

This is a long word of appreciation, but I have deliberately covered quite a few points, in case the subject comes up at some future time—as it will when I kick off, I suppose, and perhaps before that, if I'm in the limelight once more.

Thinking over some of Madden's observations on the consequences of the first person confessional narration, he decided the shift to third person was definitely indicated now, in *The Magician's Wife*. He began to revise, with this new beginning. "Around noon of a bright spring day, on Bay Street in Channel City, Maryland, a man strode toward a restaurant as though he owned it and everything in it. It was a friendly looking place. . . .

"Several girls were nearby, but his eye lingered on one a few feet away, who stood with a knot of waitresses, apparently giving them instructions of some kind. She was indeed something to see. . . ."

Three weeks later, he sent Madden a copy of *Sinful Woman*. "I look forward to the second bite of your article."

What he got, rather quickly, from Madden was his intention to expand his articles into a book-length study.

"News that you meditate a book about me . . . I find utterly flabbergasting." Warn him that you scarcely ever save clippings, old articles, and have no movie scripts, etc. "Let's let it soak a while, so you can change your mind if you want, and I can clear my decks. They're a bit cluttered now, with projects, etc."

Two weeks later, Cain hastened to set Madden straight about the Avon originals. "I don't take much pride in those books, and tend to mix them up, on account of the titles Avon asked to put on, which seemed to me like all socko titles of the promotion department, so forgettable it's hard to tell one from the other."

A copy of *Sinful Woman*, "that oddly popular little story," came from Madden, an edition that Cain had never seen before, that he could remember.

"I'll be delighted to see you next summer, and would be only too glad to invite you to stay with us, except that it would be impossible. My wife, for some years, has been a blood-pressure case, and can stave off disaster only by a regimen of absolute quiet, especially regarding people. Her trouble is that she does enter into the spirit of the thing, and after many experiences, of having to go to bed the morning after and stay there for days, she has finally accepted the inevitable, and I permit her no exceptions, ever. I try not to think about it, and don't most of the time—I don't coddle myself, or think old.

"She, incidentally, if you have occasion to refer to her, is still in *Who's Who in America*, under her own name Florence MacBeth. She's been in it for 50 years, possibly longer than any woman—I think they discovered that was true. The book is published in Chicago, where she is a bit of a legend still, as the first coloratura of the old Chicago Opera."

"Am edgy as a horse in fly-time, in the last throes of *The Magician's Wife*."

Reading the second deck of Madden's article gave him great satisfaction, he told him. The confession angle once more: It doesn't spring, as your article intimates from an obscure compulsion in the character. It's purely a technical device. "Your discussion of it led me to recast…*The Magician's Wife*, and do it in the third person. It has some drawbacks, notably in the realm of vividness. But at least the mode of telling doesn't of itself set up a roadblock, and condition the story itself. So now my tale goes through to its proper finish, which it couldn't if the man was to tell his story, as he'd have been dead…. So, for that, once again, best thanks."

He sent *The Magician's Wife* to Von Auw, who liked it and submitted it to Dial.

Tell Madden no to the summer trip—in throes of new book, put off until I had finished *The Magician's Wife*, my wife can't take it, and "most of all, there is my own wacky nature, which would infuriate you." Promise for Madden what you did for Carl Bode on Mencken: put your reminiscences on paper "as they occurred to me." But to get distance, he would write of himself in the third person. Also, it was somehow embarrassing to write in the first person about a life that to him didn't rate a biography.

Madden wanted his full cooperation. Cain didn't know whether to agree to give it or not. To him, a literary study was almost always $\frac{1}{10}$ bio and ⁹⁄₁₀ guff. Flo listened to enough of this grumbling indecision to feel a bucket of cold water was indicated: "Well, I don't see anyone else coming around wanting to write a book about you."

"I discover," he wrote Madden, "on the basis of our previous correspondence, your articles, and considerable nervous cogitation, I am quite interested in your book, so if you still are, you may expect adequate cooperation from me. Whether I'm worth doing it about, of course, I can't say."

Madden having had no luck tracking down *Our Government*, Cain located one, bought it, sent it to him.

Meanwhile, Cain was nervously awaiting Dial's decision, suspended no doubt until someone was found to replace Robbins who had left.

Cain started his memoirs about himself for Madden's use. He worked out a simple way of "slugging" them as newspaper editors called it, so he could keep track, and even back track. Cain enjoyed pointing out to Madden that several of his childhood friends and acquaintances became men of distinction in their fields, citing *Who's Who* in each instance. Even some of his small-time fictional heroes have some of the qualities Cain admired in those friends.

He wrote in late June to let Madden know he had finally begun. Your articles "delve in me deeper than I have ever been able to do, but at the same time they are in line, very exactly in line, with such conscious introspection as I have engaged in about myself. But, of course, any writer must do considerable of that, whether he admits it or not. Every story he tells is in its way one more effort on his part to catch up with the inner id that tortures him and at the same time hides under the stump."

Now about that goddamn "tough guy" label: "I have been bracketed with McCoy, Hammett, Chandler, and Traven, especially in my early efforts, before the preface to *The Butterfly* came out. But actually, I have yet to read one line by McCoy, I never read Traven until a few months ago, when I was picked to do a preface to *The Treasure of Sierra Madre*, though I liked him so little that nothing came of it. I have read but a few pages of *The Big Sleep*, by Chandler, and as for Hammett ... I have read exactly 20 pages of *The Maltese Falcon*, which was lying around the Conde Nast Press in Stamford when I would go up there on Sundays to put the *New Yorker* to bed. This reflects no particular disinterest in these writers, merely a disinterest in all fiction, no matter who writes it—though I can get my mind on it well enough, if I have a reason to, such as writing a review. But I don't read it for entertainment. . . . Yet in the nineteen thirties, on the reverse principle, I had some curious imitators." Jay Dratler's *Ducks in Thunder* opens like mine, but he catches only the surface, not "the things that I work so hard to get."

Dial accepted *The Magician's Wife*, but with a few revisions, letter to follow. He told them he wanted to change the ending again. Still waiting for their suggestions, he sent it off in mid-August and again months went by and no word came.

He sent "Beauty, Booty, and Blood" to Miss Olding. She still maintained no magazine would buy it. He could do a major rewrite, she said, and perhaps it would sell as a novel. He decided to do that. But another project attracted his attention.

In November, he finally heard from Dial's new editor-in-chief, E. L. Doctorow, who was a graduate of Kenyon where David was now teaching, gave Cain a lesson in writing, detailed in a long memorandum, with some suggestions in line with some revisions he had been contemplating himself: shaping up the four main characters, streamlining the dialogue. Cain promised the revisions by the first of the year.

Just after New Year's, he was still deep into the rewrite of *The Magician's Wife*, but he fired off a note to Madden to Kenyon College where he was now assistant editor of the *Kenyon Review* and instructor of creative writing, to alert him to expect 100 pages or so of the autobiographical memos he was writing for him.

He got a letter from Madden telling him he had driven on impulse into Hyattesville on his return to Kenyon from a week of seeing plays in New York, and had failed to find him in the phone book or track him through the police station. He had left Cain's phone number and address at home. Upset to have missed him, Cain wrote to tell him he was in the throes of another revision of *The Magician's Wife*, fighting Dial's deadline, so with the autobio memos half done, he was suspending work on them for the duration. When he resumed, he would go into the "very things you've spoken of, that is, conceptions of story, what a story should be, etc." As he and Mencken had finally dropped last names, he suggested that from now on it be Jim and David.

Cain had to tell Doctorow that he was still in trouble. He told him that in their mutual analysis of character, he had forgotten that "characters derive from situation," and that by keeping them constantly in motion, he had been fooling himself that the situation was working. He had abandoned his original situation, for no good reason, and wanted to start all over again and deliver the new version in three weeks. But silence seemed endemic to Dial. After that November memorandum from Doctorow, he had heard nothing. There was no dialogue as there had been with Silberman. Then he got a jubilant phone call from Dial. Not about the novel he had worked so hard to revise over and over, but about somebody else's writing.

Tom Wolfe, *l'enfant terrible* of something they were calling the New Journalism, wrote a review for *Book Week* of another Dial novel, *American Dream* by Norman Mailer, in which he got off some asides on Cain's work. "If we get rid of that scene, we are quickly back into a stretch of fine-paced action, almost like James M. Cain. The spell breaks in the last chapter, however. . . . Even so, once the first fourteen and a half pages of the book are out of the way, Mailer exhibits much of the best things he has going for him, his drive, his pace, his fit of narrative, his nervous excitement, things Cain and Raymond Chandler had, but not too many other American novelists . . . in much of the book Mailer moves, probably unconsciously in the direction of Cain and shows great promise. In the context of a Cain adventure, Mailer's gothic attitude toward sex which Cain shares—a great deal of a new-sentimental business about how making love to a broad is all mixed up with death and fate and how you can tell your fortune by the quality of the orgasm—all this is not embarrassing in the context of a Cain novel like *The Postman*. . . .

"Of course, Mailer cannot match Cain in writing dialogue, creating characters, setting up scenes or carrying characters through a long story. But he is keener than Cain in summoning up smells, especially effluvia. I think Norman Mailer can climb into the same ring as James M. Cain. He's got to learn some fundamentals, such as how to come out of his corner faster. But that can be picked up. A good solid Cain style opening goes like this:

"'They threw me off the hay truck about noon. . . .'"

Rafe wrote to say he thought Wolfe's left-handed compliment to Mailer was a fine tribute to Cain.

Dial accepted the latest revised version of *The Magician's Wife* and about ten days later, Cain sent in yet another ending.

For David, he was in the throes of telling his relations with Ross at *The New Yorker*, when he got from him a copy of his Twayne book on Wright Morris, the first book ever on Morris, as his book on Cain would be a first. Madden said Kenyon College had awarded a grant to work on the Cain book.

Cain wrote to thank David for *Wright Morris*, and to explain that he had not acknowledged it sooner because he was laid up with a spring cold. "I make it a practice, for considerations of contagion, not to write anyone until ten days or so have gone by, after the thing passes."

Cain asked Swannie to send Joan Crawford the galleys of *The Magician's Wife*, hoping she would fall in love with Sally's mother, Grace, as he had. And instructed Dial to send her a mint bound copy as soon as possible.

Editors had often stifled Cain's inclination to write prefaces for his books, but Dial's publicity department welcomed a comment from him, to be offered as a press release: "'There but for the grace of God,' must be our first reaction to the consequences of crime—and that it is, actually, seems probable, from the interest we show in crime, and from our bemusement by it ... Occasionally ... comes a community leader ... who does commit a crime.... The story is usually the same: success, a lot of money, lurid sex, and then the bright idea that sudden death might help....We then see the immemorial American tragedy, colored by American farce, the TV interviews, the headlines in the paper, the hot-dogs being sold, out on the courthouse lawn.... I confess myself fascinated by this show, as well as by the psychological basis of it.. ...In *The Magician's Wife*, I was careful to picture a man whose convictions on this subject coincided with the reader's, who had no eccentric traits, no secret, Freudian urges, to make the thing easy for me. And to find him I went to the meat industry, which attracts masculine, intelligent, likeable men." Tell that Flo's father had been president of MacBeth Packing Company at Mankato, Minnesota. "A man as brainy as Lockwood would certainly be capable of planning a perfect murder, and what then? It was some time before it dawned on me that perfection itself must blow up in his face . . . a theme that attracts us all gets one more development."

David somehow got it in his head that Cain's short stories and articles were for posterity. He had tried several publishers, he said, and aroused E. L. Doctorow's interest, citing as his best short stories, "Pastorale," "The Baby in the Icebox," "The Birthday Party," and "Dead Man," and his best essays, "The Battleground of Coal," "Camera Obscura," "The Pathology of Service," and "Tribute to a Hero." In his prospectus, he argued that the essays examined the American scene, character, and dream, and that they were written in a "jabbing, slicing style that can suddenly soar with 'a tough lyricism,'" that they were "witty, charming, and often quite exciting. They have the energy and pace of his best fiction," that "one feels the presence of a strong, aggressive, authoritative, egoistic, but disarmingly honest personality." He wanted Cain to write an afterword.

Cain replied. "We've had a hot spell here, that stretched me out flat. . . another reminder I'm not as young as I used to be. Actually, I turned 73 day before yesterday—something I reflected on, a little—or tried to. It seemed it ought to mean something or other, but the more I worked on it, the less I made out of it. Except for things like the heat, I feel about the same as I did 20 years ago, work the same hours, think the same thoughts, or similar thoughts, we could say. And yet, your bones know, I'm sure."

Now to his proposal for a collection of the old essays and stories. "I don't see any point in trying revive them. 'Brush Fire' I think a good story, and 'Coal Black' isn't so bad, but the rest are machine made, and could well be forgotten, no doubt. *The Vanity Fair* play was strictly no good at all.

"The stuff I am doing for you will shorten your labors immensely. If you're not sick of me, by now. . . ."

Cain received from David a long piece he had written for *The New Republic*—in the tough guy context again—to herald *The Magician's Wife*, but it was turned down, probably because somebody at *NR* had gotten around to reading *The Magician's Wife* and didn't like it, and, again seeming to take his cue from Cain's gesture at MGM, he had returned the kill fee. But he later sent a short review that ran in the *Louisville Courier-Journal*, Krock's old paper. ". . . a demonstration of the fact that he is still a master of pace, style, ingenious narrative and vivid characterization. Readers who can't forget Cain's special magic, will recognize the famous 'love-rack' plot." He said some of the dialogue suggested the Thirties.

Cain responded: "Just which parts of the dialogue suggest the thirties instead of the sixties, I don't know, but remember that I've never, but never in any circumstances, tried to use the latest nifty."

The third person again: "I spent most of my life writing newspaper editorials, stories in the first person, and sketches in dialogue ... pretending to be somebody else. I couldn't do good columns as myself, or stories in the third person, where I wrote as myself, or be natural *in propria persona* at all. I don't think that's uncommon—most people, I imagine, are terribly stilted in their own right." And actors sound absurd when trying to be themselves. "But here in the last few years, in my mind, and on the sheet as I type, there has come a new beat, or cadence, or accent ... that I fought off at first, as probably a sign of old age. But then I began to realize it was *me*, trying to push through. So I'm letting myself be me, and don't have anything like the compulsion I used to have, to put it in somebody's mouth. It goes rather deep, I think, and is already conditioning my ideas, so it seems to me, though perhaps this is illusion, that they're branching out, or enlarging, or whatever it might be called.... I feel a gain in something—depth, maybe, or freedom.... I can still do the garrulous punk, with my eyes shut, of course. But isn't it time for a change?"

"Sunday, I suppose, the book will be announced, and I feel quite gloomy about it. However, I always do. Am up to my ears on another, against a deadline, but your stuff keeps going on paper."

Reviews of *The Magician's Wife* came through the door in August.

Martin Levin, *New York Times Book Review*: Cain doing business at the same old stand. By "one of the granddaddies of this truly American folk art, Mr. Cain's horror epic is suitable recreation."

The *New Yorker*: "Mr. Cain's writing is flimsy, like the people he deals with."

Granville Hicks, *Saturday Review*: Having thrown Wilson and Frohock at his head, Hicks alerts his readers that Cain has "merely repeated himself. There is as much trash as ever.... That Cain was at one time taken seriously is hard to understand . . . at best it is only a diversion, and there are better diversions on the market."

Time: "For 30 years, novelist James M. Cain has worked a literary lode bordering a trash heap. Even his best works . . . reeked of their neighborhood. . . . Cain has at last achieved a breakthrough. *The Magician's Wife* is pure trash. The book is so bad, in fact, that it is redeemed by its own absolute sins against credibility, plot, characterization and style. Reading it becomes a suspenseful exercise in disbelief, in which the reader is sustained, as well as stunned, by Cain's inexhaustible capacity for compounding meretriciousness. . . . Who else could have executed such a perfect travesty of Cain?"

On the whole, *The Magician's Wife* was received with contempt. The reviews upset Cain more than he would care to admit.

"The only book that hurts you is no book," said Flo, "and the only review that hurts you is no review at all."

The low sales and Joan Crawford's lack of interest were knockout blows.

Even though Swannie secured another movie option for *Past All Dishonor*, many past experiences put a damper on the enthusiasm that Cain would have liked to enjoy.

Commenting on each of his novels in his memos for David, Cain thought about what went wrong in *The Magician's Wife*. "It wasn't too good an effort. It had one dreadful effect—no 3." It had a 1 and a 2, but where it went after the somewhat successful murder, Cain could never invent. "The man's suicide, at the end, was simply the confession he had no 3, for suicide is an ending few readers accept. But the ending of a tale carries, or should carry, its point, and this story didn't seem to have one. But it's a hit in Japan, where harakiri is an honorable way out!"

He went to work on a novel about the psychological conflict between a little girl who is given a tiger cub to raise and her domineering mother who refuses to allow the child to raise it in her own way. A fairy tale he knew he could do with one hand, until not even two were enough, and he was sweating through the summer with that tiger that, like a genial genie that had proven so troublesome, he couldn't get it back into the bottle. He called it *Jinghis Quinn*.

David wrote to tell Cain that he had proposed to Bill Koshland the idea that a Cain omnibus, consisting of *Postman*, *Serenade*, and *The Butterfly*, was in order, now that Chandler and Hammett omnibuses were out. Koshland had turned down the idea.

He had a sense of physical well-being for a change, and he was mentally clear-headed.

He wrote to Mostyn Thomas. "I don't get sick. I don't fall down. I don't do anything much, except get one day older every 24 hours. Every so often, my processes unexplained, I get out a book."

Flo's brief period of relatively good health had waned. With friends and neighbors, she wasn't very sociable unless they would listen to her talk about her childhood and her pets. He supposed some people found her hard to get along with under normal conditions, he supposed maybe that he did too, but his "little opera singer" was Florence MacBeth, and her slow deterioration was to be a strictly private process. Singing was her life, and when the singing stopped, she crawled into a hole and pulled it in after her, and some would say, Cain in with it. But he understood what few people had need to understand, that opera singers are a separate breed.

He took her outside one day, and she fell. Hospitals were out. She stayed with Cain. Her blood pressure got to 205 after they had a few friends in. Even he couldn't keep her company most of the time for fear he might bring up a subject that would start her blood pressure up. Their cat Mittens stayed with her, and she got in the habit of drinking brandy to kill the pain of a neuritis condition that disturbed her balance. Cain couldn't allow workmen in the house, so what started to slip was allowed to fall apart.

Cain mailed the first batch of memos on January 12, 1966. He told David that when he got up to telling how he wrote *The Postman*, he found he was freezing up on it. He promised to try again to tell "what happens in my mind when I write a story . . . if you toss your book in the ashcan, I think that would be a fine idea. . . . I'm disgusted with myself."

With the New Year came a call from David, asking when the autobiographical memos would be ready. He told him soon, soon. It was always good to hear from him, but whenever he called, Cain could never get David's rising phone bill off his mind.

It now seemed obvious to Cain that David wanted to rush something between covers to get a better job, not out of passionate conviction that James M. Cain was worth his efforts.

The Library of Congress asked Cain to donate his papers. He told Rosalie that when that happened to a writer it was a sure sign he was going to die, since recognition didn't come before.

"David sent Cain some chapters of his book, and he lent them to a friend, a woman who was a shark on fiction, to check on his impression that David wasn't rating him very highly. A little defensively, he had conceived the idea that if David rated him so poorly, there wasn't much reason for anyone to publish the book. But Flo took exception: "Perhaps there is something vaguely apologetic about that book, but I would say, the main reason for the delay is: You're not quite as hot as you once were, and he can't hot you up, no matter how he tries. You could use a hit. You're as good as your last book, always. So saw up your wood, and perhaps you can light a fire."

He mailed the last batch, except for addenda, in early March. "About writing itself, it freezes. I must have more to say about my ideas, my mode of work, and my writing aims than I set down for you, but to save my neck can't get started with it, so I say it. However, it will have to do. You suggest a conference, but I can't have one." Flo's health is more precarious, she has no sense of balance, she's fallen several times.

David sent a copy of the *Kenyon Review* that he co-edited containing one of his stories, "The Singer."

Cain worked up an addenda to the Mencken gloss he had sent David. He explained his mode of work when research was involved, which was all the time, and enclosed two cards to show how he had made notes on *Mignon*. David's story "The Singer" was, he said, a startlingly promising set of notes for a novel, with impoverished Eastern Kentucky as background. The dialogue format bothered him, though. "I can't say I went for the form it was cast in."

His books always go lousy, he told David, causing endless trouble, as with the one he was working on now. "However, I try not to weep on people's shoulders."

David wrote later to tell him he had sold a story, "Big Bob's Night Owl Show," to *Adam*, a second-rate imitation of *Playboy*.

Cain felt a compulsion to give this young writer some over-the-shoulder advice. "The best news from you in a long time is that you're now writing for commercial magazines. They're supposed to be low-class, and they're not. They're competitive, and insist on much more taxing work than college publications. Leave us face it, these reviews do a bit of self-kidding, and exist for reasons not on the masthead—actually, they are a side-alley down which mediocrity can duck, to escape the dictum PUBLISH OR PERISH. It is a foolish dictum, for if the object of the game is to teach, it just flummoxes things up to tote the score on writing. So as with so many things academic, a bit of hypocrisy is allowed to get in. . . . The worst part of your piece on East Kentucky wasn't the stuff in your mind, but the hasty, first-thing-to-come-to mind approach you took to it, and the slap-dash execution. You take a walk around the block, let the material soak, and you could come up with something memorable. And keep sending stuff to those lowbrow, commercial, in-it-for-the-dough magazines.

"I'm having a perfectly gruesome time with a novel. But if it's any gruesomer than usual I wouldn't know. Is there such a thing as an *easy* one? I hope to start it one day."

Cain had bought a copy of Hagemann's and Durham's bibliography on his work, and he sent it to David.

Despite the meticulous care he gave Flo almost hourly, in 1966 when she was seventy-six, she suffered more steadily and grew steadily weaker. May 5, he tiptoed into her room to begin another day of rituals, and spoke to her. She didn't answer him.

Because Flo hadn't wanted them listed in the phone book, no reporters called to do an obituary article. Cain tried to drum up some attention, but got nowhere. He buried her in Mankato, Minnesota, her hometown.

He wrote to Rosalie, "So it appeared as though the waves had closed over her." Of course, it was a result of her own obsessive withdrawal from the world, but to see a legend pass without even an obituary was hard on Cain. "I was hooked on her, but bad. Both of us were screwballs, but our wackiness matched up, so we got along and needed each other."

From David came a gift, an old copy of *Treat 'Em Rough* by Lardner.

After a while, he could tell his old friend Ruth Goodman Goetz that although Flo's death had knocked him apart worse than he was showing, he didn't really feel lonely. What did get him was these sudden surges that swept over him, futile strugglings to bring her back.

He fixed up the house a little, the living room especially, but the new drapes made it resemble a prayer nook in a high-class mortuary, appropriately though, because he had closed himself up in a kind of shrine, to avoid people who might talk of Flo and set him off.

Somehow, as in lesser crises, when *Mignon* failed and then *The Magician's Wife*, the work was always there to be done, and so he did it.

David wrote to say he was still trying to persuade publishers to bring out a collection of Cain essays and stories. He thought Cain's essays of a very high literary quality, especially "Camera Obscura."

Thanks for promoting me. "However, any time you get an a idea for the reprint of something I wrote in former years, forget it." I hit on something back then, but changes put that essay out of date. "I just don't care to have it exhumed. My short stories, except for a few reprinted, just are plain lousy." In *The Postman*, "my proper approach and content and style began to reveal itself." Unfortunately, when that novel smashed, I got frantic wires from the agent... and let her clean out the trunk. So those old stories got published . . . why exhume those gristly mistakes?"

"So, let it slide hereafter. . . .

"These last few years, I make heavy weather of the humidity."

David sent Cain "Lone Riding," a chapter from his novel *Cassandra Singing*, published in the *Southwest Review*. Cain wrote to tell him it was excellent and to advise him that it was vitally important that he protect his copyright.

"I am deep in a novel that is setting me insane. I don't remember the ones that didn't set me insane, but it would seem that just once you could hit one that would sail along nicely, without all this outlining and beating the bio sketches and chaptering and all the rest of it."

On September 8, David called to have a telephone conference with him, to check information for his book. Some indication that it was still a viable project.

David sent him the issue of *Adam* in which his story "Big Bob's Night Owl Show" appeared. He had moved on once again, this time to Ohio University in Athens to teach creative writing. Cain told him he liked the story, it "stays in the frame." "The discovery of a woman within a woman is a very exciting thing," something he had tried to do toward the end of *The Moth* when Jack rolled on the beach with a woman he didn't recognize as the twelve-year-old girl he had loved, now grown up. Seeing the possibilities, Cain went on for a page telling him how he could rewrite his story into novel length.

"Am in the throes of a damned novel that's setting me nuts." *Jinghis Quinn*.

In October, he received from David four chapters of the book. He responded in early November, sending back the ms. "Bombs away on the scripts—the four parts you sent me. . . . The first thing you should want to know, did it hold me?—answer yes. " The American Authors' Authority is "a chapter of my life I look back on with the utmost distaste." That "tough" label again. I am bewildered by the constant bracketing of me with Chandler and McCoy. Cut the line about my working up the dope on me for you in the third person. "Well, I confess myself quite moved, so thanks and all luck with it."

He got a second batch at the end of November and returned it with marginal notes, okaying the facts. "You handle me, my personal story, that is, very pleasantly, and I am most grateful. However, I had an uneasy feeling, the same as I had when writing my notes, that it was a story not really worth telling. But that isn't your fault." "I seriously and solemnly request two small cuts." That he left the Catholic Church at age 13, on learning that it would interdict his marriage to a Methodist girl. Cut his quotation from *Newsweek* about his father dying a "blithering idiot." "Well, finally, let me express my amazement at the thoroughness of your research. I would be incapable of it."

For Cain's comment, David sent another commercial story, "Mirage," published in *Adam*'s brother magazine *Cad*.

Cain expressed the same objection he had with "Big Bob"—the man should get the girl. "I think you write them too soon after thinking them up—or possibly don't rewrite them after their outline becomes clear on a first draft.

"A woman down the block is doing some sort of paper on me, for an M.A. dissertation at the university, or something. She keeps yelling at me out the car window, about Frohock, whoever he is—he figures in your book too. Much more about him and I'll Frohock all over the carpet. I looked him up—he exists, he actually lives! Hooray."

As a Christmas gift, David sent him *The Great Singers.*

Just after Christmas, a young woman named Katherine Gresham came to the house to do an interview. He had put on his new suit in her honor. Cain was working on the notes for David's book, and, the day after New Year's the interview appeared, with photographs of himself and his house.

"Today Cain is 74 and lives in a dimly lit, slightly rundown frame house on a quiet Hyattsville street." She called his new suit "old" "musty brown." She obviously figured him as the subject of a second-rate assignment forced upon her. "His wife died six months ago and his only companion is a gray and white cat he calls Mittens. His gentle manner does not fit the image one might expect from his novels, but his cryptic, direct speech does.

"They say I put a ladle in and stir up the violence that happens in real life. That's nonsense. I don't consciously do anything about violence. I don't give it much footage in my books." Sex is there and passion and what he calls "emotion that has a dimension that's big," but Cain says he underplays it all. When a reviewer is quoted who calls the author a "wizard of sex, action and supercharged effects," Cain insists, "I don't know what he's talking about.

"People talk about my characters being tough, but all my guys are a bunch of yellow-bellied rats. I thought if I ever met Hemingway I would ask him, 'How long do you boil them to make them so tough?'" Cain uses language that is "quick, half improvised, the way people speak. Maybe this candor begins to sound kind of tough."

Mignon: "a bust from beginning to end." *Galatea*: parallels his own loss of weight. Two novels in the works. One was *Jinghis Quinn.* The second one follows a familiar pattern of murder and sex. *Cloud 9.* "I don't write out of devotion to art." "All books are potboilers. A man who says he writes a book for any purpose except recognition and money does not know what he is saying." The interview set him fuming for days.

In March, Cain was upstairs one day when the phone rang. He reached over the banister in an awkward position that unbalanced him and over the banister he went, landing very heavily on his back. He rejected the hospital regimen and nursed himself, standing while he wrote, because the fall had set off his chronic bladder irritation.

Aileen called and they talked as they had years ago. He had written to her to tell her that with Flo gone, he could now write to her more naturally. In his letters, he hinted at a reconciliation, but apparently the idea did not overwhelm her.

He was finally able to send *Jinghis Quinn* to Von Auw, indicating its chances with the movies in view of the success of *Born Free*.

In May, Von Auw reported that it didn't work, and Cain rewrote it.

David sent him *Hair of the Dog*, episode one of a serial of his appearing in *Adam*. Cain told David the fall downstairs "was the worst personal disaster I ever had in my life." Now to *Hair of the Dog*, a real progression. "I've had the feeling that if you eased off the relentlessly artistic, and chipped some edges off to move over to the more popular side, you would at the same time be more artistic. Or in other words, by not aiming so close you'd probably hit the target you're really interested in."

Did your publisher turn down the book on me? "I should have warned you I've been out of circulation a long time." Twayne will probably reject, he thought, because they will decide Cain is beneath scholarly consideration.

In June, Dial said no to *Jinghis Quinn*, ending Cain's contract obligations there.

When he discovered he had angina pectoris, the question of Cain's living with any woman lost urgency. But the quandary gave him an idea for a novel—one he did not pursue.

Cain wanted finally to deal with the complex elements that made up the scene in Washington and nearby Maryland. So he devised a plot in which embassies, lobbyists, caterers, and real estate were entangled in violence, sex, and money schemes. He called it *Cloud 9*.

The mail brought *The Thirties*, which contained an essay by David called "James M. Cain and the Tough Novelists of the 30's." Cain realized that he finally understood what David had been saying for seven years about the pure novel. "Something I was quite in the dark about, and afraid to probe into, with you, for fear of appearing dumb, or even worse, captious. But I conclude, after reading this article, that by it you mean a novel whose point is developed from the narrative itself, rather than from some commentary on the social scene, or morality of the characters, or economic or political or aesthetic preachment. If that is what you mean, you've hit my objective directly, for I try to let the fable, or outline, or tote, whatever you might call it, deliver its own 1 2 & 3, which to me is a perfectly defensible ideal."

Cain's rereading of *Postman* in July 1967, on the occasion of its reissue by Bantam, inspired him to recast into the first person the adventure tale he'd been writing in the third, *Cloud 9.*

David sent more of the manuscript for the book. Cain provided missing dates and asked for two cuts: the early jobs, "They are utterly pointless, and a very sore subject with me. It's a long story, but I have felt all my life if I had been reared with a little more comprehension of what I was really cut out for, I would have been spared this succession of false starts." And cut out of Flo's name the name of her first husband, Whitwell.

In August, another article came from David, "James M. Cain, and the Movies of the Thirties and Forties." "Thanks for *Film Heritage*, with its entertaining article on me. I leave it out on the living room cocktail table, and it impresses my friends no end."

Part Four of *Hair of the Dog* was really a nice piece of work. "Once again: I think this is the best thing of yours I've read, and partly for the reason it's not hell-bent to be artistic. Simply trying to entertain is possibly a better ideal, when you cut into it, than more pretentious purposes are."

"Here we have dog days, and I meditate cutting my throat."

In October, Jim Silberman at Random House said no to *Jinghis Quinn.* As Cain told Arthur Hornblow, "I thought a law had been passed that when I wrote a book it sold," but that was jaunty humor kited out of an abject misery of disappointment.

Failure worked on him in two contrary ways—it depressed and it galvanized him. He sprang to his feet and went back to work on *Cloud 9.*

What might happen if a girl were to stow away on a spaceship to Mars? What he imagined never made it out of the typewriter.

Cain was shocked and saddened to learn of the death by heart attack of Laurence Stallings. Arthur Krock in his memoirs published in that year recalled an incident from their *World* days. "Stallings, as befitted a man born in Macon and brought up in Atlanta, spoke in the rich brogue of those parts. This was a constant irritant to Cain, a Marylander, who appeared convinced that any Southern accent beyond the slight tinge in the speech of the natives of the Free State was put on.

"One day the group was joined by Markey, a Virginian whom I had placed, on the recommendation of Stallings, as a reporter for the *Evening World*, and whose idolatry of Stallings, Cain concluded after listening to Markey a while, included a devout effort to imitate Stallings's Georgian slurrings. Whereupon, the future author of *The Postman Always Rings Twice*, among others, arose from the table, and, departing, announced, I have to listen to Stallings, but not to his stand-in on a road show!"

The mail brought *Tough Guy Writers of the Thirties*, edited by David Madden, dedicated to "James M. Cain, Twenty minute-egg of the hard-boiled writers." Nobody had ever dedicated a book to him before, but why did David have to carve that label in stone and hire some gal to write about him? "Man Under Sentence of Death: The Novels of James M. Cain." Joyce Carol Oates. He looked her up. She'd written three collections of stories and a novel. She taught at the University of Windsor. Thinking of the nasty cracks Dawn Powell used to get off about his work, he began to read. "These are his tricks, his gimmicks, but how cynically he exploits them as 'gimmicks' that lead his heroes to their deaths!" Mildred Pierce was "overlong and shapeless." Its flaws derived from the third-person omniscient narration. "In the sub-literary world of American popular writing, it is the 'how' that is important—'what happens next,' 'what happens finally. . . .' It is the fact that such pessimistic works are entertainment that fascinates. . . . In the end one can call him simply an 'entertainer'. . . . Is it possible that Cain did not understand what he was doing in *Serenade*? . . . . *Mildred Pierce* is the most convincing of Cain's central works in its plodding, repetitious, unimaginative progress . . . ." Veda gives the reader "access to the mystical reservoir Cain associates with music." Cain's craftsmanship "can perform dazzling tricks but it cannot make us believe in them." She was Dawn Powell reincarnated with a sharper tongue. David's gift was like a Trojan horse, inspiring mixed emotions.

And there were Hemingway, Hammett, Chandler, and McCoy, not for the last time, he was afraid. Rather ironic that this collection of original essays had grown out of Madden's background reading for his book on Cain, which he doubted would ever come out.

"Tough Guys" had spawned another book published at the same time, *Proletarian Writers of the Thirties*, a consequence of so many invited critics having seen parallels between the two types of Thirties novels. Nathanael West was missing only because the great interest in his fiction had generated yet another potential collection. All this could be traced back to David's having seen *The Postman* when he was a twelve-year-old usher at the Bijou in Knoxville, Tennessee, and to his having been fascinated by Robert Jonas' covers for *Mildred* and *Serenade* in the forties. He had not read word one of Cain until he decided on impulse to write the essay at Yale.

"Thanks for the book, haven't answered sooner because the doctor has me on digitalis, which flies you higher than a kite. The dedication touched me. The girl who wrote me up handled me very rough, which is OK, as I'm used to it by now." He reached back to a parallel with Winchell, who had attacked him in the twenties. "But why am I such a heel now, when I wasn't thirty years ago? Then, there were quite a few who took me quite seriously, and in fact I was quite a literary personage. But to this girl I'm just a bum, and a bum she seems to take personal." "Your book on me will come out when I hot up again, not before—if I do. And I may, at that. I have another one—having abandoned two or three that were too much like the others preceding—that could ring the bell."

In his response, David seemed a little irritated by his reaction to Miss Oates' essay, arguing that Cain didn't understand the often paradoxical frame of mind of the critic, and that her article consciously was ironic, full of literary assumptions, dealing also with the popular reader's assumptions in a way that may appear somewhat gleefully perverse but that was finally very complimentary, and that she shared David's own high regard for his work. He pointed out such passages as "That Cain as entertainer is entertaining his audience in a highly masterful and intelligent way is indicated by his remarks on his own writing." "Let us consider *Postman* as an example of Cain's craftsmanship at its finest." "*Serenade* is an ambiguous work"—"ambiguous" in critical works being not necessarily a pejorative word. "There is perhaps no writer more faithful to the mythologies of America than Cain." He pointed out that, as he had said in his introduction, he asked Miss Oates to write about him because he saw some similarities in his fiction and hers.

To persuade Cain to accept his approach to the tough guy label, David cited his introduction. "Ideas and attitudes are 'in the air' at any moment in history. Independently, different writers, of varying caliber, hit on similar subjects and even similar styles. Thus, Cain may rightly deny Hemingway's influence upon his style, but the similarity remains. We need to understand this process."

In his introduction, David talked about the effect of Cain's fiction: To most readers, "Faulkner is unknown, Cain is read. It is Cain then who affects the popular imagination, which is so liable to translate its imaginative experiences if not into direct action, into real attitudes that have consequences in behavior." But he also told of giving "a speech, in fear and trembling, to a group of Ohio English professors. To my surprise, that lecture conjured up in them a latent literary interest, mingled with a passionate nostalgia" for Cain's novels.

Cain shot back. "I did re-read, or at least tried to, what Miss Oates had to say about me, but found it heavy going. I'm not much upset by criticism, in fact always read it with interest, on the theory the guy could be right, and I might learn something." But Oates is "just plain intellectual jibber-jabber. She insists on intellectualizing something that isn't intellectual. . . . What the hell is her squawk? . . . . The things I ought to be praised for, at least as I see it, she finds unforgivable . . . nobody, so far as I know, goes through the mental processes she. . . seems to think requisite." One thing upset Cain. "Your assumption that I had been a novelist of the 30's and 40's but had nothing to say from the 50's on." He wasn't conscious that he was basically representative of any particular era. "What explains my dip, I think, is not the passage of time but my moving to a new locale. It was an upheaval indescribable, internally, though in his physical appearance, scarcely perceptible. What gave my other books their vitality, if any, wasn't a period, but the West, where I moved, and where I found, in actual, name-the-date consciousness, the roots, or kick, or whatever it took, that books probably need. Moving East left me blank—though I was done with the West, it having somewhat lost its taste for me. Now, though, I may achieve a comeback, as Suburbia, where I live, begins to cast its spell, or takes its toll, or whatever we would say. I'm beginning to realize it's the new frontier, and as such worth anyone's close attention.

"Can I say what I really think, about you, this piece, and other things? I feel as though I am seeing myself in a distorting mirror, just as I felt when reading Miss Oates." Hit that odious tough tag again. No influence. I never read them. "I have no kinship with them. . . . I wouldn't say this if you hadn't spoiled me with" the serial "you wrote for *Adam*. I suspect you thought they were hack, and in the sense that you probably didn't file and polish and sandpaper to any great extent, they possibly were. But they were a different kind of writing from this stuff for the think magazines that you get off with your other hand."

Give the case of a friend writing a biography as a think book. It was rejected. "A girl said to me once, repelling my pass: 'I think you want me, but not much.' That's how it is with this intellectualized stuff. I can read it, I like it a little, but not much. The real pay-off is for *Adam*, or publications out to hook readers and hold them. David, why this obsession with the literary? After all, you can go just so far on writers. On others, on the figures of history, you can go the whole way and get rich. I have to take off my hat to your research: it is thorough, it's downright exhaustive. So why not move out to the big time with it?"

"So now, I suppose you're not speaking to me. . . . I'm very glad you're off to Louisiana. . . . It will give you a big change of scene, and I have to say, I think the modern South a better climate for writers than the modern Middle West. . . . For Christ sake get out of the wading pool and dive off where the waves are big, the fish are big, and the money they bring is big. It's moula that makes the world go round—not love."

A week later, Cain mailed a follow up. "Having made myself 100% obnoxious, I send clippings from *New Yorker* and *Time* on Roger Sessions, whose sin is composing for composers, not for an audience." *The New Yorker*: "His realm is the college composition classes of America, and these have somehow become divorced from the needs of people who go to hear music." *Time*: "He had had to settle for the high esteem of colleagues and critics. . . . 'Immediate response is not what one is preoc-cupied with.'"

Tell David again. "You have a talent, far beyond what I'd suspected. You have, that is, when you write for people, not just for insiders on the faculty. It's tougher, writing for people, don't let anyone tell you different. And it's better. These academic dissertations have been bad for 100 years."

David responded with a gracious note, saying he thought Cain's comments were fine.

Tell David about Philip Goodman's effect on Mencken, how he lifted him from being a Baltimore wunderkind, who played to the local gallery, to the big stage. Goodman was "the closest friend I ever had." And that Mencken ever had. David was headed the same way as Mencken. "Let me be your Philip Goodman."

"I have to plead guilty to being obsessed with the phoniness of the university approach to writing." "Why you wrote about me at all I have no idea. . . . I've just finished a new script, but of that more when I sell it. If I sell it."

A Modern Cinderella went through a third movie transformation in 1968, when a British company remade the 1957 *Interlude* with the same title, directed by Kevin Billington, with Barbara Ferris and Oscar Wer-ner—Grant, the poor little American rich boy, had spoken with a French accent, then an Italian, now a German.

In May, Swannie wrote to say that CBS had taken an option on Cain's most-often optioned novel *Past All Dishonor*.

Good news came from Von Auw that Knopf would publish *Post-man*, *Double Indemnity*, and *Mildred Pierce* in an omnibus volume, and that Book of the Month Club would offer it. The advance was a spirit-lifting $5,000. As a selling notion, Tom Wolfe was assigned to write an introduction.

Cain had several neighbors who made good conversation, and who kept an eye on him and even ran errands or drove him around, and their children did yard and other work around the house for him. He needed a new suit, so Carol Kisielnicki, one of twelve children next door, drove him to the shopping center on US 1 in Hyattsville, where he woke up looking at blue sky and Carol's face, a crowd of people all around him. He had dropped dead. To the spectators gathered around in front of People's Drugstore, he must have looked like an old wharf rat, and he'd embarrassed poor Carol to within an inch of her own young life.

The fall did damage, but a hospital captivity was out. His own diagnosis of the problem was that the digitalis prescribed for his angina condition had blacked him out. He dropped the digitalis and became his own physician.

11

"Station to Station Does It— I'm the Only One Here"

WITH FLO GONE, HE THOUGHT HE'D LET HIS NAME AND NUMBER GO IN the phone book so people could reach him. But he got so many person-to-person calls that cost people money, he decided to have a line printed at the bottom of his new run of stationery: "STATION TO STATION DOES IT—I'M THE ONLY ONE HERE."

The September issue of *Playboy* came in the mail with a note from the editors saying that David Madden wanted him to have a copy. He had to say of David what interviewers often said of himself: he didn't look at all as he'd imagined. His story "The Day the Flowers Came" was about a man who wakes up one morning and one florist after another delivers flowers in condolence for the death of his wife and children—whom he did not know were dead. The kind of situation that appealed to Cain and kept him awake all night.

He wrote to David to say he thought it was the best thing he ever did. "It is a very distinguished job, kind of a neo-Faulkner thing with touches of Durrenmatt."

Then he wrote to Jack Kessie, managing editor of *Playboy*. "Madden is an old friend whose development I've watched with the greatest interest. He started out as a pedigreed highbrow, writing stuff for the university reviews, showing scholarship so vast it was hard to believe, even when you saw it. But lately he has been veering over to big-time publications like *Playboy*, and growing, I have felt, in stature." "The Day the Flowers Came" is a fine specimen of his more recent phase, to my taste a beautiful, simple tale with a curious subtle quality. It doesn't depart by one decimal point from a rigorous, credible reality, and yet through it peeps something weird, a glimpse of Death's horror that left me a little frightened. I do hope you work on him plenty, to get more stuff out of him, as I think you'll be well repaid. Your magazine impresses me no end."

He enclosed a carbon of this letter with his letter to David. He was now writer-in-residence at Louisiana State University.

In November, Swannie reported that Disney had not gotten excited about *Jinghis Quinn.*

Cain was watching the Huntley-Brinkley newscast, then suddenly he jerked awake. "If you're so tired, why don't you go to bed?" Flo asked, from the chair across the room. "I guess I should," he said. He wondered why she was sitting over there, where she couldn't see the news. Then he realized that she wasn't there—he was utterly alone.

Cain was happy to see *The Postman Always Rings Twice, Mildred Pierce,* and *Double Indemnity* included in *Cain X 3.* He began reading Tom Wolfe's introduction with eager anticipation. He led off referring to his earlier advice to Mailer, which had made Mailer howl. Along with Steinbeck, Farrell, Saroyan, Faulkner, and Thomas Wolfe, "Cain was one of those writers who first amazed and delighted me when I was old enough to start looking around and seeing what was being done in American literature." But he had "momentum," "acceleration" that was unique. "Picking up a Cain novel was like climbing into a car with one of those Superstockers who is up to forty by the time your right leg is in the door.

"His 'fast-paced,' 'hard-boiled' technique really is complex. It is not just the sex and violence that made him notorious in the 1930's and 1940's that explains his effect. Sexual details are never gratuitous, the violence is never a relishing of brutality, yet you feel as if you've had a long violent experience. This feat goes back as far as *Crime and Punishment.* Cain puts us in the skin of an 'egocentric' Universal Heel. Our sympathy is entwined with horror and disgust. Cain deals with the sin of betrayal, as in *Mildred.* More than Hemingway or Chandler, Cain is a master of pace. Chandler and Cain created the atmosphere of southern California. Like Hemingway, Cain immerses 'the reader in secrets of various arcane arts.'"

John Carmody, editor of the *Washington Post Potomac Magazine*, wanted to write a cover story to promote *Cain X 3*, so he came over to the house in his car on a dark winter day. Riding over to the Olney Inn for lunch, Cain talked mostly about Flo. Her illness had cut him off from the world for fifteen years. In the Chicago Opera, she was "always in the shadow of Mary Garden. In Hollywood, she was a grande dame, a personage. And I brought her back here." He confessed that he felt guilty about that sometimes.

At the inn, he told Carmody some Hollywood stories—everybody enjoys those. And anecdotes about Ross, Lippmann, Mencken, Vincent Lawrence: "And he had such plans. We both had such plans. And it all turned out so different." A half-smile, not of self-pity, he hoped.

Each day, he gets a big pile of mail. For years, he has corresponded all over the country, and has written many letters to the editor. His latest novel is about a young composer who falls in love with his father's girlfriend (or vice versa). It was going slowly. He wrote in longhand. Sitting at a typewriter had taken its toll.

Neighbors took him to only three movies in recent years: *Kon Tiki*, *Born Free*, and *Who's Afraid of Virginia Woolf?* "I have every emotional tie to California. As an idea, it's an achievement intellectually, culturally and industrially." But movies don't stick to his ribs. His memory of his flop as screenwriter is "a slight toothache."

Past All Dishonor was recently optioned. That novel was "a grand vin"— it had held up thirty-five years. His paperbacks, even in their many translations bring in money: $85 recently from the Rumanian government.

He hated much on TV. Didn't like Bobby Kennedy. Not sure about religion, but loved most animals.

He always dreaded seeing himself in the photos, and he wondered how Carmody really saw him. "James M. Cain at Twilight Time." An epigraph quoted him: "I told him: I'm world-famous without doing one of your goddamned B pictures." To a Hollywood producer. More photos than he wanted his friends and neighbors to stare at. "Jim Cain scrunched down in the front seat of the car. The brim of his old felt hat is turned up. He is wearing what he calls his 'undertaker's coat.' A ten-year-old double-breasted gray suit. A faded Pendleton plaid shirt and a solid red tie peer from the top of an old nubby brown sweater." "Wayne Morse eyebrows," and "a wide toothless smile that is almost always there." "He speaks in a gruff 'city room' voice of which he is proud." Good mimic. "He says there is a good deal of the ham in him." So that's how he looked to other people—or to editors anyway. "He turns to look at every pretty girl the car passes." Accurate so far.

Thinking of finally buying the house. His house is run down, "needs paint badly," curtains drawn. "It is that kind of an old man's house, now." Inside walls: a few framed handbills of opera star Florence MacBeth, posters advertising the *Cross of Lorraine* newspaper. He has given all his books away, except a small corner of shelves, history books, critical articles that touch on Cain's place in American literature. Out of tune Mason and Hamlin grand piano. A couch where he often naps. Upstairs: tiny study, typewriter, couch, book-case: paperbacks of Cain novels—"almost the only mementoes he has allowed himself." "He sits in his dim house, greeting the teenage kids who come by in the evenings to talk to a real novelist."

Carmody did a number on his singing in the Inn: "arms waving, the eyebrows dancing, toothless and laughing, some ghost" from the Brown Derby days, making people flee embarrassed, "amid the cackles and the profanity." One couple, fascinated, later laughed along with Cain's antics. Hoary old Hollywood stories he's told a hundred times. "You realize that this is one of those men you used to read about, who really did go to lunch with Scott Fitzgerald," who flickered through novels by Budd Schulberg, West, Fitzgerald, O'Hara. "Cain had outlasted them all out there, finally." "Cain, in person, is a lot of long sentences, punctuated with very innocent sounding gawddams, delivered in that city room voice." "Jim Cain still loves to talk. One suspects he was a consummate newspaperman."

"And almost any protracted anecdote turns, finally, into some lesson in . . . writing. . . . The novels—the big ones—creep into his conversation only as examples of how he turned personal experiences into the books." "He is easily, at the age of 76, the best of all the characters he ever wrote about on the screen or in his novels."

Carmody the old-style journalist also reprinted entirely Tom Wolfe's new journalist introduction to *Cain X 3.*

The jacket of *Cain X 3* was one of the classiest he had had in a long time. He didn't want Hammett's recommendation of *Postman*, "A good, swift, violent story," but Hammett was hot and maybe he would help sell copies.

He sent David an advance copy of *Cain X 3*, inscribed. The publicity was good, he told him, though he said he knew nothing of how the trick is done. "Don't worry about the book you did on me. If it comes out a bit later than the main flurry about me—it could keep the pot boiling in a most welcome way." His health had been bad, but it was better now.

All the attention made him meditate on how little time he had left. "So many die, it leaves you rather frightened," he wrote a friend. "I no doubt will go soon—I'm nearer seventy-seven than seventy-six, and I hardly know myself, or quite understand how I got that way."

A girl came to interview him. "How do you see yourself as part of the literature of violence?" She must have spent the whole trip thinking up that question. He told her politely he took no interest in violence.

Not far behind her came John Leonard, editor of the *New York Times Book Review*. He told him he still writes of "the wish with terror in it," and manipulates so "my algebra . . . moves . . . progressions. You wait for the hot flash. The hot flash saves you from going outside and walking around and whistling about it."

"My mother told me I didn't have the voice. She was right, but she could have kept her flap shut and let me find out for myself." She also taught him grammar. "I slip into the Vulgate every once in awhile—an affectation I only half understand. There I am speaking impeccable English, and suddenly I lingo it."

On Mencken: "Did you know he never even read *Alice in Wonderland*? Imagine: Henry Mencken never read the greatest novel in the English language." Nixon: some hope. "Syntax! Nixon doesn't dangle his participles." "New York's not even a city, it's a congerie of rotten villages." "And I came from a newspaper where the ideal was information. The *New Yorker*'s ideal was entertainment. I earned my money, but I had no pride or satisfaction."

Novel writing "has to be learned, but it can't be taught. This bunkum and stinkum of college creative writing courses—writers make their decision to write in secret. The academics don't know that. They don't know that the only thing you can do for someone who wants to write is buy him a typewriter."

Resents "using as mucilage the simplifications that the school hypothesis affords" the critic whether Wilson or Madden in *Tough Guy Writers*. Tried reading *The Big Sleep*. "That's too good. The old man who grows orchids. When it's too good, you do it over again. Too good is too easy."

"I write love stories. The dynamics of a love story are almost abstract. The better your abstraction, the more it comes to life when you do it— the excitement of the idea lurking there. Algebra. Suspense comes from making sure your algebra is right. I don't write whodunits. You can't end a story with the cops getting the killer. I don't think the law is a very interesting nemesis."

Cain paced as he talked, mimicked his characters, dipped in and out of the "Vulgate" as he explained his moves.

He rejected influences. He was wary of reading much fiction. "I like that guy Capote, but I'm scared I'll start trying to write like him. Mailer? He's good, but I wish he'd take a walk around the block and get rid of the smell of the privy that's on him."

Shakespeare: "I don't think Shakespeare wrote those sonnets in his mid-thirties to some boy." He wrote them in his teens, to himself. Narcissist. Was Anne Hathaway part Negro? "I wrote that fellow, George Steiner, and asked him to do a book on it. He disagreed." His new book turns on a similar situation to "young Shakespeare–older Hathaway" "— young composer, an older woman devouring him." Three versions so far. "But the last was too good. Like Chandler's orchids. Too easy. If you're not lying awake at night worrying about it, the reader isn't going to, either. I always know that when I get a good night's sleep, the next day I'm not going to get any work done. Writing a novel is like working on foreign policy. There are problems to be solved. It's not all inspiration."

Cain offered Leonard cigarettes and liquor, which he had to deny to himself.

He was still an editorial writer, but as letters to editors of newspapers and magazines. Elements in his fiction, "the dreadful, the impious, the shame of God," are at large and dangerous in our country today. "We are the worst violent nation in the history of man, from colonial times on. Look at what happened to registration of fire-arms—killed off by those so called sportsmen who think manliness means shooting birds and animals."

Another book: "It's about a tough-luck Susy. I've got the characters. I've started to make my moves. The next step is . . . what these people do for a living."

Other involvements: The manuscripts *Playboy* sends him to comment on, David Madden's "Flowers," growing mint in the backyard for summer juleps, counting classical allusions in Shakespeare's sonnets—only seven, which suggests a young man wrote them. Seeing the world get excited about his books again is very satisfying. "Time is the only critic. If your algebra is right, if the progression is logical but still surprising, it keeps."

Cain was glad to get his hands on the March 2, 1969 issue of the *New York Times Book Review*. The whole front page with five photographs and a review by Ross Macdonald. The Leonard interview on page 2: "The Wish of James M. Cain." Leonard was objective and impersonal, making no cracks about Cain's looks or the condition of the house he had shared with Flo so many years and where he now had to live alone and write against time.

Macdonald's twenty-first novel, *The Goodbye Look*, was coming out. Cain read his review of his own seventeenth book. The West Coast crime novels provide "our most persistent literary impression of California. James M. Cain was one of the great inventors of this form. . . . Not even Raymond Chandler" ever did better. "The human figures in Cain's landscapes are in terribly rapid motion, most of it downhill, as in a vision of judgment. . . . The intensity of this passage . . . translates the blood into symbol, the stuff of art." Cain's California is "reminiscent of Verga's Sicily. . . . Mr. Cain is a conscious and deliberate artist." The famous echo that Wilson damned in 1941, Macdonald praises as not, in context, a "fine operatic flourish ending a chapter," but "the echo of the dead man's voice hints at something out there in the void, like an echo of the voice of the ghost of God."

Cain X 3 "should make its way into the universities . . . the vernacular, and the people who speak it, are the main source of his imaginative

JAMES M. CAIN
6707 44th Avenue
Hyattsville, Md. 20782

September 3, 1972

Dear David: I was badly upset when I realized I had missed you. I was home, actually, but upstairs, in bed, asleep – I have to nap in the afternoon, else I'm no good at all at night. Next time give me a little notice, so I can be indeed with a grin on my face and a faded carpet. The end of a rather bumpy road in the book, which I've heard nothing about, my reach to many reviews. I hope I made it readable. I hope next time will be soon. All my best –

Yours
Jim

Mr. David Madden,
Baton Rouge, La.

Phone: 301 927 1963 *Station to Station does it — I'm the only one here* strength," as with Melville, Whitman, Frank Norris, Stephen Crane, Hammett. Regarding Hammett, "I can see no evidence of direct influence." Maybe Mencken influenced both Cain and Hammett. "Cain must have experienced that coming together of the already known and the freshly heard which opens the imagination to new life." In *Mildred Pierce* Cain's "language has changed, losing some of its poetic power and pace ... the two languages spoken and written, which a novelist must listen to binaurally as he writes, fail sometimes to fuse at the level of sensibility." Cain's wonderful eye for everyday detail recalls the fact that he started as a journalist. "He persists in styling himself" in *Who's Who* as "newspaperman." *Mildred*: "The concept is broad-gauged, and prophetic of our anomie, but it falls a bit short in the execution, particularly in the eccentric structure." When he wrote *Double Indemnity*, "he had learned, as few writers ever do, how to dispense with everything inessential." It has, "like *The Great Gatsby*, the effect of a rather large action boiled down to a concentration approaching that of dramatic poetry. But it isn't an action story. Its critical actions are psychological and moral." Cain, who influenced Camus, "was an important precursor of the existentialist school of fiction both in his portraits of alienation and despair, and his ultimate concern with good and evil. Like most twentieth century writers, he tends to define virtue in terms of its absence."

And in the back a full-page photograph of Arthur Krock, advertising his *Memoirs: Sixty Years on the Firing Line*, fourth place on the bestseller list.

Cain X 3 reviews:

Robert Kirsch, *Los Angeles Times*: "novelist par excellence of Southern California." The novels have not dated. "They capture and compel with all the illusion of the original experience."

William Hogan, *San Francisco Chronicle*: When they first came out, he thought Cain "was the greatest writer in the business," and now the novels read like "poetry."

Robert Sorenson, *Minneapolis Tribune*: When Cain listened to the critics, "and tried to become *serious* and *significant*, we lost an exciting, if not an important, writer."

Pete Hamill, *Village Voice*: Cain is better than Hemingway, though not a great writer, a good one, except that *Postman* "might be a great one."

Kenneth Lamott, *Nation*: *Mildred* was a serious novel. "Watching Cain at work can still give the reader that particular pleasure that comes from watching a master craftsman."

Starting with Tom Wolfe's praise, the thread that ran through these reviews that encouraged him was that his best work, at least, had not dated.

Cain knew that he ought to invite over friends who lived close enough to visit. But as he told his old friend and Mencken's, Sara Mayfield, in June, "You and your passel of friends could easily have had crisis stretched out on the floor to deal with—and you couldn't very well have gone kiting off to your car and left it lying there."

When his friend Carl Bode's *Mencken* finally appeared, he checked his own contribution for accuracy, then settled down to read what all that long labor had wrought.

What would happen if a woman in her thirties married a boy not yet out of his teens, and they lived in suburbia, in Maryland? He called it *Kingdom by the Sea.*

David called, just back from Venice, Italy, where he had started a new novel called *Bijou.* Would Cain read his forthcoming novel in galleys for comment? Yes, he would. They came swiftly, with a fast deadline. Reading long galleys was like reading a book printed on the backs of a basket full of eels. He hurried a telegraphed comment off to David's editor at Crown, David McDowell: "Madden tells it like it is. A very fine book."

To David he wrote: "I found it extraordinarily good, along the line you've been developing on, but more opened-up and freer-running. I hope you do more of this kind.

"I've been in the snow bank with one, and God only knows what comes out. . . . I wasn't born to this manor. . . should have stuck to weighing meat for Swift, the best job I ever had."

Cain enjoyed being involved in the developing fiction career of the young man who was also writing the first book about Cain himself. In November, an advance copy of *Singing Cassandra* came with a moving inscription, and David's claim that *The Butterfly* helped inspire it. Cain replied that only the guy who wrote it had any effect on it. "I am half into it once more, and it holds up even better. . . nice to hear your voice, on the phone, the other night."

David called a few nights later when Cain was in a foul mood from sleepless nights after hard work at the machine. Would he send to Twayne a photograph to go on the jacket of the book? His old fears that the whole project after ten years would fall through came out in conversation, and David got irritated with him. He wrote to explain. "So O.K. I'm a rat and an ingrate." He went into the extenuating circumstances, one going back over four years, when he took a ribbing on when this book was coming out. The other was a heart condition that "aggravates all my worst faults." Told him he sent two photographs to Twayne.

For 1969, the best Christmas present he got was the appearance at the house of a stray cat that he called Snobby.

Washington College continued to offer him honors, even after a new president came in, but Cain declined. His anger against the college for the way it had treated his father decades ago and for the library's rejection of Cain's fiction abated enough for him to donate fifty paperback editions of his foreign language reprints to the library, where they would repose in a room donated by Sophie Kerr, the popular magazine writer of the 1920s and 1930s.

He didn't know what impulse led him to say yes to a request that he participate in March in a five-day symposium on "Literature and Cinema" at Catholic University in Washington, but he did, and it wasn't bad.

Cain was glad to get a letter from Joyce Carol Oates in April saying she admired his work, and was distressed he had misread her essay in Madden's book. She wrote only about people whose work she admired. But that didn't change his perception of the essay.

In June, *Kingdom by the Sea* failed to convince Bill Koshland at Knopf. He advised he set aside this variation of the Poe theme.

A plump young woman named Robin Deck and her friend showed up one day, reminding him that they had met at the "Literature and Cinema" symposium, and they wanted to get to know him better. Robin was working on Capitol Hill and had an interest in theater. Her friend wanted to be a writer. Robin began coming frequently, until she would often stay all day, and they went out to various events in the evenings sometimes.

David wrote to say the Cain book was definitely coming out, and that he was at Warner Brothers to start a screenplay for *Cassandra Singing*, and that then, like Faulkner, he was going home to finish it. He told him that he had met Mervyn LeRoy who had had a ten-year wish to direct a movie of *Serenade*. David had told LeRoy he would like to write the script. And in the office of his producer, Tony Bill at Warner Brothers, he had met Jim Thompson who had remembered Cain when they were both in Hollywood. R. V. Cassill had written about Thompson's *The Killer Inside Me* for *Tough Guy Writers of the Thirties*.

"I confess myself quite flabbergasted, to say nothing of impressed, at your new assignment, working for Warner Brothers. I worked for them, I worked for them all, and was a complete, 100% bust. So if you do well, admiration will be well mixed with envy. Jack Warner is an old friend, a most likeable and amusing guy.... I don't place Thompson, but if you see someone else that remembers me, give him, or her, my regards."

Cain wanted to write a novel about a teenage girl and her problems with her father. He started in August 1970, calling it *The Enchanted Isle*.

The Mystery Writers of America asked Cain if he would accept a special award, naming him a "Grand Master." He didn't know whether he could make it to New York and back in one piece, but when Patricia McGerr, an attractive mystery writer living in Washington, offered to watch over him, he decided it was worth a try. The experience was enjoyable, and he was surprised at his own energy.

James M. Cain by David Madden arrived in time for Christmas with a moving inscription and a letter from David.

"I know, and have regretted, that you have not seen my commentaries, at times, in the light in which I wrote them—as tributes to a man I respect, whose work I continue to read and recommend eagerly.... I never say you read Hammett, etc. It's a matter of people just happening to be doing somewhat similar things sometimes—not in every book.... The whole project began in 1959 as an act of appreciation and that's the whole point to this day." He said he'd never make more than $250 on it.

He also sent an essay in *Papers in Language and Literature* on similarities between *The Postman* and Camus' *The Stranger*.

He ordered from the editor at Twayne as many copies of David's book as $35 would buy. "He did a fine job, I thought. I'm pleased as punch."

Then he wrote to David on New Year's Day. "I've been reading it since it came in, and like it fine actually, it leaves me rather shook. I find myself utterly astonished at the thoroughness of the research, and indeed have the feeling I'm learning more about myself than I ever personally knew. I can't thank you enough...." Go over our previous misunderstanding. "It's not how I feel now, that I've had a chance to live with this book, and digest it.... Anyway, just a detailed assurance I'm not only pleased, but pleased as Punch, and accept this book, as well as like it."

He went on television in Washington, and the host, a friend of his, held up David's book to help plug it and as proof that Cain was now a part of the scholarship on American literature. He had not yet read the book, but the next night, he called to tell Cain that he couldn't put the book down. Well, it still stuck to Cain's ribs, and he'd tell David that.

Cain and Robin had been together constantly for nine months. His affair with Robin clarified some of his ideas about love. Mencken had said that "Love is an illusion that one woman differs from another," but Cain made a crucial revision: "Love is the discovery that one woman does differ from another." Also, he believed that love without desire is nothing.

Cain sent *Cloud 9* to Bill Koshland through Von Auw.

Koshland reported that *Cloud 9* was unconvincing. Somehow Cain was so humiliated by this string of rejections that he apologized to Von Auw and Dorothy Olding for involving them in such a shoddy enterprise. "I think I'm in a new phase, so don't scrub me, just yet." He intended to be in a new phase, anyway. Looking back to 1957, since then he had crashed with three novels, and had three or four rejected. The failed scriptwriter, who left Hollywood and put all his money, time, and energy on novel writing, had not had a success since the days when he was a failed scriptwriter. And he somehow couldn't count old age as a factor. His imagination was fertile, and wasn't he productive? Well, maybe too productive, too facile.

Somehow he let himself be persuaded to participate in a creative writing seminar funded by the Maryland Arts Council with some people

he liked: Carl Bode, who taught at the University of Maryland; Jack Salamanca, a novelist; and James Backas. He remembered an exercise David
had told him he had used at the Morehead conferences: take a student's
simple plot idea and lead the class into developing a screenplay. That
seemed to work for Cain, too.

Snobby didn't come home for four days. He appeared on the fifth day
with a fractured jaw. The vet held out little hope that it would mend. One
day, they were napping together—and when Cain woke up, Snobby was
dead. He wrote to Rosalie, "Few things in my life have upset me so." As
with all animals, this one "brought me closer to God."

Publisher's Weekly ran a piece by novelist Benjamin Appel that contained some inaccurate information about Cain's AAA of the forties. He
started to write in the corrections, but didn't get around to it. In the next
issue, he was glad to see a long letter from David, setting it all straight.
He thanked him and told him that his friends continued to say pleasant
things about David's Cain book.

In October, Cain made a proposal to Philip Geyelin, editorial page
editor of the *Washington Post*. He had sent him a number of pieces for the
op-ed page and Geyelin had published a few of them. Cain would now
like to become an occasional editorial writer on such nonpolitical subjects
as he had written for Lippmann on the *World*.

Geyelin declined.

A letter from David in October suggested that like Cain in his youth,
he was firing off in all directions in an explosion of energy: a Ribald classic for *Playboy* called "Night Shift," from an Appalachian Folk Story. The
selection of his story "No Trace" for *Best American Short Stories*, 1971.
A contract for his novel *Bijou*. a long essay on Jesse Hill Ford's murder
of a black man for *Esquire*. Four new short stories written last summer,
plus a memoir of his war with the army during the McCarthy era. Warm
reviews for *Rediscoveries*, a book of essays he commissioned from well-
known writers about their favorite neglected novel.

"Give me a call sometime if you get lonesome."

Von Auw declined to submit *Enchanted Isle* to Knopf. What the hell
was wrong with him anyhow? Ruth Goetz, who had a number of Broadway successes to her credit by now, set him straight: "I think you must

come away from this idea of doing quick little situation books ... 'situation' is a hangover from Vinnie, and Vinnie's kind of storytelling is far behind us now." He ought to get back, she said, to what he'd done so well in the past, but without repeating himself, of course.

For many years, he had contemplated a sequel to *Past All Dishonor*, taking up the life of Biloxi from the point where the prospect of starting a new whorehouse with the help of a rich man blows up. She tries to open one on her own. But the old Civil War terrain finally discouraged him, and he pushed away from the typewriter for a while and gave his two index fingers and agents and publishers and domineering friends a rest.

Cain now had such a great need for money that he had to suspend the check he usually sent Rosalie, and to request an advance from Von Auw for $1,000 in November, warning that a has-been writer in his late seventies might not earn back the advance. But then, in mid-December Swannie wrote to say he thought Cain showed a rare understanding of the younger generation in *The Enchanted Isle*. "I plan to sell it by pointing out that this girl is typical of the kids who run away from home these days." Was *The Mink Coat* all right as a new title? Yes. He sent ten copies around to the studios.

And Swannie also secured another option on *Past All Dishonor*.

Neither prospect bore fruit.

Cain returned to work on the novel he had started after finishing *The Magician's Wife* back in 1965, a biographical sort of thing about a modern Don Juan that had been in his mind for years, but had always gotten hung up on a basic problem. This Don Juan's career, in which he long ago fulfilled the wish of many males, reaches a crisis when he conquers a filthy-rich widow. She is ecstatically happy, but her teenage son is not. To keep the money, the lover knows he must be faithful, and he also knows he is incapable of doing that. From friends, the son finds out about the man's past and confronts him: I know you will try to kill her for her money, and if you do, I'll kill you. The man's dream of big money had come true, but he couldn't live with it, because of his conflicting dream of making love to every woman to whom he was attracted. But Cain detected a flaw in his conception. Like Casanova, this man was contemptible, his attitudes and behavior sickening. He had the algebra, and from it had derived a detailed outline with all the explosive elements and a climax for them, but he couldn't write one word of it.

His reading interest was mostly in the area of biography and autobiography, but he also took another look at the Bible and wondered, as he told Rafe, at "the taste of the human race in accepting such stuff and enshrining it as something to live by." As for religion, Christian theology went up in smoke if you didn't believe, as he didn't, in life after death. God is life and immortality of the soul need not figure in the concept. Cats, somehow, mystically, did.

For Cain, his ten volumes of *Who's Who in America* stood up better than the Bible as something out of his childhood that continued to sustain him. The facts of lives, the records of achievements were the form of sustenance he craved.

And he was frequently asked for facts and reflections on the lives of the men with whom he had worked or had friendships: Lippmann, Ross, Swope, even Hemingway, whom he had never met. Cain responded to queries as fully as he could, perhaps more fully than the researchers expected, and looked forward to seeing what they made of his contributions, checking first for accuracy. He consulted so many sources for accurate data, he wanted his own contributions as a source to be accurate.

Some were writing their autobiographies or memoirs, as Krock had done. Why was Cain not writing his? Friends, agents, and publishers asked. He would have written his autobiography if he could justify it in a title as apt as *Up from Slavery*. He couldn't, so he didn't. Rafe could, but he didn't either. Phil Goodman had no such story to tell, but a memoir would have been appropriate. Memoirs are something else. A less grandiose goal is satisfied in the best memoirs.

A fine biography is an impressive thing, for biography is "the mother of history." American biographers struck Cain as being particularly impressive in their research and in the literary quality of their books: Kahn's *The World of Swope*, Sandburg's *Abraham Lincoln*, Nevins's *Grover Cleveland*, Van Doren's *Benjamin Franklin*, Parton's *Andrew Jackson*, Freeman's *Robert E. Lee*. A great biography requires a life worth telling and a biographer who can tell it in an interesting way, concentrating not on the work but on the life. The lives that particularly interested him were James

K. Polk, General N. P. Banks, Juan N. Cortina, a Mexican bandit who had some impact on the American Civil War, and Ulysses S. Grant, who was also a fine writer.

Out of all this interest, often very passionate indeed, came an idea for a novel that drew on all the research he had done about Maryland for the Don Juan story.

Lloyd Palmer meets and makes love to Hortense, his female equal, and they become partners in a great adventure—setting up a $22 million biography institute. Hortense's husband Richard Garrett agrees to put up the money, but Lloyd sees an opportunity to use the institute as a front for a much more lucrative blackmail scheme. A younger woman complicates the web of relationships. "I first met Hortense Garrett at her home in Wilmington, Delaware on a spring morning last year. I wasn't calling on her but on her husband, Richard Garrett, the financier, to make a pitch for money—a lot of money, twenty million or so. It was for a project I had in mind, an institute of biography, which I hoped he would endow, and, incidentally, name me as director.

". . . this girl came whirling into the room with her hand outstretched."

One afternoon Cain was watching a baseball game on television in his T-shirt. Someone knocked at the door. He said he was Larry McMurtry, a Washington book dealer and a novelist, and that he had a telephone message that Cain had called to say he wanted to sell some books. Cain took him upstairs, showed him where the books were, mostly fiction that he always sold soon after reading because he didn't like having fiction around the house, for fear he might be influenced. He went back downstairs and watched the ballgame. McMurtry came down and said, "The message said your name was K-A-N-E. You're James M. Cain." He asked if he wanted to sell his old manuscripts, versions of his novels, original screenplays, stage plays. A little irritated by the distraction from the ballgame, Cain said, "Oh, I guess so." The man gave him $500 and he was rid of them.

David wrote to say he had just given a reading of his fiction at Hollins College in Virginia and that he and Tom Atkins, editor of *Film Journal*, wanted to throw a Cain festival there next year, with showings of all films made from his novels, a production of the play version of *The Postman*, and an appearance by Cain himself.

"OK on everything but the play—that is out, and I won't have it in any way, shape, or form. It is a sore subject, mainly because I feel I made a mess of it all by my own self. Whether I attend depends.

"Everyone I send the Cain book to likes it."

Another Lippmann book came out, *Lippmann, Liberty, and The Press* by John Luskin. Cain checked Luskin's use of "The End of the World" for accuracy.

In the news, the name and the photo of a woman named Dita Beard intrigued Cain. Her inter-office memo had been made public to support a charge that the Nixon re-election campaign people had received a $400,000 contribution in return for the settlement of an antitrust suit in ITT's favor. He wrote to her in Denver where she was hospitalized with a heart condition to advise her that she had an excellent basis for a lawsuit. They began to correspond and he told her she had an "enchanting" writing style and that she was "very good looking." He became more and more infatuated with her as they continued to write.

And then a meeting was arranged. Her daughters would bring her to his house on a Sunday. He invited a neighbor couple for moral support. What he opened the door to was a woman in no way as good looking as her photographs and who barraged him with constant talk, spiked with every curse word he had ever heard. Having no use for cussing women, he faded into the upholstery, and was relieved to realize that she wasn't overwhelmed by him either.

Thomas Chastain, a novelist and longtime fan, arranged to come down to do an interview with Cain to run in *Publishers Weekly* on the occasion of his eightieth birthday. "My eyes are not on the past. I can honestly say I have no consciousness of any sense of achievement. I'm excited for the future, for the new book, the book I'm working on now." Eighty years old. "That damned day." July 1.

Jack Nicholson planned to star in *Postman*, he told Chastain. The new book is called *The Institute*, an "adventure of sex." And "I still work as long as I ever did. The only change in work habits is that I made myself get off the typewriter. This will be the first novel I've written in longhand." Set in Washington. "California is a kind of wonderland, now, and Washington, D. C. is another kind of wonderland." Two different fable climates. Cain's method was to write and rewrite, four versions of this one in the past year. "But that doesn't bother me. I remember that I made about 50 different starts on *Past All Dishonor* in 1946. It had the biggest trade edition sale of all my books. That taught me not to give up." He didn't like to set deadlines for himself. "Not long ago, some of the publishing people talked to me about writing my autobiography, but the idea doesn't interest me."

"I was just trying to tell stories, to get them down in informal, colloquial language and I found that I could get the bite and the kick I wanted by writing in the first person....To me, writing is the scrim through which the reader sees the story. If the writing is too fancy, or has pattern in it, there's a conflict in the scrim. It disturbs the reader and he doesn't see the story clearly."

Hollywood: "But I want it understood that I consider I had a record of failure unmatched in Hollywood's history."

He got hundreds of letters a year, mostly people, young ones, reading him for the first time: "The kids and I have an affinity, and they're reading my books and writing me about them."

He re-read Conan Doyle, he read little other fiction, from fear of imitation. Didn't re-read his own, had seen only three of the movies made from his novels.

Publishers Weekly came in the mail. "At the eminent age of 80, the author of 'The Postman Always Rings Twice' looks back on a celebrated career and forward to his new novel."

"Cain-in-person is something of a surprise," after the book jacket photos over the years. "Actually, James Cain is six feet tall and big-framed, the hair and memorable bushy eyebrows are still gray rather than white, giving him, overall, a bit of the look of a Southern colonel." "A shelf full of autobiographies could scarcely contain the many lives James Mallahan Cain has lived." He listed them. His recurring theme is the wish comes true, "the secret wish, the hidden dream—with a seed of evil in it—which becomes reality with terrifying consequences."

"One wonders as the day of talk draws to a close if he's aware of the impact and influence of his novels. Of the art of a very high order indeed that was at work behind the writing of 20 or 30 years ago that reads as if it had just been put down on paper this minute. Of how one knows from years of conversations that James M. Cain's name and books have touched the nerve endings of a diverse reading public" from bartenders to professors, "some of whom couldn't tell you the name of another book they'd read recently, nor the writer." Cain leans forward: "It's a very vain remark," softly, "but the question always is: 'Is he out of date? Or does he keep?'" His head nods. He knows, he knows. Reading Tom's ending, Cain smiled.

Word came from David that once again he had missed him. He'd come to his very door this time and even talked to neighbors. Passing through Washington on his way home in his car from Bread Loaf Writers' Conference in late August, he had impulsively left the superhighway and swooped into Hyattsville. He enclosed an advance copy of his Avon paperback original, *Brothers in Confidence*, another parallel to Cain's own career.

"I was badly upset when I realized I had missed you. I was home, actually, but upstairs, in bed, asleep." Give notice next time, "so I can be on deck with a grin on my face and a fatted calf at the end of a sabre."

In January 1973, David called to say he planned to attend a gathering of writers at the Library of Congress in February. Could he come out to Hyattsville and spend a few hours with him? Cain said, yes, he would fix lunch for them. He was always shy meeting people with whom he had had a long friendship by mail and telephone, so he asked Robin Deck to provide a little moral support.

David arrived in a taxi, and although he had seen a headshot of him in *Playboy*, he was totally unprepared for the short, blue-eyed boyish man who had just turned forty and spoke in a soft voice. He had expected at all, lean Tennessean with Texas overtones about him, as all Texans came from Tennessee originally. He liked the real David Madden much better.

The book was out, so the meeting was a little anti-climactic on that score, and David talked as if he were just another fan, showing great interest in the pictures on the wall, the few books, and he asked to see the study. Cain told Robin to take him upstairs and show him the work place. For lunch, Cain made his own recipe of Hollandaise sauce for the broccoli. David went back to the Library of Congress activities, and it had been a pleasant meeting.

A week later, David wrote to thank him for lunch, but added that he would have preferred to talk with him alone. He said the people at Hollins College were extremely disappointed that Cain wouldn't be attending their spring literary festival honoring his work, but that he had made them understand Cain's point of view about such events.

Cain told David that Robin had sensed that David would have preferred to see him alone. "Superficially, she's a screwball that likes to crack jokes, but actually a competent, well-schooled girl who knows how to do things, and I asked her to stand by to back me up in case I needed such backing. She's left me now, gone off to meet a guy she ought to marry, but she liked you enormously, and spent her time her next trip out bawling me out for not having told her more about you. I told her if she'd only shut her trap long enough, I'd tell her a lot more about everything—and so on and so on."

For the third year, Cain honored a rash commitment to participate in the Creative Writing Seminar with Bode and Salamanca, but he got a bad case of the doubts about the whole project. These young writers shouldn't be encouraged. Next year, he would refuse to join in.

Cain was dismayed to learn through Von Auw's office that Bill Koshland had rejected *The Institute*, without direct comment to Cain. That made five straight rejections over the past several years.

Ruth Goetz suggested one possible problem: The dialogue was dated. What could he do? "I have to write as I write, and can't young it up."

David had made that charge again for *The Magician's Wife* in 1965. A famous hijacking incident gave Cain an idea for a new novel. Davy Howell's wish has already been fulfilled. He lives the good life in rural Ohio solitude with his mother, whom he loves. Then a hijacker parachutes into his life, $100,000 rich in ransom cash, with a beautiful stewardess as hostage. Davy now wishes to be rich and to have the stewardess. He goes on the love-rack with the stewardess—and with his mother. "It was the same old Saturday night Mom and I had been having off and on since my father died—or at least the man I had thought was my father. . . . But don't get the idea that things were slow or that time dragged. Plenty was going on, a little too much, for my taste, and too lively. The first part—in the early evening—wasn't too bad, just screwy, which, of course, there's no law against.

She'd begin talking about how rich we would be by and by, pretty soon, one of these days, and tonight was extra special on account of the rainbow she'd seen late in the afternoon, after the rain when the sun came out.

"And you know, Dave," she whispered, "what's under the end of that bow—a pot of gold, that's what."

Out of the mountain mores and his use of it in *The Butterfly*, he took a cue for an element of forbidden sex. The mother has a letch for the boy, but she turns out not to be his mother after all.

To get up the dope for the novel, he took a trip to its setting, Marietta, Ohio, just across the river from West Virginia. He fell in love with Malinda Howes who interviewed him for the *Marietta Times*, but got nowhere. Researching the novel and the way Malinda affected him got his energy up, and the trip proved to be quite exciting.

Tom Chastain called to tell Cain he had talked with Thomas Lipscomb of a new publishing house called Mason and Lipscomb about the possibility of considering a new Cain novel for publication. They had accepted one of Tom's novels. Cain told him that Knopf had rejected *The Institute* and that he was well into a new one called *Rainbow's End*.

Lipscomb contacted Cain, saying he'd read *The Institute* and wanted to come down to meet him. When he arrived, he admitted he was not very enthusiastic about the novel, but asked to see some of *Rainbow's End*. Cain told him he never showed work in progress, but told him the story, and Lipscomb was enthusiastic. Here was a new house, with few writers, and all possibilities open. Cain also unloaded on Lipscomb some other ideas he had for books.

Back in New York, Lipscomb called Cain to tell him he had discovered a vital interest among movie people and reprint houses in any new book by James M. Cain. He offered him a two-book contract, $7,500 each, the highest price Cain had ever received, *Rainbow's End* to be published first. So, he said, finish *Rainbow's End*.

By the end of the summer, Cain submitted it and went immediately to work on revisions of *The Institute*.

Lipscomb responded quickly. *Rainbow's End* was very good, except for the unconvincing happy ending.

Setting *The Institute* aside again, Cain started revising *Rainbow's End*.

Cain received from David an off print of a piece he had written on him for a library reference volume, *Contemporary Novelists*. "In their total commitment to each other, severing all ties to other people, Cain's lovers experience a blazing, self-consuming flash of self-deceptive purity and hideous innocence." Was that true of the characters in the *Rainbow*? In some ways, yes.

"*Double Indemnity*, based on Raymond Chandler's suspense classic." That TV commercial infuriated Cain as a humiliating irony. Not only did he receive no money for this television remake, the credit went to the man who wrote the first Paramount script. It was directed by Jack Smight, starring Samantha Egger, Richard Crenna, and, in the Edward G. Robinson role, Lee J. Cobb.

When David told him his *Bijou* had been taken by the Book of Month Club, Cain was delighted for him. David thought it had sure-fire mass appeal.

"You've entered Writer's Valhalla.... *Serenade* is on a sure-fire theme, though I didn't know it at the time I wrote it. I was a little ashamed of it. It has consistently been my one big bid for critical acceptance. Acceptance and merit aren't quite the same thing. In case you talk anymore about it.

"Once more: I'm green with envy."

1973 had been twice as good as 1972, for his income had doubled to $13,000.

Finished with the revision of *Rainbow's End*, Cain wrote to Lipscomb on February 9, 1974. "I'm pleased to report that though I'm generally nauseated by what I write, in this case I realized it was holding me—I have done better than I realized." Convinced that the ending was what it should be, he had not changed it.

"Thanks for *Bijou*—the first few pages gave me a kick. Robin Deck, the assistant hostess and chief cook and bottle washer of the Cain household, whom you met, took off for Guam to get married, then changed her mind, I suspect in favor of a more advantageous alliance. It's all I can do to keep up with her."

As a board member, David asked Cain if he could come to Milwaukee to receive an Achievement Award from the Popular Culture Association.

Lillian Gish had been the first recipient, and Cain would be the second. He replied, no he couldn't make such a trip.

David wrote to say he had accepted the award for Cain. "You're much loved and admired among these people." Cain wrote a few weeks later.

Thanks for accepting the award. "My obligations to you mount up. I don't quite know why I was singled out, and in fact don't quite know what popular culture is. As I get the idea... the kind of thing no one can remember who wrote it—and I suppose, alas, that means me.

"I've been whipsawed between a job of writing I picked out for myself and some press appearances downtown," so he hadn't read *Bijou*. "It's long, but I like it fine so far.

"Robin is still on the island of Guam. She always asks about you."

A few weeks later came a lecture from David on the importance of Popular Culture as a new field of study, and the value of PCA's promotion of writers like Cain. He also wanted Cain to know that in *Bijou* the movies made from Cain's novels and the paperback editions of the early novels were important elements in his autobiographical novel.

Lipscomb changed the dialogue so that the characters no longer spoke mountain, and rewrote the ending of *Rainbow's End*. Cain wrote to Dorothy Olding, "In fifty years of writing, for newspapers, magazines and book publishers, I never had anything like this to happen to me." Cain did eliminate the double wedding of the son and the "mother." But Lipscomb wrote that his idea that the boy lose the girl in the end "is so fantastically wrong I've discarded it." Reluctantly, Lipscomb agreed to Cain's version.

But Lipscomb had left the firm. The new name was Mason and Charter, and they wanted Cain to make an appearance at the American Booksellers' Association convention in Washington in June, and would he submit to interviews? He said he'd try.

Larry Swindell came up to him and told him he used to see him around Hollywood when he was a kid, and asked if he could interview him for the *Philadelphia Inquirer*. Sure. Re *Rainbow's End*: "The title sounds valedictory but I'm working now on another book, about a love affair ... a funeral starts it." *The Cocktail Waitress* is based on his strong-woman theory. "Women run things in this world. And they rule the politics of this country, say by 99 percent." "Well, she teases him along, and I let him bathe her naked, yet he never gets her until the end of the book."

At a press conference, when asked about his work habits, he said, "I lie on a couch and write longhand and a girl types it for me."

In a rather hurt tone, David wrote that the St. James Press in London had asked him to update his essay on Cain because a new novel was coming out. He had not heard of the impending publication of *Rainbow's End*. He was working on a new novel himself, *The Suicide's Wife*. It had a familiar ring.

For the *Washington Post's Potomac Magazine*, Cain wrote, "Christmas Past—'Silent Night, 1918'"—another memoir vignette.

He had lunch occasionally with the editors and writers for *Potomac*. They liked to listen to his stories about Hollywood and writers. Carmody had become a good friend, and Cain hit it off with another editor there, Marian Clark, who chauffeured him around now and then. It was understood that more of his pieces would be welcomed at the magazine.

His 1974 income of over $10,000 was a drop, but not a disastrous one.

Cain was sad to hear of the death of Walter Lippmann. Carmody asked him to write a tribute for the *Potomac* to a fast deadline. So at eighty-three, he was looking back, with the intention of achieving a balanced view, on one of the five great influences in his own life. He wanted to tell about the Lippmann who is not written about. First, the personal angle, with a series of incidents featuring Cain's own direct relationship with him. "I never heard a dull word from him." Then the misconceptions. Then: "So what did he add up to?" What were his convictions? "I shall now astonish you. It became my belief, when I'd come to know him well, that he didn't have any." Give examples, key issues, and his failure to take a stand. "It turned out however that when the occasion arose, he could write bugle calls, and that his were better calls by far, than the calls most people wrote. The best writing of his life, as I personally think, was the series of columns he did against the Vietnam War, at the end of his career. They made the general point that it is not up to the United States to be the world's policeman, a big, profound observation, a real contribution, which, if remembered, could save millions of lives in the future. It was in connection with these columns that I heard myself say one night to guests in my Hyattsville home. 'He can't be frightened and can't be bought.' I think it is a very high tribute and the fact that it was true justifies everything else, and indeed puts a laurel wreath on it."

Word came from Andy Logan at the *New Yorker* that he had passed Cain's Lippmann piece on to Richard Rovere, Arthur Schlesinger Jr., William Shawn, to Victor Nasby at the *Times*, and that all were very impressed. Carey McWilliams liked it too, and asked Cain to contribute to the *Nation*. "The old fire horse could still jump to the sound of the bell, and send it out in two days, that being *Potomac's* deadline they slapped on me." But he said he didn't think he could write what the *Nation* required.

Advance copies of *Rainbow's End* came in. The cover showed a rainbow, a briefcase spilling cash at the end of it, against yellow, red, and blue lettering. The quotes spanned the decades: Tom Wolfe, Edmund Wilson, Ross Macdonald, Max Lerner, William Rose Benét.

Cain inscribed and wrapped *Rainbow's End* to send to David. "*The Suicide's Wife*, the title excites me. . . . Get it done, and get it out. I would say it's more up your street than how many movies some boy went to see, as in *Bijou*." "I'm not getting any younger, I'm sorry to say."

In March, the *Rainbow's End* reviews came in, each reviewer competing with Cain in getting off witty, tough phrases in praise or condemnation.

John Barkham Reviews: "Tough, realistic, stripped to the bone, with every word carrying its own weight." Happy ending suggests he's mellowed. Cain still thought it worked, though it had a few kinks.

Philadelphia Bulletin: "Like *The Postman* ... this one rings the bell—loudly."

Richard Fuller, *Philadelphia Inquirer*: "Cain has the old momentum, and you keep turning the pages to find out what in thunderation is going to happen."

Boston Globe: "could have been a cracker-jack novel were it not for too many goodies at the end."

Charles Willeford, *Miami Herald*: "vintage Cain, and it's all here—the big money, the unusual circumstances, the spare, tight style and the staccato dialogue."

The *Detroit Sunday News*: "What most novelists couldn't accomplish in a 500 page book, Cain has done in 191 pages. The rich characters of 'Rainbow's End' could move gracefully to Broadway or film."

Seattle Post Intelligencer: "The old punch is still there, and Cain is still able to put more sexuality and tension into what people imply rather than say or do than all the Mickey Spillanes and Harold Robbins."

Using the movie *Chinatown* as a springboard, the *New Republic* published a piece called "It's Chinatown," by Kevin Starr, city librarian of San Francisco, author of *America and the California Dream, 1850–1915*.

"If you have the courage, take a look this summer at James M. Cain . . . of an entire generation of tough-guy writers—James M. Cain is possessed of the most brutal, elemental, and intrinsically pessimistic view of human events and possibilities." Only Robinson Jeffers "matches Cain's abysmal bleakness." Didn't he see the comic element in some of his work, especially *Career in C Major*? "He was on the way to becoming just another hard-drinking Irish-American journalist with baffled aspirations in the direction of literature. As a production writer working on the Hollywood assembly line, he was too stubborn, too touchy regarding his integrity, to do anyone much good." *Postman*: "one of the finest moment of depression literature." *Serenade*: "ritualized lust."

"He triggers in us an act of imaginative cooperation. Convinced that Cain's fables of lust, murder and money are true to the epic structure of life in the urban-industrial complex, the reader amplifies and visualizes the details, like a director working from the bare bones of a story line: visualizing. . . . Reading Cain, then, is a mixed media event, to which you bring," etc. Jean-Paul Sartre was among the first to take him seriously. Cain was primarily a writer of the 1930s and 1940s. *The Magician's Wife* "suffers from an element of time displacement," while his best work has "an element of laconic timelessness."

"I think it's your best in some time," David said of *Rainbow's End*. David himself was involved in a new enterprise, a short story textbook for Holt, Rinehart.

Cain suggested that David, now looking for a fiction publisher, write to Orlando Petrocelli, "the big enchilada" at Mason Charter. "They seem to be loaded with money. At least they treated me quite handsomely."

Having finished revisions on *The Institute*, Cain started to sharpen his focus on *The Cocktail Waitress*. This will be, he thought, the third novel I have written while in my eighties. The pride he felt in that was diminished by the prospect of not living to finish it. It had an autobiographical basis in his own angina, which had made him wonder if he could still make love to a woman.

What if a girl's husband died in an auto accident and she had to take a job in a cocktail bar? A man she met at the funeral comes in; they are attracted to each other. He leaves a big tip. Then the man sends his car to bring her to his house. He comes outside, hands her through the window an envelope containing $45,000. That night, in the bar, she asks him why he doesn't approach her in a more conventional way. He tells her he is crazy about her, would like to marry her, but has a heart condition, and sex would kill him. But now what? Cain wondered. If he married her, without sex, the story draws a blank. If they marry, and they make love anyway, and he dies, what next?

Cain tried it first in the third person for about one hundred pages. It didn't work. Mindful of David's caution years ago, he decided he would never attempt the third person again. As soon as he let her tell it in her own lingo, the thing came off the floor astonishingly.

In the fall, a man named Roy Hoopes called to say how much impressed he was by Cain's piece on Lippmann. By way of credentials, he said he was a journalist who had published books on politics, on the steel crisis, the Peace Corps, had been an editor for *National Geographic*, the *Washingtonian*, and *Newsday*, and was working on a book about the American home front during World War II. He wanted to interview Cain for a possible biography of him. He assumed Cain was working on his autobiography. "No, I don't believe in 'em. I don't believe any man should write his autobiography unless he can give it a title as like Booker T. Washington's *Up from Slavery*. Unless you can say that, you've got no story to tell. I am planning a book about my early life, contrasting it with the present day, but it is definitely not an autobiography." May Hoopes have an interview? "Yes, if it we hit it off alright. But the sessions will have to be after dinner. . . ."

Hoopes came out, armed with a tape recorder. Cain said he hated microphones—his voice needed no amplification.

"I seem to have a zest for writing. I can't say I enjoy it. Anyone who enjoys writing can't write. It's laborious and frustrating. But it excites me and possesses me, no less today than it did fifty years ago." He sounded off on Knopf, Mencken, and Ross.

His background: "Anyone who talks about 'the good old days,' doesn't know what he is talking about. Make no mistake about it, allow for the oil shortage, Depression, everything, the world we got now is so much better than the world I was born into that there's just no comparison."

Reaction to *Rainbow's End*: "It entertained quite a few reviewers. They liked it and thought that at the age of eighty-two it was amazing that I would write such a book—or any book at all."

"How does your day go?" He got up at half past seven. Read the paper. "Then I just sit here, intending not to work. I owe it to myself. I always intend not to work. Then I do work. I go upstairs at about eleven, although sometimes I sit down here thinking about what I'm going to write, clarifying my dialogue. That can often be more laborious than what I actually do at the machine." For a year or two, he'd been writing longhand. But "my writing is not as sharp when I sit at the machine. I used to work standing up, with the typewriter on the piano, but it gave me a touch of bladder trouble. . . . I get about six pages a day now at the typewriter and that poops me out, but six pages is about two thousand words and that's what any writer regards as a day's work." The bladder trouble faded out. He finished at 2:00. Came down, sat "twiddling my thumbs for twenty minutes, then fix lunch." Slept two hours. 5:30, watch Mike Douglas, for guests like Totie Fields, a good-looking number. Joe McCaffrey, a friend, on Channel 7. He often went out. Taken down to Jim Youniss's, professor of child psychology, at Catholic University, the Dunklees up the street, very old friends. He leases autos. Friends next door, Kisielnicki, twelve children, very close. Cynthia is a semi-secretary for Cain. Mr. and Mrs. Harry Piper are close friends. He's a professor, she's assistant to the dean of the graduate school at University of Maryland. Alice Piper takes him to concerts and film showings.

Regarding research on *Mignon* and four years on another novel, not published: "When you take two or three years on one that didn't come off and two or three on one you couldn't publish, it's a heartbreak, and expensive, too."

Why not return to Hollywood? "We stayed here. And it was not a good decision. I should have gone back because it's a neck of the woods that everybody is fascinated by, and I understand it and could write about it. I don't know who gives a goddamn about Prince George's County politics. I started a book that was supposed to have a background in county politics and I did a lot of research but couldn't make it come to life. A book came out of it—*The Cocktail Waitress*—which I am finishing now, but it is completely different from the book I started to write." National politics? "I just have never been able to get interested in politics or politicians. The labor movement, yes, but not politics. I have no idea what the reason is and don't particularly care." Why nothing on newspapermen? "I couldn't do it. I instinctively shy away from those novels in which the writer is writing about his business. It would be a transparent thing about myself. Also, I have no impulse to write about the issues and decisions a newspaperman has to make."

Why did he fail as a scriptwriter? "Even working in a whorehouse, the girl has to like the work a little bit, and I could not like pictures." Although movies have improved.

Why not an autobiography, why no sense of accomplishment? Madden did a literary biography of him, he told Hoopes. "You've had a fascinating life." "It may be to you but it's never been interesting to me. There's something very peculiar about me that I don't understand. I cannot write in the third person—and it seems to have something to do with this sense of a lack of accomplishment." Writing editorials I pretended to be the "corporate" awfulness of the paper. "There's something left out of me. I can't figure it out." Ever wavered from your decision to be a writer? "A hundred times."

Hoopes talked Cain out of his reluctance to let him take a photograph of him sitting on the bench where God had told him he was going to be a writer back in 1914. They drove out there to Lafayette Park, and Hoopes caught the historic moment, as he put it.

In October, his neighbor, Alice Piper, one of the four ladies who drove him around and looked in on him, took him to the American Film Institute for a retrospective of the movies made from his novels. Hoopes showed up with his camera, and got another shot of him.

And he came out for more interviews. The piece appeared in the *Washingtonian* on a Sunday in November, an impressive layout, with Hoopes's photographs, and there Cain was on that park bench sixty years later. God had still not made up His mind whether Cain was really going to turn out to be a writer as promised. "JAMES M. CAIN, AMERICAN NOVELIST, 83 YEARS OLD, WRITING EVERY DAY, LIVING IN HYATTSVILLE, STILL FEELING MISUNDERSTOOD."

It led off with a long detailed account of his life and works, drawing a good deal of material from David's book, with the interviewer's comments mostly at the end. There was much in the opening about how Hoopes came to get interested in Cain. The immediate inspiration was the "beautiful piece on Lippmann in *Potomac*, which made him feel he knew all about Lippmann." Hoopes had collected Cain first editions. He had read a profile on him in 1969 when *Cain X 3* came out. There was his own interest in journalism and politics, and his desire to do the biography of a writer, a journalist like himself. In some ways, his background was closer to Cain's than David's had been. "It was . . . a pleasant surprise to find that Cain was still alive and well—a surprise he apparently shares." He enjoys being Washington's dean of letters. Cain "has turned out to be one of the most interesting and enjoyable personalities I have met in some time."

A week later, Hoopes had interviewed Mr. Cain again. "And he has agreed to work with me on the biography. So maybe, as I try to pull the story of his long life into a book, I will come to understand what makes a man who has accomplished so much feel he has done so little—and why it seems to him to be related to his inability to write in the third person. Why, in his writing, does he have to pretend to be someone else? What's wrong with being James M. Cain?"

Finished with *The Cocktail Waitress*, he sent it to Dorothy Olding, and while Petrocelli at Mason-Charter was reading it, Cain wrote to tell him he was still not happy with the ending. "If you're dealing with me, you may as well get used to it. I work on an ending ceaselessly, believing it to be the most vital part of a story."

Two months later: Petrocelli read the new ending, but returned the novel to Miss Olding, who decided not to send it to another publisher.

In 1975, Cain's income had gone down drastically.

E. B. White told Cain how well his children's books had sold, so Cain thought he might have more success with a revision of *Jinghis Quinn*, aimed directly at the children's book market.

Rainbow's End had sold well enough to keep up Mason-Charter's interest in *The Institute*. Berkley had bought paperback rights. Cain was convinced that the controversy worked into the novel over the question, "To whom did Shakespeare address his sonnets?" would draw to the novel a great deal of interest. Orlando Petrocelli, his editor now, had agreed with Cain that *The Institute* was more important, and should have come out first. But there were flaws, and he suggested changes. Cain went to work on them.

Peter Brunette and Gerald Perry asked to come to the house to conduct an interview about Cain's experiences in Hollywood. He turned on his porch light and set out a supermarket cardboard box so they could distinguish his from his neighbor's house. At precisely 7:30, they rang the bell. At the end of four hours, he felt as if he had dredged up enough detail about those days to fill a book.

The May-June issue of *Film Comment* carried Brunette and Perry's long interview: "Tough Guy." Right off, the old label, and there he was, old, in front of his old house. It opened oddly with the pair of them fantasizing they are in a film noir, like the lovers in *Double Indemnity*, going to see James M. Cain.

Jinghis Quinn bounced around from one publisher to another for six months, prompting Dorothy Olding to decide it should go no further.

The reviews of *The Institute* came out in August.

John D. MacDonald, *New York Times Book Review*: The old Cain was great and he influenced many writers, including Hammett and Chandler, but this one is only "a faint and embarrassing echo."

Mark Stuart, *Hackensack Record*: "You've got to be kidding."

In the *Louisville Courier-Journal*, David said it was the best of Cain's more recent novels. It "does not have the force that made Cain the most powerful of the tough-guy writers, but he is still in command of all his most effective qualities. The force of character and personality electrically discharged in the first-person narration produces a pace few other writers can sustain. We go with Cain for the ride.

"The ideal Cain reader enjoys watching him do again what he has done so well many times before." Palmer shares his knowledge of many areas. "Those procedures are as suspenseful as his dangerous love affair.

"One of the novel's problems is the outdated tone of much of the conversation. The time may as well be the '30s. It's probably best to read the novel as if it were. The way the characters behave with each other, especially the lovers, seems off. Similar problems of style, of anachronisms, plagued *Rainbow's End*, published last year, but they are less disruptive here.

"All Cain's best qualities keep uneasy company with faults that come naturally when one is no longer in the midst of the action, watching and listening. But what we still see and hear so vividly in *The Institute* are images and sounds that are the creation of Cain's distinctive imagination and craft."

The reviews were sparse, and they were generally humiliating.

In the Bi-Centennial edition of *Who's Who in America*, Cain and David were happy to be listed together, David for the first time.

Cain's income for 1976 was frighteningly low.

On January 7, David Zinsser came to the house to interview him for the *Paris Review*. "So this is where you grew up?" "I was born in Annapolis," etc.

A hint that he might become a writer came when he sent cigarette coupons of his father's for fountain pens, filled each with an eyedropper at ten or twelve. "Today, whenever I take out the clinical thermometer to take my temperature, I think of those pens and the eye-droppers. So the succession of fountain pens may have been an omen."

On not going with a whore at eighteen: "I guess the things you didn't do. . . ."

"I talked the way my father had beat into me." Then he mixed in the Vulgate.

The New Yorker: "a job that I was weirdly unqualified for temperamentally. I wasn't a flop at the job, but it meant nothing to me. I couldn't take pride in it. I did well enough."

"One personal reason for being pleased at being in California was that I couldn't seem to write about New York. Those funny New York taxi drivers weren't funny to me. I couldn't manage the New York idiom. If you can't write like New York, you have no business living in New York and making New York the locale of your stories. There would be a falsity to it. When I got out to California, I found the people there spoke my lingo."

"Do you work from a story or a situation?"

"I don't know what I work from."

"But there are devices one can use to set up a story, aren't there? Such as the love-rack, or the algebraic analysis of a story?"

"Devices, yes. Like the old switcheroo. I used quite a few in *Past All Dishonor*...I was able to top it, and that's always what you try to do when you have a situation: you pull it, you switch it, you top it, which is the old Hollywood formula for a running gag." When Roger shoots Morina: "Quite a switcheroo. Well, now I've gone and admired my own book."

Butterfly: "would be even better for the screen than *Past All Dishonor*, especially these days. I'm still a member of the United Mine Workers."

"Which of your own books would you say stand up best?"

"The book that stands up for me is one that sold the most copies. That's the only test for me and that one was *The Postman Always Rings Twice*. There's the silver kangaroo over there on the shelf that Pocket Books gave me when I passed the million-copy mark. That must have been thirty years ago."

"How did you react to Albert Camus's praise of your writing?"

"But I never read Camus. In some ways I'm ignorant. In other ways I'm not. At fiction I'm not. But I read very little of it. I'm afraid to because I might like some guy's book too well! Another thing: when you write fiction, the other guy's book just tortures you—you're always re-writing it for him. You don't read it just as a reader. You read it as a guy in the business. Better not read it at all. I've read a great deal of American history."

"How related is style to your objectives? You are so well-known for your 'hard-boiled' manner of writing."

"Let's talk about this so-called style. I don't know what they're talking about—'tough,' 'hard-boiled.' I tried to write as people talk. That was one of the first arguments I ever had with my father—my father was all hell for people talking as they *should* talk. I, the incipient novelist, even as a boy, was fascinated by the way people *do* talk." His father "had Ike

Newton put in a brick walk and I would sit out there while he worked, listening to him. He was a stocky man, rather nicely put together."

"Did you ever hear praise about your books . . . that you felt appreciated your intention?"

The producer of *Postman*, Carey Wilson, said, "What I like about your books—they're about dumb people.. .. I can believe them and you put them into interesting situations. After all, how the hell could I care about a hobo and a waitress out there in that place you put them I . . . for Chrissakes, I couldn't put the goddamn thing down for two hours!" Just enough time to read it, as *Liberty* used to say.

As he worked on *The Cocktail Waitress*, he worried about the dialogue, and in January wrote to David for help. "May I ask a very big favor? Your review says my dialogue is dated and other reviews do, too. This is a new sin for me to be committing, but I don't know what you're talking about. So, would you, by page number, give me some clue to what you mean? The publisher, with no permission from me, let a woman step in and edit me.... The whole book is a botch, for that reason, and I can't make myself re-read it, to know what this dated fault is—whether I am guilty, or it's part of what was done to me. So, if you'll particularize a bit, I'll be truly grateful.

"I never had such a nightmare as my relations with Mason-Charter, and the fact the book has made me more money than most of my books have, and that I have it in the bank already, doesn't help. The damned book is a nausea to me, but I ought to know what this 'dated' stuff means. Thanks in advance."

Thanking him for the inscribed copy of *The Institute*, David promised to send a list of dated expressions later on. He was setting out to Clark University as visiting writer for three weeks.

But it was two months before the list arrived. "I'm not saying these two lovers never heard these expressions nor would never, never use them— but if speech typifies characters and should be typical of them, these, and more, expressions seem off—so does their relentlessly CUTE love-antics, anger antics, and other behavior patterns with each other. But I especially like Lloyd's put-down of the senator, especially the statement that he's the most important person in the world because he is an American citizen.

That's vintage Cain. I'm preparing a little present for you, my friend. Be well, productive, and content." It was a devastating list.

Just back from giving a dramatic reading at the Spoleto Festival in Charleston, David wrote in June, "I was talking about you and your fiction with some people recently, and just got to thinking about you and the fiction you're working on now, and I simply feel that I want you to know I wish you well in your work and your health during these hot summer months."

All summer Cain was writing pieces for the *Post* and the memoir vignettes, but he felt more depressed than usual, and sometimes disoriented. He was aware that his neighbors, especially Alice Piper, Dorothy Youniss, Leona Dunklee, and Thelma Kisielnicki kept close watch on him.

"For the first time in my life," he told Thelma, "I feel the undertaker breathing over my shoulder."

He put up signs around the house: "IN CASE OF DEATH, PLEASE NOTIFY THE MARYLAND BOARD OF ANATOXY."

He persuaded Alice Piper to be the executrix of his estate.

Cain lay in bed until noon one day, and Thelma who had a key to the house, as they all did, appeared in the doorway. "I just don't know what's happening to me. I can't seem to get the distance between here and my feet." She called the doctor.

For his latest piece for the "Style" section of the *Washington Post* Cain wrote about bunions in turn-of-the-century America. Since he had started writing these pieces for the *Potomac* magazine and now the "Style" section, he had racked up fifteen pieces, enough on animals alone, the pieces that had by far stimulated the most mail, especially "The Raccoon," as such pieces on the *World* had, to make up a collection. He had also written a piece on music, on how to sing the "Star Spangled Banner," and on one of his long-favorite subjects, "Treason." He had been working on his memoirs in the form of a series of vignettes, and some of the pieces for the *Post* might fit into the finished opus: "Remembrances of Cain's Past," "Nostalgia," and last summer, the piece on "Charles Laughton," and this fall on "The Gentle Side of W. C. Fields."

He put "America My Foot" in the mail.

His stepson Leo called from California and said he hoped to come east and have Thanksgiving dinner with him. Cain said that was a good idea, but he felt tired and weak. "Leo, I'm losing out to them."

The Maryland weather that had set its teeth deeper into him every season since 1947 was a cold rain the next morning.

Looking down at an unopened box of books that had come in the mail from a rare book collector, Cain felt he just could not open it and sign all those first editions of his books. He dialed the dealer's number. His wife answered. Cain asked her to tell her husband that he could not sign the books, and that he wanted him to come and get them, please.

The man showed up and Cain stood with him looking down at the unopened box of books. "I can't take on a job like that. I'm too old." While confessing to one sin, he knew that he was committing another, for his voice was too gruff.

The dealer was sincerely apologetic for the imposition.

"If I promised to sign those books for you, I'm sorry to break the promise. That's my problem—I have a flaw in my character. I let people down."

After the dealer had left, Cain realized he still had the $3 return postage, so he wrote him a note, enclosed the stamps, and put it out for the postman.

At about six o'clock, Thelma and Ted came over with his dinner on two trays. Sitting in his chair, he watched them arrange the trays in front of him. As usual, he tried to force Ted to have a drink.

When they shut the door as they went out, he realized he had not stood up when Thelma entered the room. He would apologize when she came back for the trays. And the dishes would be washed. He rose from the chair and took the dishes into the kitchen. When the dishes were clean, he turned from the sink. . . .